BLACK MAMBA WHITE SETTLER

A NOVEL BY

Ken Tilbury

Books by Ken Tilbury

TOM OWEN SERIES

BAREFEET and PAPERTHORNS

BLACK MAMBA WHITE SETTLER

THE GOLDEN HORN

ON the RUN

OTHER BOOKS

UNFINISHED BUSINESS

For more information about the author and the books he has written,
please visit
http://www.kentilbury.com

BLACK MAMBA WHITE SETTLER

First published by KTC Publishing in 2010

ISBN: 978–1699789926

CONTENTS

Map of Zimbabwe (Rhodesia)

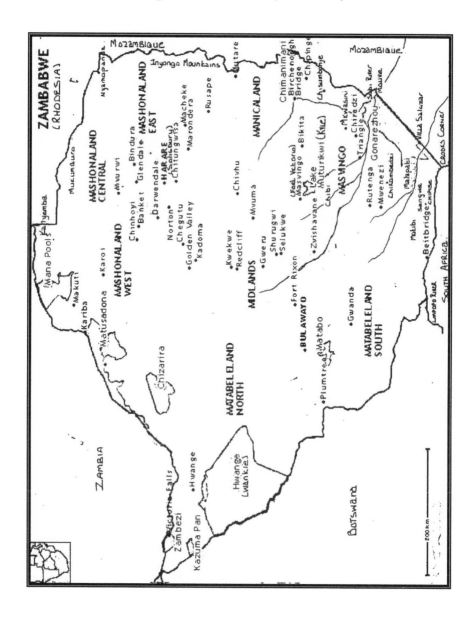

DEDICATION

This book is dedicated to all those brave people who have suffered as a result of political land reforms in Zimbabwe - including the farm workers. Like my family, they too have lost their land, their homes, and all their possessions.

Perhaps it will help to touch the hearts and souls of those who do not understand, and that one day something will be done about it. We can only hope that in the end justice will prevail, and some normality can be restored to the lives of those who have been misplaced and suffered so greatly.

DEDICATION

FORWARD

It is over thirty years since ZIMBABWE became an Independent state within the Commonwealth of Nations. Many historical accounts have been written of the painful birth of this now troubled and financially crippled country.

This story depicts the various degrees of goodness and hope before Independence when the country was prosperous and peaceful. The dark days, of the so-called war of liberation, which lasted twelve years, eventually dragged the people of all races and the country, into an age of darkness and fear.--

The author describes the period of darkness and fear and the eventual consequences to both the victor and the defeated. Neither was a winner, and neither gained, but both were losers.

It is hoped that eventually some form of sensibility will prevail and the beautiful country that so many people loved and respected will again return to a prosperous and peaceful society. A country, once again, that will be welcomed into the Commonwealth of the world.

Peter John Russell (ex BSA Police 1962-1980)

BLACK MAMBA

The black mamba, averaging 2.5 meters in length, is the fastest most deadly snake in Africa. If threatened it can become highly aggressive and will rear its head and advance rapidly while balancing on the rear third of its body, jaws open to reveal the black inside of its mouth before striking. Not many have survived the venom of a black mamba.

Certain individuals, who think they have the same frightening characteristics and wish to terrorize others, adopt the name of Mamba.

Prologue

A week after their arrival at the ZANU military camp in Mozambique from the training camp in Tanzania, Mamba and his unit were given their first mission. Their instructions were to go to the Mrewa district in Rhodesia and launch an attack on a white farmer in that area. At the briefing, they had been told where the 'friendly villages' were, and where staging positions with food and ammunition could be found. They would have to find a way to conceal their weapons and maps when entering the country.

Wrapping their AK47 rifles in blankets, then tucked into hessian bags and loaded onto the roof, they boarded the bus travelling from Tete to Salisbury. They crossed the border at Nyamapanda and entered Rhodesia without any problems. To avoid being seen as a group and attracting the attention of the driver or the conductor, the five men boarded the bus separately and did not sit near each other.

They all got off the bus when it stopped at the road to Hoyuyu, in the early afternoon, 150 miles from Tete and only 80 miles from Salisbury. After gathering their precious luggage, the group split up and made their way individually to a spot 10 miles along the road to the south. They met up where the road crossed the river and took cover in the hills to the east of the bridge.

Mamba had been given the location and name of the farm, as well as the name of the farmer they were to attack. The farmer was known to be very hard on his labour force, and they suspected that if compromised, they would not be reported. The group of freedom fighters was on the way to teach this white settler a lesson. Besides, his farm was close to a large Tribal Trust area that would help them to escape after the attack.

Selecting a secure spot well off the road, they settled down to rest. Mamba sent two of his men off to the nearby store at Hoyuyu to get rations for the following two days.

They returned within the hour, and they ate a good meal. Mamba planned to move off as soon as it was dark. Their target was only 5 miles further to the east across the next river.

As the sun went down, they moved off and followed the road until they found a signpost indicating the entrance to the farm they had been told to attack. Walking in single file, they continued another five miles down the farm road, until they saw the homestead lights. Staying well away from sheds, and far enough away from the farmhouse so that the dogs would not get a sniff of their scent, they found a small hill where they could take cover until the following night.

Feeling quite secure and taking turns to keep watch, they slept. Mamba was pleased; it was all going according to plan.

It had been a long haul to Tete from the base camp near Honde in Mozambique; followed by the delay with the bus from Malawi, and the nervous sweat of getting the weapons across the border without being caught. Now they must rest because from tonight they would have to move very fast to get away from the scene, and make for the border, more than 100 miles away. The terrain they would have to travel through was rough with mountains and rivers to cross. It would not take long for the Military forces to be on their tail.

Early the following morning, the farm activities started. The tractors were fired up, and hitching up trailers and implements, set about their work for the day. Workers rushed about doing their work, and the white farmer went off to the lands in his pickup truck with his dog. Cocks crowed, and dogs barked from time to time. It was a normal working day on the farm.

Knowing that the next few days would be hard going, the five freedom fighters settled down to rest, and get as much sleep as they could, keeping one man on watch at all times. Mamba took his dark glasses off, pulled his hat over his eyes and dozed off. As the sun climbed up into the clear blue sky, the temperature rose in their hiding place in the shade of a clump of small Musasa trees. The day passed slowly as they lay hidden in the undergrowth, but the rest was a welcome break from the hectic activity of getting to their destination. The men were all used to the heat, and only the insects buzzing around them, and the ants crawling on them were a nuisance. They had to take care not to make any sudden movements for fear of being spotted.

"The security fence around the house is about thirty paces from the building, so we will have to attack from the outside of the fence. I will take up my position in the middle, facing the front of the house, with one of you on my left and the other on my right and five paces from me. Robson, you will move to the left side of the house, and attack from there. Tsotsi you will attack from the right side of the house." Mamba instructed at their final briefing late in the afternoon. "We will commence the attack just after 8 o'clock."

"What about the dogs? They will alert the *Mabhunu* (white settler) that we are here." Robson said.

"The wind is coming towards us, and our scent will not be carried to the house. When I give the signal, we must move fast and quietly to get into position before the dogs are alerted. I will start the attack when I open fire on the house. You will then all follow suit shooting at the windows where lights are on. Kill anyone you see moving inside the house. When your magazines are empty, change them then wait for me to start again," Mamba ordered.

"When must we break off the attack and escape?" Robson asked.

"I will call to you when the time is right. If any of you run away before I give the signal, I will shoot you myself, and leave you lying there like a dog. Is that understood?" Mamba said, giving a stern warning. All four men nodded in unison.

Two hours after the sun had set, they made their move. They crept slowly in the dark until they arrived in their positions, behind the bushes at the end of the garden, and directly in front of the house. According to their information, all the farmers watched the television news at eight in the evening, and at that time they were distracted and vulnerable.

It would also give them most of the night to make their getaway. Mamba suddenly cursed himself for having forgotten to cut the telephone lines but then realized that if he had done so, it would alert the farmer.

Mamba was excited by the possibility of, at long last, being able to kill a white man. With adrenalin pumping through his veins, he started to shiver in excitement and anticipation of the imminent action.

Glancing to his left and his right he checked that his men were in position, then at five minutes past eight, when all was quiet, Mamba opened fire on the house, shattering the silence with a long burst of automatic fire. Aiming at the windows where the lights were burning in the right-hand side of the house, the rest of the group followed his lead also firing bursts into the windows.

While they changed their magazines, after the racket of the gunfire and of breaking glass, all that could be heard was the sound of a dog barking inside the house.

Suddenly, as they waited, a large dog came bounding around the right side of the house, barking as it searched for the intruders. Still, they held their fire and waited. Two booming reports from a shotgun, fired from one of the windows at the left end of the house where they had not concentrated any of their initial attack, made them put their heads down as pellets scattered in the bushes around them.

This told them that someone was still alive inside the house, and was retaliating. Mamba fired a short burst in the direction of the window, and the two men on his left did the same. The house was plunged into darkness as all the lights went out.

After a short lull, with only the dog barking and sniffing around, a flood light was switched on; temporary blinding them, and they immediately came under fire. A man appeared from the right side of the house, firing in their direction as he ran towards a large tree in the garden, with the dog at his heels. Mamba heard a grunt from one of the men on his right.

Squinting through the bright light, he switched his attention quickly to this threat and fired a short raking burst at the running figure. He saw the man stumble and fall before reaching the safety of the tree. He fired another burst at the man lying on the ground, who remained motionless.

The dog started rushing around barking frantically as it tried to protect its master, and at the same time searching for the attackers; the high security fence around the house prevented it from getting to them. Mamba fired a burst at the dog and heard it yelp as it collapsed in a heap and started to whine.

The firing stopped, and a deafening silence replaced the din and rattle of gunfire. The air was filled with the smell of cordite. The crickets and cicadas screeched, the occasional tinkle of glass and the whining dog were only sounds. The attack had lasted less than thirty minutes, and with the farmer lying dead on the ground, their mission was complete. It was time to move.

Signalling for his men to retreat they took off as fast as they could.

As they retreated, Mamba noticed that one of the men was missing, but having planned their escape route in advance, expected him to catch up in a little while. Ten minutes later, he called a short stop for them to regroup.

"Where is Tsotsi?" Mamba asked.

"When the lights came on, the man came out of the house shooting at Tsotsi as he ran to the tree," Robson said. "Must we wait or go back for him?"

"No. We have already been too long and must move now. If he is not dead, he will be captured. We must not concern ourselves with him any longer. He is a casualty of war."

"Must we just leave him and not try to help him?"

"I said leave him! Now move out."

Although the night was dark and there was no moon, the group found it easy to follow a road leading to the east, and away from the farm; the direction they wanted to go. By the morning they had covered about 20 miles and were passing through the tribal trust area, so pressed on until mid-morning before stopping to rest and eat, about 40 miles from the scene of their attack. Mamba felt it would be safe to stop and rest there until nightfall. His men were still a little surly about leaving one of their comrades behind, but they would have to get over it.

As the sun was setting, they moved on. Knowing that the Rhodesian Security forces would be searching for them, Mamba pushed his men as hard and as fast as they could move. Only being able to travel in the dark to avoid detection, he hoped to be able to cover 20 to 30 miles every night.

As dawn was breaking every morning, they found high ground where they could hide while they rested for the day, and plan the route for that night. When they stopped, it was essential for them to have a good view of their back trail, so that they would be able to see if any soldiers were following them. They would need plenty of time to set an ambush for pursuers; if they came after them.

Skirting around Nyangombe village, they made their way towards Madioma, at the foothills of the mountains along the border. They made good time, but by the third day had run out of food, and were all starting to get very hungry. Water was not a problem as they topped up their water bottles whenever they crossed a stream or river. They were using a lot of energy and needed food.

On the morning of the fourth day, they reached a group of huts in the foothills of the high Inyanga Mountains, along the eastern border of Rhodesia. At their briefing, they had been told that the people in this village were sympathizers and supporters of the freedom fighters and would be willing to feed them. As it was still too early for anyone to be moving about, Mamba decided to hide in the trees, and watch the kraal for an hour. Not long after the sun lit up the mountains, he sent one of his men forward to check the occupants, while they covered him from their hiding place. With the all-clear being signaled, they all moved into the kraal.

The only people in the kraal were an elderly woman and her grandson. She had seen them approaching and did not appear to be disturbed by their presence. After greeting her gruffly, Mamba questioned the old woman.

"Where is your husband grandmother?" he asked

"He has gone to see his uncle in Umtali. He will be back next week," she said.

"You can see that we are soldiers of the liberation army. Why is it that you are helping us, and feeding us your food?" Mamba asked.

"Because my husband said we must do so. It is not my place to argue with what he tells me to do," the old woman said.

"Who is the boy?"

"He is my grandson and the child of my eldest daughter who lives in Salisbury,"

"If you inform on us I will come back and kill you and your grandson and your husband," Mamba told her.

"Nobody will know that you have been here," she responded pulling the boy around behind her protectively.

"We are going to rest for the day over there in the trees. But we are hungry and will need food," Mamba said pointing in the direction of the path leading to the hills. "You will make food for us, and when it is ready send it to us with the boy."

"I will prepare some hot food for you. Please, you must not hurt the child."

"As long as you do as you are ordered he will not come to any harm."

"He will take the goats out to graze, and in the afternoon he will bring them back to the kraal. Then he will bring you food."

"You must have something we can eat in the meantime," Mamba said.

"There are some few scraps in the pot."

The four insurgents squatted down in the hut, and the old woman gave them what little food she had left over from the previous day, and some tea.

Slightly refreshed and taking care to cover their tracks, they moved off into the forest on the far side of the kraal about 100 paces past a large Marula tree. Finding a suitable spot in the dense undergrowth, they took cover to rest. It was a good spot where they could keep watch on the path they had been following to the kraal; they could also keep an eye on the old woman and the young boy, as well as being able to see the area behind the huts, the direction from where their enemy might come.

Mamba felt confident that they had escaped, and avoided any pursuit. They had taken cover close to the path they would follow when it became dark after they had eaten their meal. With no sign of rain, the last leg of their flight should be easy. This was going to be the last night march during which they would safely cross into Mozambique. His only regret was having lost one of his men; it would be a black mark on his leadership ability.

The young boy herded the goats out onto the cleared area to graze, then went to play under the Marula Tree where he could watch them. The old woman could be seen shuffling around between the huts carrying out her daily chores; sweeping and grinding the corn for their meal into powder on her stone. The day wore on with the temperature rising.

As the sun was sinking towards the horizon, Mamba heard the old woman call the young boy who got up, gathered his small flock of goats and herded them back into the kraal. He disappeared into the kitchen hut with the old woman, and emerged a few moments later carrying a bag and walked along the path in their direction. When the boy reached the edge of the forest, Mamba gave a low whistle to guide him to their hiding place. The boy handed them the packet of food and retreated a little way before squatting down with his back to them, where he could watch the path and the huts through the undergrowth.

After having enjoyed the food, the packet with the empty utensils was handed back to the youth, who returned to the huts and his grandmother. The four men settled back to wait for the sun to set and dark to close in before moving.

Their stomachs full and feeling well rested; the freedom fighters were relaxed and confident that they would be back in Mozambique before the morning. They had escaped the Security Forces; there had been no sign of them being followed, and the chance of being caught now was very slim.

Two hours later Mamba got up, signaled to his men then led them off along the path toward Mozambique and safety. Mamba was very pleased with himself; he had killed his first white man and had got away with it. It was a good start.

****

Part One - Rhodesia
(1962-1977)

Chapter 1

Tom grew up on his father's farm in South Africa. The farm had been awarded to his father by a grateful South African government in recognition of his services as an officer in the South African army during the Second World War. It was one of the many farms that had been destroyed during the Anglo Boer War. Winterbourne farm was a cold, windy, barren, miserable place.

After the NATS (Afrikaans Nationalist Party) won the elections in 1948 and took control of the country, Land Bank loans were difficult for English speaking farmers to obtain. As Tom's father was unable to borrow against the value of the property, he had to supplement the family income by doing a number of other jobs.

He managed a timber sawmill in the area, bred and trained two racehorses running on the Reef racing circuit, and had a wattle stripping contract in Swaziland. The family learned to be resourceful and completely self-sufficient in order to survive.

Being so isolated and surrounded by hostile neighbours, Tom, his older sister, and his *umfaan* (young black companion) Themba were constant companions and did everything together.

He remembered gathering mushrooms in early misty mornings; the bright red 'Turks Head' flowers dotted like pom-poms in the veld; picking wild Cape gooseberries and masobo-sobos (little wild blue berries) to make jam. They helped to compact the sheep's wool in the bales during the shearing season, emerging dripping with oil, and also remembered how they stung when they had a hot bath after sliding down haystacks all day.

They learned to swim in the Usutu River, which ran through the middle of the farm and were taught how to ride horses at an early age. The family did not own a motor car, and they depended completely on horses, which were an essential part of their lives, and their only means of transport.

As they got a little older, they learned how to 'break in' and train their own horses. Once every two or three months, the few English speaking people would gather on one of their farms to enjoy themselves and catch up on their news. Tom and his family all used to ride to these gatherings. Telephones were a luxury. In all the time the family lived on the farm they had neither electricity nor running water.

The family was constantly being threatened and intimidated by their Afrikaans neighbours: Their sheep were stolen; haystacks of winter feed burned and their dogs were poisoned. With the build-up to national elections, the NATS increased their intimidation and did everything in their power to prevent people from voting for the mainly English, United Party.

Because of the transport problems, and the remoteness of where they lived, from an early age Tom was sent off to boarding school in Natal. Although the school was an English medium school, there was an Afrikaans medium school not far away. The 'Boer War' continued between the young boys.

Eventually, after years of struggle, the farm was sold, and Tom's father bought a farm in Swaziland; a British Protectorate. Everyone in the family seemed to relax and settle down into a much more pleasant lifestyle in a country run by English speaking people and headed by a British Resident Commissioner. Tom and his sister moved to a school in Mbabane and assisted his father with farming operations whenever he had the chance.

From their home high up on the mountain, they had beautiful views of the town and the Ezulweni valley. Ezulweni in the SiSwati language means Heaven. Tom remembered Albert Dlamini, the farm foreman telling him of a Swazi man, who had been up in the hills around Mbabane attending a meeting, to drink beer made from millet.

On his way home he decided to have a sleep on the wayside. Clouds descended to the level just below the mountain tops on either side of the valley with Mbabane above the cloud level. When the hungover bleary-eyed fellow woke up in the morning, he was above the clouds. Thinking that he had died and gone to heaven, he cried out "Ezulweni" (Heaven).

Wattle trees had been planted on the hills surrounding Mbabane and along all the streams on the farm, and when they were in flower, it was quite beautiful. The dark green leaves contrasting with the bright yellow blossoms that filled the air with their lovely scent.

Tom played rugby for the School First Team. On a rugby trip to the Eastern Transvaal accompanied by the girls' hockey team, he met and fell in love with a beautiful girl with long dark hair who played hockey for the Convent. After the games were finished, all the players met in the school hall for refreshments. One of the girls in the school hockey team introduced him to Julia who played for the opposing hockey team.

She was the most beautiful girl he had ever met. She had long dark hair and an outgoing, happy personality. They got on well from the outset and agreed to keep in touch. He fell head over heels in love with her. After returning to their respective schools, they corresponded daily and met up whenever the opportunity arose.

Apart from meeting up at inter-school sports functions, during the holidays they met up at Julia's mother's ranch where they swam in the river; they met up at her uncle's farm in Ezulweni where they frolicked in the pool and lay in the sun; Julia came to Tom's home, and they went riding together.

They went to dances and played tennis at the Country Club and went swimming in the pools at Mantanga Falls at the foothills of the mountains near Ezulweni. Whenever they were together, they had a lot of fun and were oblivious to others around them. They only had eyes for each other. Everyone loved Julia she was such a lovely happy person.

Their romance was so intense that it began to affect their schooling, so their parents kept apart as much as possible. After passing their exams at the end of that year, Julia was sent off to finishing school. Although she objected and told her parents that she did not want to go, they were adamant. Vowing to keep in contact with each other and to meet up whenever the opportunity arose, they parted.

By the time she finished her year at the finishing school, Tom had hoped to be launched on a career. Both of them were heartbroken but knew that they would soon be together again. A year was not too long to wait. Time and distance played its part, and with Tom moving around from place to place with his work and Julia a long way away, they eventually lost touch with each other.

Tom saw a recruiting advertisement in a careers magazine for the British South Africa Police in Rhodesia. Although Tom's ambition was to become a successful farmer, it looked like an exciting career to pursue, and he sent off an application. He also heard that young farmers were wanted in that country. Joining the police force would be a good starting point in his quest to get a farm of his own. If he moved to Rhodesia, he would get Julia to follow him there.

Shortly after applying to join the Rhodesian Police Force, he was offered a job on a cattle ranch in the Lowveld of Swaziland. He gladly accepted the offer and in next to no time settled into the work with gusto. He thoroughly enjoyed what he was doing. His duties included dipping the cattle, maintaining the fence lines, assisting in the farm store and shooting four head of impala a day to keep the butchery supplied with meat.

A temporary construction camp had been built on the ranch to house all the workers building the railway line into Swaziland from Mozambique. The ranch supplied all the food required to feed the 200 hungry workers housed in the camp.

Dipping the cattle, to prevent tick infestations, was always an exciting time on the ranch. Sitting outside under the trees the evening before dip day, the whistles of the cattle herdsmen could be heard as they wandered around the camps calling their cattle. Each herdsman had a different whistle - all made from cow horn. By the morning all the cattle had arrived at the dipping tank and herded into the plunge tank.

After being dipped, those cattle with wounds had them treated. The young animals with horns starting to show were de-horned, to prevent them from hurting other animals, and then branded with the ranch brand using red-hot irons. The young bullocks were castrated.

At the end of the day after the cattle were all returned to their camps the beer drinking and party started in the compound. The women beat the drums, and the men danced around the fire leaping high and stamping the dusty ground with their bare feet as each one told a story of his achievements and conquests. The party went on most of the night and was typically the sound of Africa.

Although Tom was still pining for his lost love, Julia, life in Swaziland was good. During the season Tom played rugby and polo and went to parties most weekends. Most of the young men just out of school were away at University or College, so a young man was in demand and kept busy on the social scene with far too much drinking.

All in all, life was pretty hectic, but he was enjoying himself. He met his beloved Julia after playing in a rugby match against Nelspruit. Her family had moved to Malelane which explained how they had lost touch with each other. He was over the moon and very much in love with her again.

Six months after applying to join the police force, Tom received a letter from the BSA Police inviting him to report to Salisbury to attend a selection interview. Having now settled into his new job, Tom did not know what to do.

He had not told his parents that he had applied to join the police force in Rhodesia and wanted to spring it on them at the last moment to prevent any obstacles being put in his way. He knew that his father would be happy for him knowing that his son had matured early and had been doing a man's job for the past two years, but his mother might not want her boy to go off into the unknown world and so far away.

He had a burning desire to own his own farm and could not see how he was going to achieve this in Swaziland, and certainly not in South Africa. Although Tom was settled into a job on a ranch whose directors all owned farms in Natal, and he enjoyed working for them, the prospect of venturing into an unknown country excited him. He decided to discuss his predicament with Mike, his boss.

"Listen here lad, you go up to Rhodesia and feel the water. If you don't like it, there will always be a place for you back here on the ranch," he advised. "I will let the directors know what is happening."

"Thanks very much, Mike. I really appreciate what you have done for me," Tom said happily shaking his boss by the hand.

The decision was made for him, and with the blessing of the directors, Tom resigned two weeks before he was due in Salisbury. He was delighted and relieved to know that if he did not make the selection, he would still have a job on the ranch.

When Tom broke the news to his parents, who had moved to Mozambique and lived in a cottage at Catembe, they were delighted and agreed with his decision to move out of Swaziland. They even assisted him in making the arrangements for his journey. His father bought him a rail ticket, and his mother fussed around thinking of all sorts of things he might need to ensure his comfort.

He was so excited that the days to his departure dragged by and he could hardly sleep a wink as he tried to visualize the kind of life he was going to lead and what the country and its people were going to be like. His one regret was leaving Julia behind again.

****

Chapter 2

In a cloud of dust and with a neck-jarring thump, the car came to rest up against a large rock on the verge ten paces from the side of the gravel road. They had been rushing to get the next checkpoint ahead of the competitors in the Castrol Rally, and after leaving the border control post into Mozambique, Vince lost control of the car rounding a sharp bend, and they careered off the road.

"Dam it all. I was going much too fast. This is all we need now," Vince shouted slamming the steering wheel with his fist.

"You're bloody right. I've got a train to catch this evening. Let's hope there isn't too much damage. The border post is about to close, so I don't think we have a hope in hell of getting a lift," Tom said as they leaped out of the car to check the damage.

The front headlight was smashed, and the wing on the driver's side was pushed onto the front tire which was flat. Luckily there was no other damage and with the aid of a fencing-standard Tom found nearby they managed to bend the mudguard away from the wheel. After changing the wheel, they were soon on their way again.

Vince had asked Tom to assist him with his marshaling duties on the Mbabane to Lourenco Marques section of the rally. It had been such a busy, exciting day for them with all the competitors flying through their checkpoints that Tom hardly had the time to think about his decision to move to Rhodesia.

Arriving at the finish later than they had planned did not leave Tom much time to spend with his family who was in Lourenco Marques to see him off. After a quick meal and a few words of advice from his father, he was bundled onto the train and sent on his way.

Tom sat on his own in the compartment, gazing out of the window, trying to deal with his emotions. The steam engine gave a long whistle now and then as the train picked up speed leaving the outskirts of the city behind. It soon settled down to a steady clickety-clack, clickety-click, clickety-clack, as it rocked back and forth, traveling into the sparsely inhabited cattle and game ranching areas of southern Mozambique. The train was travelling passing through open grassland with Leadwood, Acacia, and Marula trees dotting the vista.

As it progressed, the train passed the occasional village where the inhabitants were busy corralling their cattle and goats at the end of the day. Their plots of maize adjacent to their mud huts shone a bright emerald green in the twilight. The train was heading north-west into Rhodesia and ultimately, via Bulawayo to Salisbury; the only way to travel from Lourenco Marques to Salisbury was by train.

Not long after leaving Lourenco Marques, just as the sun was setting, they crossed the Limpopo River, and there, on the banks, a small herd of elephant could be seen slaking their thirst before the moving off for the night.

High in the darkening deep blue sky, a few wispy clouds were turned a bright pink by the setting sun. The rest of the passing county side was bathed with a golden yellow light with the tops of the taller trees painted orange and yellow. The shadows cast by the trees became longer and longer as night set in, as the temperature dropped.

With nothing more to be seen out of the window, Tom stirred out of his reverie. Organizing his bedding and stowing his blanket roll, he locked his compartment and made his way forward to the dining saloon.

A group of five English speaking young men were propping up the bar, and two high ranking Portuguese Army Officers were seated at a table having dinner. The group at the bar seemed to be having a wonderful time, with laughter and jokes flying among them. Tom eased himself into a corner of the bar and ordered a beer just before the largest of the group at the bar turned to greet him.

"Hello there, young fellow. You look like a man from the bush," he said, commenting on Tom who was wearing a khaki shirt and trousers and tire soled shoes. "Why don't you come over and join us?" He made room for Tom who smiled eagerly and moved over. Tom needed the company.

"Where are you headed for?" the big fellow asked.

"I'm going to Salisbury," Tom replied, happy to be included in the merriment.

"My name is Bobby; we're the remnants of a cricket team from Triangle. We've been on a cricket tour to Mhlume in Swaziland. The rest of the team returned home two days ago; we stayed behind a couple of days to see friends," he explained introducing himself and the rest of the party.

"I'm Tom. I was working on Mlaula Ranch, right next door to Mhlume, until a week ago. I heard that there had been a cricket match. I'm on my way to join the police force in Rhodesia," Tom explained. They all agreed that the BSAP was indeed a fine police force and nothing at all like the South African Police.

Most of the group were sugar cane growers from the Lowveld in Rhodesia and certainly seemed to know how to have a good time. Many beers later they all decided to play 'Bok-Bok', a game where the players are divided into two teams with one team leaping onto the backs of the other team. The 'horses' then try to buck the 'riders' off. The game is only played by men who are very drunk. The bartender and the now drunk Customs and Immigration officer were also included.

After much laughter, and a few more drinks they decided that it was time to 'hit the hay.' Assuring the wild bunch of farmers that he would visit them in the Lowveld as soon as he had completed his training, Tom staggered off to his compartment to get some sleep.

A few hours later Tom was awakened by the stillness, and lack of movement of the train. He raised the window blind and looked out onto Malvernia station. It was just getting light, and a few people were leaving the train with bundles of goods. The two army officers, who had been in the dining saloon the night before, also left the train disappearing into the railway station.

The guard was standing on the platform, shouting in Portuguese, and waving his arms at the departing passengers. The train had pulled up at the border between Mozambique and Rhodesia. As it pulled off again, Tom saw another sign reading, 'Vila Salazar. Welcome to Rhodesia'.

The train picked up speed and settled down to a steady rhythm. The sound of the wheels on the track reminded Tom of his school day journeys home. The sound seemed to be saying 'clickety-clack don't go back, clickety-clack can't go back.'

The Immigration Officer moved through the train, checking tickets once again, and this time, passports. They had entered Rhodesia. When asked to see his passport, Tom asked about the two names on the station. Apparently, at the time of building the railway line from Lourenco Marques to Rhodesia, Salazar had been the president of

Portugal and Lord Malvern the Prime Minister of Rhodesia. In recognition of the two leaders, the town on the Portuguese side had been named after Lord Malvern and the Rhodesian village named after Salazar. His curiosity satisfied, he settled back in his bunk and dozed off again.

Two hours later, when the train stopped at Mbizi siding, Tom leaned out of the window to wave goodbye to his Triangle friends, who were getting off there. The sun was starting to climb up into the sky, and the surrounding countryside was bathed in warm light orange. It was springtime, and all the trees and bushes were showing off their new foliage. Tom had never seen such an array of colors on trees; a mixture of greens and ochre's, with touches of almost pink, red and burnt orange everywhere he looked.

Shortly after leaving the small siding, Tom saw a herd of wild dogs moving off into the bush on the side of the rail track. They looked beautiful with the early morning sunlight lighting up the yellow and white patches on their dark brown coats, and showed off their long fluffy tails and big rounded ears.

The train was passing through countryside that was quite different from the Swaziland Lowveld. The terrain was fairly flat terrain with a number of large granite domes, and small hills sprinkled with massive boulders. Mopani trees and Mopani scrub in masses mixed with Musasa, Acacia, Leadwood, Pod Mahogany, and Marula trees filled the vista. In the distance, he could see a range of blue hills.

Tom spent the rest of the day gazing out of the window enjoying the passing scenery. He was heading for a new part of the world where he knew nobody and very little about the country that was to become his new home.

****

Chapter 3

With a long, loud whistle, the train slowed down as it entered
Bulawayo. It was early evening by the time it pulled in to the station
and stopped, and with a tired sigh, the engine released clouds of white
steam. Picking up his blanket roll, Tom jumped down onto the
platform and went in search of refreshment. He had three hours to kill
before boarding the train to Salisbury.

As he strolled around the station, looking for a tea room, Tom
bumped into Phil, one of his good friends from school.

"What in the hell are you doing here?" he asked incredulously. They
were both a long way from their homes, and in another country.

"I am on my way to join the Rhodesian Police. And what are you
doing here? I thought you were still in Swaziland," Phil replied with a
broad grin.

"I'm also on my way to join the Police," Tom laughed.

"That's incredible. Last I heard you were working on a Ranch in the
Bushveld. Were you anywhere near Balegane and old man Foresters
farm?" asked Phil referring to their old headmaster at school.

"Yes, but about 50 miles from there and closer to the Lebombo
Mountains. The ranch was next door to the King's Country where we
used to help capture impala for Mlilwane Game Reserve," Tom
explained.

They spoke fast. Having not been in contact for over two years,
both were amazed at the coincidence of meeting on the station in the
middle of nowhere, and at the fact that both of them were heading for
the same destination. They were pleased to have the company and
chance to share this adventure. It brought confidence. They had a lot
of catching up to do.

Early the following morning a mule cart with the driver, met them
at Salisbury Station. Sitting in the back of the cart with their luggage,
gaping around, they were driven slowly along First Street in the middle
of the city. The people in Salisbury, being well aware of the regular
monthly police intakes, caught sight of the mule wagon, with the two

young men perched on the back, leaned out of office windows and stood in shop doorways to wave and to greet the newcomers. It made them feel welcome in this friendly young country.

They progressed slowly through the city and into the residential areas where wide avenues were lined with Jacaranda trees in full bloom. Their fallen blue and purple flowers formed a richly hued carpet; as if laid out especially for them. This glorious sight made their arrival seem even more welcoming. An hour after being collected at the station, they were delivered to their hotel in the avenues, to wait for their interviews.

While Tom was unpacking, a brown paper bag fell on the floor. It had been given to him on the eve of his departure from the ranch by Danger, the ranch mechanic, with strict instruction not to open it until he arrived in Rhodesia. He opened the paper bag, and inside were half a dozen pieces of tree root used for cleaning teeth, and a photograph of Danger dressed in a tuxedo, after winning the Natal Sugar Mills heavyweight boxing tournament.

To fill the time, Tom and Phil visited the museum on the west side of the Salisbury Koppie, to do some research into the country's background. Financed by Cecil John Rhodes, a Pioneer Column consisting of 130 ox-drawn wagons with 200 settlers, 200 policemen and 200 men from the Pioneer Corps set off from Mafeking in South Africa, to establish a British Colony in the north.

After a long, hard journey taking five months, the column eventually stopped in the middle of a vast, mainly uninhabited, grassland plain. There was ample water in the Makabuzi River and a high Koppie (small rocky hill) for a lookout post. The Union Jack was hoisted on the 13th September 1890 and Salisbury founded. The country was named Rhodesia.

At the time of the occupation of Mashonaland, large tracts of land were desolate, and the people were very poor. Slave traders had taken millions of people, resulting in many tribes vanishing completely. The estimated black population in the country at the time was 275000 with sufficient land for everyone.

In 1896 there were uprisings by the Ndebele and the Shona people who protested against white rule. Peace settlements were reached with the Ndebele, but the Shona chiefs would not sign any treaty and had to be defeated in some vicious battles and skirmishes. Rhodesia was established by right of conquest. Road and rail links were built soon afterward.

Other prospective recruits from South Africa and the outlying areas of Rhodesia joined Tom and Phil over the next few days. Not knowing what to expect, they all waited nervously to be interviewed by a panel of Police Officers. The prospect of returning to Swaziland so soon did not appeal to Tom.

Being one of the first to arrive he was the first to be interviewed. He was questioned about his upbringing, what his reasons for wanting to join the police force were. Tom heard with sheer delight that he had been accepted, amazingly along with the other applicants, and they all moved from the hotel to the Police Training Depot - their holiday was over.

The first morning a Sergeant called them all out of the barracks, and ordered them to 'Fall In' on the 'Hard Square'. After milling about trying to locate the hard square, they finally gathered on the hard surfaced parade ground.

"Wot you fink this is? A Debutante's Ball?" the Sergeant bellowed at them.

"Form up in three lines and be quick about it," he ordered then marched up and down the lines eyeballing them, one at a time.

"'Ave you 'ad a shave today?" he asked Tom

"No sergeant, I only shave once a week," Tom replied.

"Well you're a man now, not a boy, and you will shave every day. Do I make myself clear?"

"Yes Sergeant."

"Get yourself down to Shamrock Barbers and get an 'aircut. Short back and sides will cost you three shillings and sixpence," he ordered Tom, who had had a haircut the day before leaving Swaziland.

"You lot had better get to know the bugle calls. From now on the bugle calls will run your lives."

Two days later the recruits from the UK arrived. They had spent two weeks on an ocean liner to Cape Town and then a three-day train trip to Salisbury. Tom considered them a funny looking bunch with pale white skin and accents that were difficult to understand.

The next six months was one long nightmare which none of the recruits had been expecting. The instructors chased them around, shouted at them, and chivvied all day long, with everything being done 'On the Double'. They had drill instruction, known as 'square bashing', equitation instruction, life-saving, riot drill, musketry, law and policing, unarmed combat, assault courses, cross country runs. It was not unusual to hear a recruit after another hard day say, "I thought we had joined the police force, not the bloody army." The Squad Instructor pointed out to them that as the BSA Police were the first line of defense in the country, they had to be equipped with all the necessary skills.

At the end of the six months, those who had completed the training course performed a passing out parade. This consisted of two separate parades; a drill display performed on the 'Hard Square' followed by a Mounted Display on horseback and carried out on the large grassed field, half the size of a rugby field, and in the middle of the Training Depot. This was the hallowed 'Green Square' and only used for passing out parades. It was a big day for the recruits with family and friends being invited to attend.

Tom applied himself and performed well in all the disciplines. He was the leading file in the equitation school and right-hand marker on the parade ground. With his experience of hunting, he easily qualified as a marksman with a rifle.

After 'Passing Out' the recruits moved to the driver Training Depot where they underwent motorcycle, motor vehicle, heavy duty, and high-speed driving instruction. Once qualified and with the necessary licenses, Tom was posted to Salisbury Central, where he was to 'walk a beat' for the next two months, before being transferred to Harare Police Station in the southern suburbs or what was known as the 'Black South'.

Language and cultural backgrounds were so diverse in Rhodesia that it was necessary for a white policeman to be paired up with a black policeman. This worked very well as each team developed a bond of understanding and assisted each other with investigations, interpretations, and support. They also witnessed to each other's actions during their duties. This was very important as suspects were quick to try and accuse policemen of assault and other misdemeanors.

For the two years that Tom was stationed at Harare and Stodart satellite station, his right-hand man was Constable Lucas Mpofu who was a Shona from Chiweshi Tribal Trust* area to the north of Salisbury. They learned how to trust and understand each other, always reacting quickly to situations without the need for unnecessary discussion.

Before reaching the age of 20, Tom was investigating crimes ranging from petty theft to murder, rape, and stoning. He became efficient in his work and was well respected by his peers. Although he enjoyed his work as a police officer and was having a good social life in Salisbury, the prospect of working in uniform and having to salute officers for twenty years before being able to retire on a meager pension did not appeal to him as a long-term career.

Tom saved up and bought a second-hand car. This made life a lot easier for him, and he was able to explore the surrounding countryside and farming areas. During his travels, he met some farmers and in next to no time had friends who were managers on tobacco farms. Being a farming boy, he fitted in easily. Many a weekend was spent on these farms with Tom finding out more and more about the farming industry in Rhodesia.

As promised, Tom took some leave and went to visit his friends from the Lowveld that he had met on the train. Taking Basil, a friend who was also stationed in the 'Black South,' with him they headed south. Stopping for a day at Lake Kyle on the way, they spent time exploring the Zimbabwe Ruins. The ruins were fascinating with their neat, precise stonework and obviously built by Arab Slave traders. Lake Kyle was a huge stretch of water and had been built to supply water for irrigation schemes in the Lowveld.

Around the shores of the large lake were some Chalets and camping grounds for fishermen and water sports enthusiasts. The whole area was surrounded by granite hills and rocky outcrops and Musasa forests; a place of quietness, and natural beauty.

From there they traveled on to the Lowveld (so called because it is less than 800 feet above sea level) and the vast fertile areas of emerald green Sugar Cane fields with the 'tshick, tshick, tshick' of overhead irrigation sprinklers spraying silver arcs of water onto the crops. The bright red flowers of the Flamboyant's and yellow flowers of the Cassia trees were a blaze of glory; a welcome sight after traveling for miles on a corrugated dirt road through the hot, dry surrounding countryside. It reminded Tom very much of the Swaziland Bushveld.

There they were hosted and wonderfully entertained by Bobby, and the other friends Tom had met on the train, on his way up to Rhodesia the previous year. They spent four days in the Lowveld being shown around, and partying in the Country Club, watching polo followed by more partying. The Lowveld is an extremely hot part of the country where, with water, everything grows well. The un-irrigated sweet veld is very good for cattle ranching, producing some of the best beef in the world.

On the ranches, large herds of impala, wildebeest, zebra, and buffalo roamed freely. Because of the extreme heat, people in the Lowveld drink a lot, and all houses are air-conditioned. Tom was impressed by the happy, carefree lifestyle of the sugar growers and the ranchers.

"When you leave the police force, if you still want to go farming, you must come and work here," his friend Bobby told him.

"I might just do that," Tom replied earnestly, as he said goodbye.

His visit to the Lowveld had given Tom a lot to think about. Although the lifestyle and the people in the Lowveld tempted him into considering getting a job there after he left the police force, the farm managers on tobacco farms in the Highveld were earning good production bonuses that made it possible for young farmers to buy farms within a few short years. When the time came, he decided, he would look for a job on a tobacco farm.

****

Chapter 4

Rhodesia at the time was entering the same political landscape that was sweeping through the sub-continent, with the black population wanting their 'freedom.' They looked to the countries in the north that had won their independence from colonialism and which in some countries had been handed to them on a plate. Unrest and dissatisfaction was on the increase and was being stirred up by the political leaders. Incidents of violence were taking place all over the country. The police were kept fully occupied monitoring political gatherings and meetings.

During their working relationship, apart from the usual police investigations, Tom and Lucas were involved with riots and political disturbances on a weekly basis. The waiting, at political meetings, knowing that riots were about to break out, was always a nerve-wracking time with 'butterflies' in the stomach and adrenalin starting to pump. Once the action started, with people running around and sticks and stones flying in all directions, the nervousness disappeared.

"Watch out sir! They have got petrol bombs," Lucas shouted to Tom during one of the riots.

"Don't let any of them near the Land Rover. They will put a stone on the door handle then set us on fire with petrol bombs, and we will be trapped inside the vehicle," said Tom.

The youths had learned this tactic in the early days of rioting.

They were chasing a group of about thirty youngsters who were particularly aggressive. Their leader was a tall young man wearing dark glasses who seemed to have his gang well organized. Tom recognized him from other incidents of violence, and he always seemed to be able to avoid being arrested.

"Lucas, we must try to apprehend that man wearing dark glasses and a blue shirt. He is definitely a ringleader," Tom said.

"Yes, Sir. I will make inquiries and try to find out where he stays," Lucas said.

Not long after this incident, all meetings of a political nature were banned and 'Operation Cordon Sanitaire' was carried out. The army surrounded the location while police screened the residents resulting in hundreds of known agitators being arrested and detained in remote camps under the emergency regulations. The rioting stopped, and they did not see the young youth leader again. He seemed to have disappeared or had possibly been detained.

....

Although Tom was kept fully occupied performing his various duties as a policeman, time seemed to pass slowly. Had he been posted to a rural station in a farming area things might have been a lot better for him. He would have been working in the farming community, and the farmers would have got to know him well. He had applied for a rural posting but as was the normal case those who applied for rural postings were sent to urban posts and those who applied for urban were given rural posts. He had to make do and bide his time.

He was, however, enjoying the carefree life he was living. Living in a city with its fast life, and having access to the variety of entertainment and pleasures, was a new experience for Tom. He played rugby for the Police Club and rowed in the police fours. There was motor racing, weekends on farms, parties to attend, and a host of girls were always available to assist and accompany him in these pleasures. Life on the social and sporting side was extremely good for him, and he was having a lot of fun.

On the social side, he had met and had some casual affairs with girls but was still carrying a torch for his first love, Julia. They had made contact with each other again and corresponded regularly. Tom suggested that she join him in Rhodesia, so she agreed to come for a short holiday. He was waiting nervously for her at the station when the train arrived from Bulawayo in the early morning, they had not seen each other since he left Swaziland nearly two years ago, and he did not know what to expect. His heart almost stopped when Julia stepped down onto the platform. She had matured into a beautiful woman with the same lovely long dark brown hair. When she saw him, a big happy smile spread across her face as she rushed into his outstretched arms.

"Hello, Tom. It's so good to see you at last. I've been so excited that the train trip seemed to take forever. But I am here at last," she said.

"I thought you might've changed your mind and not been on the train. It's wonderful to have you here at last. We haven't seen each other for two years. I've missed you," Tom said hugging her tightly.

"I've missed you too," Julia gave Tom a long kiss. "I've been dying to be with you again."

"Well you're here now, and we only have a week, so we must make the most of it. I have lots to show you. This is such a wonderful country," Tom said picking up her suitcase.

"Goodness me, but you look so smart in your uniform. I hardly recognized you," Julia teased.

"And you are even more beautiful than before. Come along let's get you to your hotel. I have the rest of the day off. We'll just go via my digs so that I can change before getting you settled in." Tom took her hand and led her to his car.

Tom took a few days leave to be with Julia. She was only going to be there for a week, and he intended spending every minute of the time with her. They stayed together at the hotel in the avenues and every day went exploring; the first day he took her up the Kopje where they had a good view of the city and surrounding areas and then they went on to the museum.

The second day Tom got the hotel kitchen to prepare a picnic lunch for them, and they went off to spend the day at Mermaids Pool. Located 30 miles to the east of Salisbury, it was a delightful picnic spot where a small river cascaded over a series of flat granite rocks before splashing into a deep pool. Being a weekday, they had the place to themselves.

"Come on, let's jump into the water and have a swim," Julie suggested.

"I am all in favor of that. After all, that's what we came out here for," agreed Tom, going behind a tree to get changed then stood guard while Julie donned her bikini.

They had great fun climbing to the top of the rocks then sliding down in the water to plunge into the pool at the bottom. Tom chased Julie around in the water eventually capturing her in a bear hug that turned into a long lingering kiss exciting them both. The next thing they knew, they had both lost their costumes and were making love in the water. Tom felt a great tenderness for Julia as they recovered their costumes, and lay down on a rug they had spread out on the grass. It was the first time they had made love together, and he felt that his heart was going to burst as he gazed into her green eyes. Julia smiled back at Tom and put her arms around him.

"Do you still love me, Tom?"

"More than you can ever imagine. You mean everything to me," Tom replied, squeezing her tight.

When they had warmed up, they came together again and this time made love slowly under the African sky with the sun on their naked bodies. On their return to Salisbury Tom moved into Julia's room.

The next day they went to see the 'Balancing Rocks' to the south of Salisbury. Wandering around hand in hand they were dwarfed by this impressive display of gigantic granite rocks, stacked precariously on top of each other without any support. Some of these rocks were the size of small houses. They then went north out of Salisbury to Mazoe dam built on the Mazoe River and around the corner from there they found a small hotel near Jumbo mine where they had lunch.

They spent a day at Lake Maclwane, a large dam west of Salisbury. They had lunch at one of the hotels around the Musasa lined shores of the lake after driving around the perimeter visiting yachting, boating and fishing clubs. The dam had been built to supply Salisbury with water and was a popular recreational venue.

In the evenings they had intimate dinners at restaurants and went dancing at nightclubs always ending up making love until the early hours then sleeping till mid-morning. Their love for each other was as intense as it had been before and grew stronger by the day as they enjoyed being with each other. Julia told Tom all about her year at finishing school in Natal and her job in the bank in Durban. Tom told her about his training and life in the police. He showed her around the Training Depot and took her to have lunch at his quarters where he proudly introduced her to his colleagues.

Time went by all too quickly, and suddenly it was the day before her departure back to South Africa. Phil was going on leave and Julia was getting a lift to Johannesburg with him. She would get the Pullman from there back to Durban. Back in their room after a light dinner, Julia started to pack.

"Julia this last week has been wonderful. I know you have to, but I don't want you to go. I love you very much, and I want to spend the rest of my life with you. Will you marry me?" Tom asked her.

"Yes, Yes, Yes, of course, I will," Julia said turning to kiss and hug Tom tightly. "I was worried that you were just going to let me disappear again."

"Why are you crying when you should be happy?" Tom teased her.

"Because I am a woman and women do these things when they are happy."

"Are you sure you will be happy to come and live here in Rhodesia with me?" Tom said pushing his luck.

"Yes, my darling, of course, I will. I love it here. We can start making plans as soon as you have my parent's permission," Julia said with an evil grin.

"I was afraid you were going to say that. Shall we phone them now?" Tom asked.

"Do your parents know that you are here with me?"

"Yes, they know I am here, and yes let's phone now. I'm so excited," Julia said.

Julia spoke to her mother first and primed her before getting her father on the line and handing the phone to Tom.

"I am sorry to spring this on you, sir. Julia and I would like to get married, and I am asking you for your permission," Tom blurted out after the usual greeting.

"This is not really a surprise, Tom. You and Julia have loved each other for some time and are both adults now. Although you are both young, you know your own minds and what you want. Let me speak with Julia before I give you my decision," Mr. Preston said.

After a brief conversation with her father, Julia handed the receiver back to Tom.

"Tom, it seems that Julia is very happy and wants to marry you. Her mother is standing beside me and nodding her head, so it is our pleasure to give you our blessing," Mr. Preston said.

"Thank you, sir. I promise you I will look after her," Tom assured him hanging up.

Knowing that they would spend the rest of their lives together, parting in the early morning was not too painful. They planned to get married within six months and in the summertime.

****

Chapter 5

Titus Ngopi at 18 years of age was tall and slim. He was bigger, stronger and older than the rest of the boys in his class. He lived with his parents in a village not far from the Mission School he was attending near Kyle Dam outside Fort Victoria when things changed for him.

The Priests at the Mission, where Titus was educated, had sowed the first seeds of being opposed to white Government in his head. Their teaching made him believe that black people should be running the country and not the whites. Why should he have a white education, leave school and find a job working for a white man and obey white men's rules?

During the last school holidays, he had been introduced to a man in Fort Victoria who had impressed him. He spoke of taking the country back from the white oppressors who had stolen the land from the black Shona people. His name was Ndabaninge Sithole, and he was the leader of the Zimbabwe African Nationalist Union (ZANU). He gave Titus his address in Harare Township on the outskirts of Salisbury and told him that he should visit him when he had finished with his schooling. He promised money, smart clothes, a nice house and all the women he needed. What did he need a white education for when he could have all that?

Up until his last year at school, he had been a good pupil, and his grades were better than average. The last year, however, he changed. He disobeyed the teachers and gathered a group of boys around him who terrorized the younger children and leered at the girls. He had taken to wearing dark glasses as he thought they made him look superior.

There was one girl though, who stood up to him and was not intimidated by his taunting. Her name was Maria da Silva, and she got under his skin, always seeming to get the better of him. The fact that she was white annoyed him even more. She was in the same class as he was, but was always better at everything she did; she made him look stupid. She was prettier and better developed than the other girls in the school, and he was tired of her humiliating arrogance. He did not like her at all and would have to find a way to teach her to respect him.

He studied da Silva's daily movements around the Mission. Every afternoon after the classes were over, she would take herself off with a friend up into a small rocky outcrop behind the mission. The two of them would sit in the shade of a mango tree and study there: well out of earshot and isolated from the school. It was a perfect spot to ambush her and to stop her arrogance forever.

One hot sunny Friday afternoon, Titus and his four followers, sneaked up on the two girls, surrounding them they cut off any possible way for them to escape. Two of his gang grabbed hold of Maria's friend, gagged her, and dragged her off around to the other side of the rocks. Titus and the other two boys gagged da Silva and pinned her to the ground. She struggled and kicked as hard as she could but was no match for the stronger boys. Titus raped her while the other two boys held her down.

"That will show you that you are no better than me. If you ever give me any more trouble I will not be so kind," Titus said when he had finished with her.

Titus urinated on her, then leaving her lying in the dirt sobbing, he disappeared with his gang. It was the first time he had raped a girl, and it gave him great pleasure. He would remember the hatred he had seen in her eyes for a long time but the power he felt was overwhelming.

Titus knew they had to run away from school. They would be hunted by the police, and he would go to jail for a long time. He left the others to their own devices in Fort Victoria and made his way to Salisbury where he disappeared into Harare Township. He had no intention of finding a dull regular job preferring the exciting life on the streets. He soon became a member of a gang in the township and was recruited by the Zimbabwe African National Union (ZANU) youth organization. It did not take him long to establish himself as a leader.

He never returned home during the three years he stayed in Harare. He never contacted his family or friends to let them know where he was. He had just disappeared. He did not care; they meant nothing to him and were puppets to the system.

Titus organized attacks on homes of opposition supporters and supporters of the government. His gang would surround their houses at night then throw stones through the windows and at people in or near the house. Passing cars on the main road to the South being driven by white people were also an easy target. They marched into the beer halls in the evenings when the workers were having a drink, and ordered everyone out in the name of ZANU. It always gave him a feeling of power, when the weak workers put their drinks down unfinished and left without offering any resistance or even objections. They barricaded the entrances to the schools and ordered the scholars to return home as there was to be no schooling that day.

Most of all, he enjoyed helping to agitate crowds after political meetings. This usually resulted in riots with sticks, bricks, stones, petrol bombs and any other suitable missile that could be thrown at everyone and anything, including the police Land Rovers and policemen. He operated in the Stodart area and had a few close shaves with a tall young white policeman and his assistant who were stationed there.

The two policemen were well known in the area as a team not to tangle with. He made it his business to study these two men carefully from a distance. He would not forget them and would target them when he got the chance.

Titus was forced to flee the country when the police and army surrounded parts of Harare and began to search all the houses. People known to be involved in political activities in the country were being arrested. He was a prominent leader of a group of youths involved in political activities and at risk of being caught in the net.

As soon as the army surrounded the Stodart area in Harare Township, he managed to slip through the cordon posing as an office worker. He contacted his cell leader who gave him money and put him in touch with another wanted man, Robson. Following the cell leader's instructions, the two of them were able to travel to Mozambique, then on to Tanzania for military training.

At the training camp in Tanzania, the Chinese instructors advised him to use a nickname and not his real name. This would make it difficult, if not almost impossible, to be identified if he was captured: he was on the wanted list in Rhodesia. Titus decided to call himself 'Mamba' as it suited his character; he was like the king of snakes and had used the nickname at school. He carved his name into the butt of the AK47 rifle he was issued.

Mozambique was a colony of Portugal and supported the white Rhodesian Government. Their struggle for independence had been going on for years. Most of their army consisted of conscripts from Portugal who had no real interest in the country, and were known to have an appetite for black women and beer; with the help of a little money, there was no shortage of either.

Because of the lackadaisical attitude of the Mozambique forces, the opposing Frelimo Freedom fighting forces were almost in complete control of certain areas where there was little danger of attack by the military patrols. Bases were set up as staging posts for the comrades preparing to launch attacks into Rhodesia. These bases were close to the border and well-guarded by the Frelimo. One such post was located near Catandica, in a heavily forested area just north of the Pungwe River, not far from the border.

During his training in Tanzania, Titus had shown good leadership skills, dominating the rest of his group. After six months of hard physical drills and indoctrination, he was made a platoon leader. He and Robson, with four others, were sent back to Mozambique to await orders.

When they arrived at the base camp, just 30 miles from the eastern border of Rhodesia, the freedom fighters were kitted out with boots, uniforms, and ammunition. They already had their AK47 rifles.

Despite being kept busy at the base camp, training, cleaning their weapons, learning the latest techniques in the laying of landmines and booby traps, Mamba was eager to get back into Rhodesia and to have the chance to attack soft targets and white farmers.

More than ever, this freedom fighter was ready for action.

****

Chapter 6

When Julia had gone to finishing school, four months after Tom moved to Rhodesia, she had lost contact with him and had been worried that their relationship had ended. She never dreamed that they would end up together again.

When at last she heard from Tom a year later, and he had invited her to visit him in Rhodesia, she had jumped at the opportunity and hoped that their feelings for each other would still be the same as they had been before he had left Swaziland.

The handsome young policeman waiting for her at Salisbury station, with a broad, welcoming smile on his face, was the young man with whom she had fallen in love. They had a wonderful time together and while Tom showed her the sights around the city her love for him grew even stronger.

She also fell in love with the country, and when Tom proposed to her, she accepted without hesitation and was the happiest person alive.

After leaving Tom in Salisbury and returning to Durban, Julia set about making plans for the wedding. She was so excited that she could hardly concentrate on her work, and time seemed to drag by slowly.

They had decided to get married on her uncle's small game ranch in South Africa, not far from Rhodesia. The wedding was to be in early spring.

. . . .

Six long months later, Tom and Julia were married. Julia was beautiful. Her gown was amazing, and she looked radiant and happy. It was her day, and she was marrying the man she loved. Phil was Tom's best man, they had a police Guard of Honour, and they all wore their Number One uniforms and looked very smart. Tom had been given permission for them to wear their uniforms in South Africa.

The bushveld setting was magnificent with panoramic views of the surrounding countryside and the occasional impala and kudu grazing among the thorn trees beyond the garden. The weather was kind, and it was a lovely warm day with a light breeze keeping the temperature down.

The following morning after a good breakfast, they motored north back to Rhodesia for their honeymoon. After a long hot drive, as they approached Victoria Falls, they could see the mist created by the waterfalls rising like smoke out of the bush in the distance. After checking into their hotel and needing to stretch their legs, they decided to go for a walk to see the world-famous waterfalls.

Tom and Julia were dumbstruck by the beauty and magnificence of this natural wonder. Within minutes of entering the 'rainforest,' they were soaked by the spray coming up out of the gorge. Totally mesmerized, they watched the waters of the mighty Zambezi thundering over the edge to crash into the gorge way below. The roar of the falls made it impossible to speak, and so they stood; arms linked; in silent wonder. It was no surprise that the Falls were called 'Mosi-oa-Tunya' (The Smoke That Thunders) by the local inhabitants.

"Oh Tom just look at that rainbow over the gorge, and you can see the bridge underneath it. Isn't that too wonderful," Julie exclaimed as they reached the end of the rainforest.

"What a magnificent sight that is."

"The rainbow is caused by the sun reflecting on the mist coming up out of the gorge. Isn't it amazing to think that the engineers were able to span the gorge with such a marvelous bridge all those years ago? I believe the bridge was built in 1904." Tom said.

Elephants wandered around freely everywhere, and one large bull even spent a morning in the hotel garden. After a week exploring the Falls, the gorge below the falls, the river above the falls and a couple of trips upriver on the 'booze cruise,' Tom and Julia returned to Salisbury and moved into a garden flat.

Tom served the last six months of his time in the BSA Police stationed in one of the 'white' suburbs close to where they lived. After the hectic pace in the 'Black South,' where he had spent the previous two years, Tom found the posting to be very tame.

Tom was offered and accepted a job as the manager of a tobacco and dairy farm 50 miles east of Salisbury in the Goromonzi district. He was anxious to make a start with his new job and to learn the intricacies of growing tobacco.

It was a dream come true for him, as it meant that he was one step closer to creating the life that he and Julia planned. They wanted children, and if he worked hard in a few years, he would have enough money to start a farm on his own.

They moved into their rustic cottage on the farm, and a new phase of Tom's life began. The farm was diverse, and he had a lot to learn. Because he had worked on his father's dairy farm, he was able to pick up the dairy side quickly, but tobacco was a delicate and complex crop to grow and took some time to master.

The seed beds had to be sown, the lands plowed and harrowed. Ridging, fumigating, fertilizing and planting were carried out when the seedlings were ready. The crop then had to be reaped, cured, graded and sold before any bonus was paid.

At the top end of the farm, there was a high koppie with huge lichen covered granite boulders and a cave. The cave had been inhabited hundreds of years ago by Bushmen tribes. Their well-preserved paintings could quite clearly be seen all over one of the rock faces. They depicted scenes of hunting.

From there the farm sloped gently down to the Nora River which created the eastern boundary. The homesteads, dairy, workshops, and barns were located almost in the middle of the farm which was 3000 hectares in extent.

Baboons were a constant problem. During the day, they would sit on top of rocks and observe the workers toiling and from time to time they barked their advice. As soon as the workforce had finished for the day and disappeared, the baboons would climb down and mimic what the workers had been doing. They caused a lot of damage, with areas having to be replanted or repaired the following day. In the maize lands, they would eat all the young ears of corn. Crop guards had to be employed to keep them away from the lands

It was a typical tobacco farm with 18 tobacco curing barns, a bulking shed for the cured tobacco and grading shed where the leaves were graded, tied in hands and compressed into bales ready for sale. During the reaping season, each barn would be at a different stage of the curing process. They had to be constantly checked and monitored every two hours, day and night, with temperatures and humidity settings changed at just the right time. A mistake with the process could mean the loss of a whole barn full of tobacco.

The work was hard and required long hours. With the dairy producing 300 gallons of milk a day, and an early crop estimate indicated that they would reap 200,000 pounds of tobacco, it seemed that Tom was going to receive a healthy bonus.

Tom was happy with the way his life was going. He was married to the girl he had always loved and was doing what he had always wanted to do; farming. The possibility of owning his farm within five years now seemed tangible.

****

Chapter 7

Soon after starting work on the farm, Tom had joined the Police Reserve as he felt it was essential to keep in contact and up to date with the security situation in the country. With reports of possible terrorist incursions, everyone was constantly on the lookout for tell-tale signs of their presence.

It was reported that there had been an attack on a farm in the north, which had been successfully repelled. The attackers had been driven off, followed and eliminated. Although somewhat disturbing to hear that the terrorists had started to attack farmers, it was encouraging to hear how quickly they had been dealt with.

There needed to be a quick reaction to any attacks on farms, and so the Police Anti-Terrorist Unit (PATU) was formed. Made up of farmers who were all good shots and had used rifles most of their lives. Middle-aged and elderly men were excluded because it required lengthy foot patrols and prolonged tours in the bush.

Volunteers for this unit were commissioned, and training began in earnest. It was an exciting development because it meant, at last, the reservists were going to be used for duties other than roadblocks and bus searches.

They were to operate in 'sticks' of five men, consisting of a Section Leader, a scout, a medic, a radio man and a rear rifleman. Once their initial training was completed, the unit or 'stick' was dispatched on various one-day mock patrols and follow-up duties that taught them the basics of operating as an efficient team.

The kit they would need, food and water to carry, the arms they needed as well a few small details that all needed to be sorted out before being ready for an extended exercise. Members of the Game Department taught them tracking skills.

Again, because Tom had police experience, he was made a Section Leader and he and his unit were deployed on a five day 'settling down' exercise. Because of the time they were likely to spend in the bush, they all purchased light-weight backpacks to carry everything they might need; rations for ten days, sleeping bag, poncho, mess tins, cooker, plate, mug and knife, fork and spoon, a change of clothing and toiletries. On the webbing they were issued, they hung their water bottles, two hand grenades, pouches in which to carry four spare magazines for their FN automatic rifles they carried, map pouch with map and compass and a sheath knife. They also carried medical supplies and a heavy portable two-way radio.

As keen as mustard and excited by the prospect of having to navigate their way from the drop off point to a given destination, the team set off to test the skills they had learned. They were going into an area where none of them had any local knowledge.

The area was sparsely populated, and the terrain was extremely rugged with steep hills and deep valleys. John, a National Parks Game Warden, was selected to be the lead scout and was followed by Tom, with Tony the radio man and Terry the medic on either wing. Jim was the rear guard.

As soon as their transport had disappeared down the road in a cloud of dust, they slung their backpacks, adjusted their webbing, took compass bearings, and set off from the foothills of the Inyanga Mountains. The sun was halfway up into the sky, and they had five days to get to the Troutbeck Inn, beyond Inyanga Village.

The route they planned, with the use of a 1:50000 map, did not look too far, and they reckoned they could get there in less than four days. The patrol would give them ample time to settle down, re-organize their loads, and get a basic idea of what a bush patrol was all about.

They had to walk about three miles through open grassland to where a valley cut a path down through the high mountains. Tom chose a route leading up through the steep valley that would take them to where he planned to camp for the night.

They followed a small stream that meandered down the valley through a mass of Msasa trees in the glory of their spring colors. The new leaves were a mixture of crimson, soft reds, browns, ochre and bright green turning to the darker green of the fully developed leaves.

Wearing police issue blues (navy blue denim trousers tucked into gaiters and boots with a grey shirt and navy blue jacket) and although there was ample cover and plenty of shade, they felt that they were highly visible even to the most casual observer.

Within an hour their packs began to get uncomfortable. Unaccustomed to the weight, the straps cut into their shoulders, and the packs often snagged on branches and thorns. This was a problem because both arms needed to be free to use the rifle without restriction. Two hours later they stopped to rest and were happy to flop down in the shade of the Msasa trees and remove their packs. After a drink of water, they fiddled with their pack straps to try to make their loads more comfortable.

"This is a total ball's up. Do we really need all this stuff?" John asked, wiping the sweat from his red face with the back of his hand. "I've never before been in the bush and carried so much."

"We'll each have to work out exactly what we want to carry for a two-week patrol and cut out as much as possible. Then we can make a better plan on how to carry it," Tom said.

"Well I sure as hell won't be going out again carrying all this crap," said Jim. "Even if I have to go hungry."

"I agree with you guys. These bloody packs snag on everything you pass, and it's almost impossible to move quickly with them on our backs," Terry added his piece.

Tony, who carried the radio as well as his pack, was far too hot and bothered to pass any comment, and just sat there grunting and nodding his head in agreement.

It had been hot when they set off, but as they climbed higher, it became cooler. By the time they made the night-stop, it was late afternoon, and they were thankful for their heavy clothing. After their evening meal and with the night watches allocated, they spread out and settled down for the night.

In the morning, they were on their way again just as the sun began to bathe the hills around them with warm sunlight. The higher they climbed, the harder the going became. Thick undergrowth of wild ferns and heather hampered their progress. As the object was to keep well away from farms and kraals and to try to avoid detection for as long as possible, they stuck to the denser forest areas.

Although their loads became lighter as they consumed their rations, the discomfort of lugging so much kit was depressing and painful. Every day their backpacks were got more and more uncomfortable. To make matters worse, the packs continuously snagged on branches as they passed through the forests. Fortunately, they were in an area with plenty of water and only had to carry sufficient for a day at a time. Water bottles were topped up at the streams they came across.

On the third day as they hurried across a valley close to a farmstead, a dog started barking. Before they could scurry for cover, they were spotted by the farmer's wife. Tom quickly doubled back to speak to her; before she raised the alarm and patrols were sent out investigate.

"Good morning. My name is Tom Owen. I am the section leader of a Police Anti-Terrorist Unit. We are on a training exercise in the area. I am sorry we have trespassed on your farm and hope we didn't alarm you," Tom said, identifying himself with his dog tags.

"Good morning Tom. Have terrorists been seen in the area?" she asked concerned.

"No," Tom reassured her. "We were hoping to pass your farm without being spotted or alarming you as part of our exercise."

"Well our dogs are wide awake and gave you chaps away," the woman smiled.

"If you speak to the Member-in-Charge of the Inyanga police he will verify our presence," Tom said.

"That won't be necessary Tom. I can see you are who you say you are. Good luck and take more care in future. We don't want any terrorists catching you," she said, waving Tom goodbye.

Weighed down by their heavy loads, and not being accustomed to this type of operation, it took a lot longer to reach their destination than they had anticipated. Instead of arriving early on the fourth day, they staggered in late that afternoon, hungry and exhausted.

It had been a very useful exercise proving that backpacks were not a good idea and would not be used on future patrols. They would have to trim their loads and their clothing and work out a way to reduce the weight of their food. Something also had to be done about changing from the police blues to some sort of camouflage clothing.

After a couple of well-earned beers in the bar at Troutbeck Inn, their kit was loaded into the Land Rover, and they headed home. A good shower, a decent home-cooked meal and a comfortable bed were badly needed.

Apart from the need to reorganize their kit, Tom was happy with the way the training patrol had gone, and he was confident that they were almost ready for call outs and action. A few days after their debriefing they were all presented with their 'Leopards Paw' badges; the insignia for PATU and they were proud to wear it on the shoulders.

****

Chapter 8

In spring that year Julia fell pregnant. They were delighted with the news, and couldn't wait to celebrate and share their news with their friends on a nearby farm. Having a dairy to run, Tom could only get away from the farm between the milking hours, which was from 9 in the morning until 3 in the afternoon on a Sunday.

Two months later, on the 11th November 1965, after negotiations between the British and the Rhodesian Government had failed; Ian Smith declared independence unilaterally, thus severing Rhodesia's Colony status with Britain.

Christmas came and went with little change in their lives, except that Julia was starting to show her pregnancy as the child grew inside her. Tom loved to put his ear to her belly and listen to all the gurgling and grumbling noises going on inside her. The tobacco crop was ready to harvest, and the reaping and curing of the leaves had begun. The grading would start a few weeks later.

By Easter time, Julia had started to waddle around as her tummy grew and protruded out in front of her. The baby started to kick inside her, and she suffered from tremendous back pain. Tom did his best to help to rub it for her whenever she asked.

"If I had known that being pregnant was going to be so uncomfortable, I don't think I would ever have decided to have a baby," Julie said after a particularly uncomfortable night.

"Well, I am glad I can't fall pregnant. I wouldn't be able to go through what you are suffering. I just wish I could help you more," Tom said sympathetically.

Between getting up at all hours to check the barns and massaging Julia's back, neither of them got much sleep.

Sanctions imposed by Britain were biting and with sanctions-busting operations put into place by the government, tobacco sales continued as normal except the prices were a lot lower than they should normally have been. Tom enjoyed attending the tobacco auctions, and never tired of listening to the sing-song chant of the auctioneers as they moved up and down the rows of tobacco bales.

In Autumn Julia gave birth to a bouncing boy who they named him Stuart after his grandfather. Tom was over the moon and extremely proud of his son. When he was able to, he spent as much time playing with his young son as he could. Julie's backache disappeared but was soon replaced by Stuart's constant demand for food, and the sleepless nights continued with the child waking up at all times of the night to be fed.

In the afternoons they would go on walks, before milking time, accompanied by their dog and the cat. In between milking times on a Sunday they would get together with their friends for a braai (barbeque) and a few drinks. What more could a man want in life, except for a big bonus and his farm?

Because of sanctions and the shortage of fuel in the country, sympathetic farmers in Australia and New Zealand contributed towards a shipload of oil, which arrived in Beira and offloaded the oil. Patrolling British Warships were quick to blockade the port preventing any other oil tankers from docking.

The blockade effectively stopped fuel from reaching Rhodesia via the oil pipeline from Beira. South Africa came to the rescue when hundreds of farmers initiated fuel convoys to Rhodesia, and this motivated the South African government to step in and assist. After all, Rhodesia was a buffer between them and the black tide spreading down through the continent from the north.

Between Police reserve training and farming, Tom had little time to relax. They had been on the farm for a year and, after a short holiday to the coast in South Africa he was back to start preparing for the next tobacco season. Land preparation was on the go, and the seedbeds had to be made ready and fumigated.

International sanctions against the landlocked Rhodesia were tightening. Tobacco quotas were reduced, and prices looked set to plummet. The days of big bonuses were over, and a large number of tobacco managers were forced to seek work in the town and cities.

Little Stuart was growing fast and getting more and more interesting. He was learning to walk and continually strayed out of the garden. Their Alsatian dog never left his side when he went wandering and guarded him carefully; barking whenever he felt his little charge was in danger. Stuart was trying hard to talk and had started to put words together. Julia was content to sit in a chair in the shade of the mulberry tree and watch them playing together.

In August that year, Tom received some shocking news. He was at home having breakfast when he received a phone call from his grandmother in Natal. She told him that his parents and sister were missing at sea. They had sailed from Durban two weeks earlier, bound for East London and had not been heard from since. Tom was told that they were believed to have sailed south into gale force winds off the notoriously dangerous Transkei Coast.

An air and sea search had been set in motion by the South African Defence Force. Shackleton and Dakota aircraft were used, and after five days of searching, hampered by bad weather, and with no sign of the missing yacht, the search was abandoned.

Tom felt as if he had been hit by a train. He could not believe that this had happened; it seemed like a bad nightmare. How was it possible that they might have drowned at such a young age? Why had it happened to them when they were only in their mid-forties, and his sister barely fourteen? His mind jumped from one thing to another with the shock of this tragic news.

Tom, Julia, and Stuart motored to Durban to find out what had happened and to speak to the Port Captain. He also wanted to find out why he had not been told earlier.

From Durban they traveled to Swaziland, to help put his father's affairs in order in case they were never found. They stopped for a night with Tom's old employers on Mlaula Ranch. It was good to see his old friends again.

Tom and his family returned to Rhodesia. He was devastated. He had been very close to his parents, and it was going to take a long time to come to terms with their probable demise.

. . . .

Six months later, just as Tobacco Sales Floors were about to open, another bombshell was dropped. Overseas buyers were prevented from attending the auctions, and there was no way of selling the tobacco.

With sanctions against the country, the tobacco would have to be bought by the government at basic prices, stored until buyers were found and the crop sold via a back door; it was a major setback and a national disaster. How was the country going to survive without the largest foreign exchange earner?

The immediate future looked bleak. With a stroke of the pen and with a reduced quota coupled with deflated prices, Tom had lost a potential £2,000 bonus. With a monthly salary of £40, this was a lot of money and a huge setback to his plans. But he was still earning a reasonable bonus from the dairy sales.

It had been a bad year, leaving Tom very downhearted and disappointed. He was, however, like so many others, still convinced that an agreement would be reached with Britain, sanctions lifted, and everything return to normal.

****

Chapter 9

Lying flat on his stomach undercover in a thicket of Mopani scrub, and taking great care not to allow any reflexion from the lenses of his binoculars, Tom studied the village in the clearing below them.

He was looking for some sign of the four insurgents they had been following for the past four days. They were getting careless now that they were close to the border; Their badly covered tracks led straight to this small village, where they must have made their daylight stop.

The village consisted of four large huts, a small granary hut on stilts, and with the usual goat's pen off to one side. A group of four or five mango trees grew on the edge of the path leading into the center of the huts. A small patch of young green corn was growing around an anthill between Tom's position and the group of huts.

Further off in the near distance was a line of high, dark blue-green Inyanga mountain range that ran along the boundary between Rhodesia and Mozambique.

Tom was hoping to see a villager carrying food to where the terrorists might be hiding. It was known that they used local inhabitants to supply them with food. He was sure they were not hiding in any of the huts. They would be far too vulnerable surrounded by open ground and not being able to keep a lookout, let alone escape if attacked. He rather suspected that they were hiding somewhere in the dense bush on the northern side, about fifty paces from the perimeter of the clearing. From there they could make a hasty escape if it became necessary.

His eyes watered from the strain of trying to look into the bush around the village in his effort to spot some sign that would give away the terrorist's position. The remainder of the stick were covering the sides and the rear of their position, making sure they had not been spotted earlier, and avoiding the danger of being ambushed.

Half a dozen bare necked chickens wandered around among the huts scratching for insects, bits of Sadza and maize chips to fill their crops. A scrawny brindle dog was lying on its side, panting in the shade under the roof of one of the huts. Nothing else stirred; it was quiet with hardly a breath of air.

The sun was high in the clear blue sky, and it was sweltering hot. A heat haze shimmered in the distance, where a young goat-herd could be seen resting in the shade of a large Marula tree and watching his keep graze in a cleared area beyond the maize. It was too quiet.

Smoke seeping through the roof of one of the huts drifted lazily upwards. A gentle breeze stirred, moving the blue smoke to the south and in their direction. This was good for them; insurgents generally were known to have an acute sense of smell, and could easily detect the scent of a white man when the wind blew in their direction. (For this reason, none of the men in the PATU stick carried toothpaste, soap, deodorant or toilet paper).

Tom knew that the terrorists would want to move on as soon as it became dark. They preferred moving at night to avoid detection, and it was almost impossible to be tracked in the dark. Tom would have to be patient, and wait until the afternoon sun started to set. Then there was sure to be movement in the kraal, and he planned to pounce on the unsuspecting victims, while they were off guard and busy eating.

'Where are the buggers hiding?' he muttered to himself.

The stick had picked up trail four days ago but had only just caught up with the fleeing insurgents. They were going to make damn sure that they did not get any closer to the border. Their pursuit had led them in a direct line to the Mozambique border, and by the following morning, if they did not stop the terrorists, they would be out of the country. If they were allowed to escape, they would be able to rest and resupply before-entering Rhodesia to attack another unsuspecting farmer and his family. The stick could not let that happen.

After leaving the Fuller's farm in the Mrewa district, it had been a hard, fast chase. The terrorists had launched an attack on the Fullers in their homestead in the early evening, while they had been watching the television news and were distracted. They had heard the dogs barking a warning, but as this happened at that time most evenings, they had not heeded them.

Suddenly the glass shattered in the window of the lounge where they were sitting, and they were almost deafened by the sound of automatic gunfire. Mrs. Fuller and her teenage daughter dropped flat onto the floor, and George Fuller scrambled off to the bedroom to fetch his FN rifle leaving his terrified wife and child in the lounge.

It was the first time anyone had experienced an attack on their home in the district, and the unsuspecting family was caught completely off guard and unprepared. George, with his nerves making him shake, acted on instinct, and instead of returning the fire from inside the house, decided to counter-attack from outside. Before going outside, he fired two shots from the bedroom window with his shotgun. Then dousing the house lights, he switched on the security lights putting the house in the darkness behind the bright lights.

With the adrenaline pumping into his blood and calming him down, he quickly slipped out of the back door before the attackers could adjust to the light.

As George crept around towards the front of the house, he must have seen the muzzle flashes from the attacker's firearms and started to return fire in their general direction as he dashed for cover behind a tree in the garden. The attackers turned their attention towards him and under a hail of bullets; he staggered and fell to the ground.

The attack ended as suddenly as it had begun and silence took the place of the loud racket of gunfire. Too frightened to move, and without making a sound, Mrs. Fuller and her daughter stayed where they were for some time before deciding that it was safe to move around. Eventually, worried that she had not heard from George, she plucked up courage, and then after instructing her daughter to telephone the police, she went in search of her husband.

Not knowing whether the attackers were still out there or not, she picked up the shotgun from the bedroom, reloaded it, then with weak knees and every nerve in her body jumping, she very quietly and cautiously went outside. She had heard him shouting, and the sound of his FN firing from the one side of the house so started her search there.

Mary Fuller found her husband lying in a pool of blood on the front lawn with their faithful dog, Brutus, lying near him whining. He was alive but badly wounded. Screaming to her daughter for help, the two of them managed to drag George back into the house, but by the time they got him inside, he had passed away. They were distraught. While Mary wept over her husband's dead body, her daughter went outside and carried the injured dog back into the house.

The police arriving on the scene half an hour later found Mary and her daughter in the living room. The two women were sitting together on the couch, hugging each other and crying as they tried to console one another. All the windows were shattered, the curtains were torn to shreds, and the walls were full of bullet holes. George was lying on the floor in the kitchen, where he had died, covered with a blanket. Brutus, the dog, was lying on a blanket next to his master.

The police helped the two Fuller women pack a suitcase; then after loading George's body, they took them to stay with friends on a neighbouring farm. Four Police Reservists were left guarding the Fuller farm and had the unenviable task of putting the dog down; it was too badly wounded to survive.

Within a couple of hours, Tom and his PATU stick were called in and taken to see Mrs. Fuller. They had to find out as much as they could from her before setting out in pursuit of these monsters. She looked pale and haggard with red rims around her eyes from crying. She was twisting a handkerchief around in her shaking hands, and her bottom lip could not stop quivering while she spoke to Tom.

"I know this is very painful for you at this time, and I am very sorry that I have to do this. But if we are to catch these monsters we need all the information we can get," Tom spoke to her as gently as he could.

"I know. I'll help you as much as I can. You must try to get them. They have to pay for what they have done," Mrs. Fuller replied trying hard to stop the tears.

"Were all your employees on the farm loyal? Were any of them disgruntled or had your husband fired anyone recently?" Tom asked

"Yes most of them have been with us for years. George has always been fair with them. He hasn't fired anyone for ages," Mrs. Fuller said.

"Why did you decide not to use 'Bright Lights' to help guard you at night?" Tom asked.

"We did consider using them, but the accommodation was a problem. In any case, we didn't feel the need to have someone getting in our way all the time. We felt quite secure on our farm," she said.

'Bright Lights' was a new unit made up of men from the cities, who came in to protect farmers and their families, while they got on with the lives and the business of farming.

The pursuit began at first light. Tom and his men arrived at the farm and scouted around the outside of the fence surrounding the homestead. Here they found the body of one of the attackers. George must have shot him before he was killed. Tom, after seeing Mary Fullers suffering, and having been in the police force and had seen a number of dead people, felt only anger when he looked at the dead man. Informing the police of their grisly find, they picked up the spoor of the fleeing attackers and were soon on the follow-up trail.

The terrorists must have started their flight at about 9 o'clock the previous evening, and so they had a good lead. In the afternoon the stick came across signs indicating the insurgents had rested. The grass under a Marula tree was flattened, and an empty sardine tin was half hidden under some leaves.

The unit decided to move on while it was still light enough to keep on the trail even quickening their pace. They wanted to close the gap between themselves and the terrorists. Two hours later they made their overnight stop. At first light, they were on the move again.

The terrain in that part of the world was undulating grassland scattered with clumps of scrub and Musasa forests with the occasional Wild Olive, Marula, Sausage and Wild Fig trees, making the going reasonably easy. They used the single file formation with John leading the way, followed by Tom with the other three behind him, enabling them to move along at a good pace.

When they moved through more dense forest areas, they opened up into the arrowhead formation with Terry and Tony slightly behind, and five paces to either side of Tom. Jim brought up the rear.

In spite of only moving in the night, the terrorists were able to cover a fair distance between dusk and dawn. Tom, however, was confident that they would be able to catch up within a day or two, or even earlier if the terrorists were going to make a food stop before reaching the border. The PATU stick was able to cover a longer distance during the day, in spite of having to follow spoor and avoid possible ambush positions.

It soon became apparent that the group of four insurgents were in a hurry to get out of the country. They would know they were being pursued, and to avoid being spotted, would only stop to rest during the daylight hours so that they could watch their back-trail.

Other than what they had found on day one, there was no further sign of them having had any food; they must be getting hungry. Despite this, and the fact that the stick did not rest for more than was necessary during the day, it had taken them three days to catch up with the fleeing terrorists, not two as had been expected.

Tom and his men had followed the spoor into the village where they now lay, silently watching, yet there was still no sign of any unusual movement around the huts, nor any sign of them having moved on. The 1:50000 map showed two paths leading away from the village, which John and Jim crept around to check as soon as they had stopped.

The path leading into the hills did not have any sign of fresh footprints, and the path leading out to the left of the kraal led back in the direction from which they had come. The terrorists would have to use the path leading into the hills. There was no sure way of knowing whether or not the terrorists were waiting for food or if they had moved on in the daylight without using the path.

Although they did not want to lose their quarry now and allow them to escape over the border, waiting was a gamble they had to take. It was going to be a long wait in the hot midday heat, and they dare not move around for fear of being seen.

"We must stay put until we know exactly where the terrs (terrorists) are before we move. If we try to attack them when they are eating, they will see us coming and they will either counter attack or will escape. We will have to set an ambush position. We know they must be here somewhere and we don't want to risk exposing ourselves or walking slap into an ambush. So we must know where they are before sunset," Tom said as they discussed their plan of action.

"I go along with that. When we went around for a scout, we found a good ambush spot on the path leading away up into the hill. It is not far, and we can easily get there in about a quarter of an hour, without being seen from the kraal," John said.

"Good. Then we will just have to be patient, and sit tight until something happens. If we do not see anything, we will move into position anyway and set up an ambush just before the sun sets."

"We hope like hell that they don't move before we are ready for them," said Jim.

"I agree with Tom. It is the only option we have got. If they didn't stop then by now, they are over the border already. If they are being given food they will move before it gets too dark," said Terry.

"No, we mustn't blow it now. It has been a long, hard chase. We've got this close we don't want to screw it up now," said Tony.

Time dragged by slowly. Tom began to have doubts and thought that they might have been outsmarted and that the terrorists had moved on or not stopped at all.

A lonely yellow-billed kite circling above, in search of a meal; swooped down towards earth every now and again, to take a closer look at something that had attracted its attention, then soaring back up into the dark blue sky. There was not a cloud to be seen and even in the shade of their cover it was sweltering hot. And they waited with sweat was pouring off them, and running down their backs. The Mopani bees were a constant irritation, trying to get moisture from the corners of their eyes, their nostrils, and from their mouths. It was difficult to keep still as they crawled around on their faces tickling and getting into their eyes. But they dare not move.

Tom's thoughts wandered back to the first trial patrol he had been on, and he was grateful that they had stripped down their loads and clothing to the bare minimum. In this heat, it would have been a nightmare carrying everything they had originally used.

Now they were kitted out in black rugby shorts, camouflage short-sleeved shirt, floppy hat or cap, camouflage net scarf, webbing and veldskoen shoes (tough ankle-high shoes made from cowhide) worn without socks; arrow-like grass seeds stuck in socks and made sores on their legs.

On the webbing they hung two grenades, pouches holding four spare magazines, a water bottle, mess tin, small gas burner and knife, a plastic bag containing small tins of fruit and pronutro (nutritious dry cereal) mixed with milk powder and sugar. The sleeping bag with hip pad and poncho was all strapped onto the back of the webbing, above the belt.

It was all they needed, providing they were able to get to water every second day. They could move a lot faster than they had been able to with the old bulky backpacks.

It now seemed that a firefight with the terrorists was inevitable. How were they all going to handle themselves when the action started? None of them had previous battle experience and had never been under fire. Would any of them freeze or run when the time came? Tom was sure that the same thoughts were going through all of their minds. It was up to him to keep them calm and focused.

All of a sudden a woman emerged from the hut with smoke coming through the roof. She called to the young herd boy who got up from his position under the tree, rounded up his herd of goats, and herded them back to the kraal. It was almost 5 o'clock, and the sun was sinking quickly; it would not be long before dusk.

Once he had secured the goats in their pen, the boy went into the hut with the woman. He emerged a few moments later carrying a plastic bag, and set off briskly along a well-worn path leading towards the distant hills and beyond the tree, where he had been sitting earlier, and disappeared into the undergrowth. Tom was convinced the bag contained food for the terrorists.

Reacting to Tom's signal, the stick quietly and carefully eased back from their positions, and gathered out of sight of the village, to plan the next move while Terry kept watching. They knew they had very little time if they were to stop the terrorists. An ambush had to be set on the only route that would lead them to the northeast and Mozambique.

The stick retreated a little way further, then after notifying HQ of the situation on the radio, they quickly and quietly circled around, in the bush, to the right of the huts. This course brought them onto the path well beyond where they suspected the insurgents to be lying up.

Hoping that they would be distracted by the youth and their eating, the stick moved toward their ambush position. Tom had selected the position with the assistance of John and Jim after their earlier recce that confirmed on the map, was a good place to set an ambush. They had to hurry.

The path led up through a valley towards the summit of the low hills they had seen from their observation position earlier. At one point it passed between a fairly steep wooded slope with a stream on the left-hand side and a high vertical wall of rock on the right. The gulley was about 100 paces long and 20 paces wide; it was an ideal place for an ambush.

Crossing the path and taking care not to leave any spoor or sign of their crossing, they took cover in their positions on the slope overlooking the path. With the stream and rock wall as a backdrop on the other side of the path below them, it was perfect. The only escape would be forward or backward.

Setting the ambush using only hand signals, Tom placed a man at either end of the killing ground, one as a backstop to prevent retreat, with himself in the center with the medic and the radio man on either side of him. They would be firing down onto the pathway, so there was little chance of ricochets from the rock face opposite.

He checked their positions, making sure that they were well hidden. He instructed each one quietly to wait for his signal before they opened fire. Then he settled down into his position in the middle of the others to wait, well satisfied with the trap. It was almost dark now and beginning to cool down after the heat of the day.

They didn't have long to wait. It was still just light enough to see when suddenly out of the corner of his eye, Tom saw movement. With the adrenalin starting to pump around his body, his nerves started to jingle, and his stomach was in a knot in anticipation of what was to come. He dared not move a muscle as he waited nervously. Their targets were relaxed, walking quickly with their AK47 rifles slung over their shoulders.

The first man to pass Tom's position was tall and slim; the second man was about five paces behind him and was followed almost immediately by the third. As the second man was directly in front of him and he could see a third person following him, Tom opened fire, and with that, all hell broke loose.

The terrorists, who had not been expecting an ambush so soon after their stop, did not have a chance to return the fire. After a long burst of intermittent gunfire from the men in the PATU stick, all firing ceased as each man emptied his magazine.

"Hold your fire! Reload," Tom called out as he quickly changed his empty magazine for a full one.

The silence was deafening, and the air was filled with the smell of cordite. The attack had felt as if it had happened in slow motion, but in reality had only lasted less than a minute. All their senses remained keen as they waited; straining their eyes and ears in the dark. Their ears were still singing from the racket of the gunfire echoing off the cliff.

They waited, for what seemed an eternity. And still, they waited, expecting retaliation. But none came.

As the singing in his ears stopped, the only sound was of someone groaning as if in pain. At last after about 15 minutes, when he felt that it was safe, Tom quietly called to each of his men. All confirmed that they were fine and that none had been injured.

"Stay in your positions. I am going to check the killing ground," Tom instructed as he cautiously and somewhat nervously got up and went to check the path in front of his position.

He almost fell over the lifeless body of one of the terrorists lying face down across the path right in front of his position. Tom returned to his position, and called to the other men to check the killing ground in front of them, and then to return to their positions.

Another terrorist was found lying in the path. The groaning that they heard was coming from the last man to have entered the killing zone. He was badly injured with a wound in his shoulder and another in his groin. After checking him for concealed weapons and taking his

AK47, he was handcuffed with cable ties and left in the path. The leading man must have got away.

After calling HQ on the radio to report the contact and the kills, Tom told the men to settle down for the night. They would stick to the usual watches, but Tom reminded them to be extra vigilant. The man who had escaped could still sneak back and counter-attack them. It did not look like the wounded terrorist would last long but if he survived he would be useful to Special Branch who would be able to interrogate him.

Tom who had been exposed to death many times before, and had been hardened to it during his years in the police force, and so he felt very little. These were people who had murdered in cold blood and had now been killed in a war situation. It was going to be interesting to see how the other four dealt with it. He knew that none of them would sleep a wink.

Not long after settling back into their positions, Tom heard Tony on his right-hand side puking as the reality of having killed hit home. He was normally a man full of bravado, and had been keen to "cull the terrs". Tom had seen a tough Irish policeman reacting in the same way after shooting and killing a rioter in Salisbury, and so he was not surprised. The 'tough' guys always seemed to be a little soft inside.

As soon as it was light in the early morning, they confirmed that the injured terrorist was still alive. Tom and John followed the tracks of the one who had escaped. They found where he had left the path then, a little further along where he had re-joined it and made off into the hills. He would be over the border by that time, so there was no point in pursuing him.

"Well, we got most of them. It's a pity the one fellow got away. I think he must have been the leader, and probably the worst of the lot," Tom said to the others as they examined the bodies of the dead terrorists.

"These sods were just bloody animals. We hunted them down and destroyed them like the vermin they are," said John showing no emotion at all as he prodded one of the dead men with his foot. Tony, watching him, turned a grey colour and looked as if he were about to be sick again.

"Okay let's get them to the clearing where we will be picked up by a chopper," Tom said.

They carried the two dead and the injured terrorist to the cleared area near the huts where they would be airlifted by helicopter back to base. Jim, who seemed to have been fine, reacted as they dumped the dead terrorists in the clearing and puked his heart out. Terry on the other hand, who had travelled the world and worked in rough conditions with tough people, showed no emotion at all.

Special Branch moved in to interrogate the woman and youngster who had fed the monsters. The injured man survived long enough to be interrogated before he died. It had been their first sortie into Rhodesia. They had come in undetected on the regular bus service from Tete in Mozambique.

Mary Fuller employed a farm manager, and she and her daughter Susan returned to their farm and were carrying on. They now had two members of the 'Bright Lights' force guarding them while they tried to come to terms with what had happened, and the loss of a husband and father.

Although they had not culled all four of the terrorists, Tom and his PATU stick were pleased with themselves. It had been their first contact, and it had gone exactly as planned. It had been a successful follow-up mission. They had been blooded.

During the interrogation of the captured terrorist, he revealed that the escaped leader went by the name of 'Mamba'.

****

Chapter 10

Mamba was seething. He had made the fatal error of relaxing before completing his mission and reaching safety. Setting off on the last leg of their escape just after dark with full stomachs and feeling refreshed, they had marched along the path in single file about five paces apart. Suddenly a hail of bullets, with the accompanying racket of semi-automatic gunfire caught the unexpectedly.

Mamba, who still had his AK47 slung over his shoulder, realized in an instant that he would not have time to return fire and sprinted away along the path leaving his men to fend for themselves. He stopped two hundred paces further along the path to wait for any survivors, but none came. He cursed himself for being caught completely off guard. The firing had stopped and the night was still.

After stopping briefly to wait for his men to catch up, he moved quickly along the path, knowing it was too dark for any pursuit. After ten minutes, he moved off the path and finding high ground he hid behind an outcrop of large rocks. From where he was hiding, he could only just make out the path below him and would be able to see his men if they did come along.

With no further sound of gunfire and no sign of pursuit, he lay there waiting in the stillness of the night. If he was being followed, he was in a good position to ambush his hunters. The night sounds of the bush started up again as he waited.

He pondered if the old woman had somehow managed to get a message out to inform someone of their presence but soon dismissed the thought, knowing that the kraal was miles away from any other settlement, and it would have taken a long time to get the word out.

After waiting for an hour, Mamba knew his companions would not be coming, and he would have to hurry if he was to get over the border before morning. With the Security Forces right behind him, he had to get out of the country fast. If there were any survivors from the ambush, they would have to make their way back to Mozambique and their base by themselves. Leaving the safety of the rocks, he made his way back to the path.

He would find out who had betrayed him, and who was responsible for killing his men. He and Robson had trained together and worked well as a team. It was war, and men were expected to die, but he had failed to get back to their base with all his men. He would make sure that those responsible would pay. He had learned a valuable lesson.

On his return to the base camp at Catandica, Mamba was received with mixed feelings. On the one hand, he was congratulated for having achieved success in his mission. The news on the Rhodesian Broadcasting Corporation confirmed that a farmer in the Mrewa district had been killed by insurgents in a vicious attack on his farm. His wife and daughter had escaped unhurt. It was also reported that the farmer had killed one of the attackers, and three had died in the follow-up mission.

No mention was made of one of them having escaped. On the other hand, Mamba was criticized for having led his men into an ambush; that was careless and should never have happened. This made him angry, and he could not understand their concern; after all, he was the important one, the only man he regretted having lost was Robson. He would have to wait for some new recruits to arrive in camp from their training in Tanzania.

"How did you allow yourselves to be caught?" the base commander asked.

"I did not see anyone tracking us. They must have been warned. We moved very fast during the night, and I am sure we were not seen during the day when we rested," Mamba said.

"Do you think the people who were feeding you reported your presence?"

"No. They did not have a chance to get a message to anyone. I was watching them the whole time," Mamba replied.

"Well, how were you were caught in an ambush if you were so careful?" the commander asked.

"One of the men must have been careless and left some sign of our presence along the way, and a stop group must have been dropped off by helicopter ahead of us," Mamba said wondering why he should be subjected to this interrogation.

"According to the report on the news broadcast, your men are all dead."

"They were soldiers in the war against the white men in Rhodesia. If they have died it is necessary," Mamba answered defiantly.

After his de-briefing, Mamba was told that he would have to wait for new soldiers to work with before being sent on another mission. In the meantime, he needed a drink and to have a woman. In the base camp, there was no shortage of either of these requirements.

He sat under the fig tree near the bar with one of the 'working women', got drunk and went off into the bush where he brutally had his way her. He did not like women to submit easily to him; he preferred to beat them into submission. He was aware of his weakness for women and drink. Everyone had a weakness for women, but he had taken to wearing dark glasses most of the time to hide his bloodshot eyes. He also thought he looked superior with them on.

For the next two years, Mamba and his men were used to enter Rhodesia and to set up staging posts for teams being deployed deep into the country. He would cross over the mountains from Mozambique with one or two men: locate friendly, sympathetic villagers in remote areas who were willing to feed the freedom fighters; find suitable, safe hiding places where weapons, ammunition, and tins of food were stashed and supply lines were established.

These re-supply routes and staging places could also be used as escape routes. Once established, these caches of food arms and ammunition were to be replenished by special courier operatives on a regular basis. This was a vital part of their strategy, enabling prolonged operations within the country. Mamba was getting frustrated at not being deployed on more active 'forward operations' instead of his courier role.

"I am fully aware that our job is to re-educate the people in the rural areas and to persuade them to support our cause, but is it not time for us to be more positive and attack more farmers? The more whites we kill, the more likely it is that the rest of them will pack up and leave the country," Mamba said to the political commissar in their camp while sitting together under a tree.

"No. We must convert the people first and avoid direct contact with the enemy where possible. Once they are on our side, then we can concentrate our efforts on getting rid of the whites," he replied.

"Well I think we could speed up our take-over of the land if we were more aggressive with our attacks," Mamba said getting up and walking back to his hut.

Moving to the South East, he recruited some Makaranga fishermen to act as spies along the Lundi and the Sabi rivers. These cells of information gatherers were established near pumping stations, bridges and other farming centers where they could gather what information they could. They were armed with AK47 rifles and given strict instruction to hide them. These rifles were only to be used when they assisted the regular freedom fighters.

It would be very useful to have information on the movements of the whites in the developed farming areas.

****

Chapter 11

One of Tom's farming neighbors whose father was Chairman of the Grain Marketing Board and in the know told him of a project that was being considered for settling farmers in the Lowveld. He decided that it would make sense considering the current situation, to change direction and move away from tobacco and to find work in the Lowveld.

Sugar sales were not affected by the embargoes or sanctions. This move would put him in the area of the proposed development and give him a better chance of acquiring a settler farm.

Tom was offered a job on Mpapa, a section of Triangle Sugar Estate that was growing diversified crops of wheat, cotton, rice, citrus, and maize. He accepted the position and the family moved to the Lowveld.

Their house, situated on the banks of the Lundi River, was just below the confluence with the Tokwe River, and 40 miles from the village. Tom and Julia enjoyed sitting in the garden under the shade of a large wild fig tree where they could look out across the sandy river bed, which was about 300 paces wide.

From their look-out spot they could watch the small pod of hippos wallowing in the pools below them and, on most days, at least one large crocodile could be seen basking on the rocks in the middle of the river. Now and then they could hear the shrill, haunting 'Weee-ah, hyo-hyo' answered by 'heeeah-heeeah' of a pair of Fish Eagles perched on dead trees above the weir. Theirs was the call evocative of the essence of Africa.

"We must watch the dogs. If they go down to the river to play, they are likely to become a meal for one of those crocs. They love dog meat," Tom said one afternoon as they sat under the trees enjoying a beer.

"Surely they will see a croc approaching them and be able to get away?" Julia replied.

"Our dogs are from the Highveld, Julia, and they are not aware of the danger. Crocs are very cunning and will stalk their prey for a while before attacking them."

"Do you think you could arrange for a fence to be put up at the bottom of the garden? We don't want Stuart wandering off down to the river."

"Sure thing; I'll get it done tomorrow with a gate so that we can get down when we want to. It will also help keep that hippo out of the garden at night."

Tom had seen the crocs following the dogs when he took them with him to fish for bream. Standing at the end of the garden looking down on the river one afternoon, they had seen an Egyptian Goose honking loudly when it escaped from the jaws of a crocodile that lunged at it. It had been circling in the pool watching the goose as it waddled to the water's edge for a drink.

The whole farm was covered in lush green young wheat with three or four huge Baobab trees standing in the middle of the fields. The spray of water from the irrigation sprinklers made it all a pretty cool picture in the heat of the Lowveld. It was a low rainfall area in an extremely hot part of the country.

Some felt the heat was unbearable, but Tom was used to it from his time in the Swaziland Bushveld, and the air conditioning in the house gave them some respite. He had three horses to use for transportation around the farm; one he rode in the early morning, one after breakfast and the third in the afternoon. On really hot days the horses were dripping with sweat before Tom even mounted them.

The summer rains started in earnest with heavy downfalls in the higher parts of the country upstream from the farm and the Lowveld. Within a day the water arrived down the rivers, and the levels rose alarmingly fast. The pumps were winched up on their rails out of the river just as the raging water arrived. The low-level bridge was soon under water, and the farm was cut off from Triangle. The only access was via the railway bridge, which was high above the rapid flow.

Tom received an urgent call for help from a local fisherman. Five of his fellow fishermen were trapped on an island in the middle of the river; the water had risen too fast for them to escape to the bank. He decided to contact the police and pass the message on to Phil, who had recently been promoted and transferred to Triangle police station and was now the Member-in-Charge.

"Phil, there are about five fishermen sitting up in trees on an island in the middle of the Lundi. I'm told they have been stranded there for about five days; since the river came down in flood. I don't know what you want to do about them," Tom said over the phone.

"Can we get anywhere near them?" Phil wanted to know.

"The bush is too thick, and they are about a mile below the rail bridge. The only way would be by boat."

"Would we be able to use your boat?"

"Yes, that will be okay. I will have to meet you on the other side of the river where the road disappears under the water," Tom said.

"Thanks. I will be there in an hour."

Tom launched his small boat and crossed over to the other side to collect Phil. The river was turbulent making it difficult to get the boat up on the plane as they headed downstream. After about five miles down, where the river narrowed as it headed for a series of rapids, they saw the island and the stranded fishermen.

"We are too heavy for us all to go any further. I'm going to drop you on the bank. You will have to walk to a point opposite the island," Tom told Phil as he steered towards to side of the river.

"That's fine. I will set up the rope and when I am ready will signal to you, and you can approach the island. If you get into trouble, wave your arms, and I will shoot the line across your bows. We are getting too close to the rapids for comfort," Phil said as he leaped onto the bank with his equipment and headed downstream.

Once Phil was set up on the bank opposite the island, Tom took the boat out into the mainstream and headed for the island, he could see people perched up in the branches, hanging on for dear life. The island was totally submerged with only a few Acacia trees sticking up above the water, and so this was their only refuge.

As Tom got close to the island, the propeller snagged in the reeds under water, stalling the engine and the rushing water began to pull the boat towards the rapids. Tom knew that if he got into the mainstream without the engine, he was doomed.

On the bank, Phil saw that Tom was in trouble and using the .303 rifle with cup discharger and using a blank round, he fired a wooden block with a line attached to it across the bow of the boat. The block went sailing over Tom's head and landed on the island, but the wet line snapped. Luckily Tom had managed to grab hold of a clump of reeds and pull the boat to the island, eagerly assisted by the fishermen.

After clearing the reeds from the propeller, he ferried two of the fishermen and the block back to the river bank where Phil attached it to the line once again, and this time fired it successfully onto the island, the rope was pulled across and attached to a tree by one of the fishermen. The rest of the stranded men were rescued, the rope, untied from the tree, was then used to pull the boat to the bank.

As the fishermen were dropped off on the riverbank, they saw the policeman and took off as quickly as they could without even a thank you. They had been fishing illegally, and obviously thought they were going to be arrested.

"Did you see if those grateful bastards had any fishing gear with them?" Phil asked.

"No. When I got to the island, they were all just huddled up in trees."

"Well, I was just wondering if they were actually fishermen, or have we just rescued a bunch of bloody terrs."

"No, I don't think so. They just looked like ordinary Makaranga (local tribe) fishermen to me," Tom replied.

"I am not so sure about that. They looked very furtive and took off into the bush as fast as they could without so much as a thank you," Phil said.

"If they are terrs, surely they would have weapons stashed somewhere?"

"Yes more than likely. But I don't think they would have taken them onto the island with them when they decided to go fishing."

"Well, we've gone and let them bugger off now. They could have gone anywhere, and we don't have the time to chase aftr them; it will be getting dark soon," Tom said.

"I will get a couple of my men to come out this way and have a look around. Perhaps they will be able to dig something up. We can't be too careful," Phil said.

Gathering up the rescue equipment they headed back upstream. Goijng against the flow of the river, the boat was able to speed along on the plane. As they passed under the railway bridge, there was a loud thump, and the boat almost capsized. It was not the sound of hitting a rock or a tree stump, and the engine was still running perfectly. Knowing immediately what they had struck, Tom kept the throttle wide open to get away from there as fast as possible. Turning to look back they saw an angry hippo pop its head above the raging water. It could easily have snapped the boat in half and killed them.

Dropping Phil off at the road where he had left his vehicle, they saw tracks in the sand made by a large crocodile. Somebody was looking after them that day.

Two days later, Tom received an urgent call from the police. Some fishermen were again stranded in trees in the middle of another flooding river. This time it was in the Mtilikwe Weir nearer Triangle. The police came to the spot where the road disappeared under the water of the Lundi River, loaded the boat onto a trailer they had borrowed, and off they went with Tom to the Mtilikwe Weir.

The level of the water in the weir had risen when the river flooded, and the fishermen caught unexpectedly had climbed into a tree. The three fishermen in the tree were terrified. Two very large crocodiles were circling, waiting for them to get tired of hanging on and drop into the water. The rescued fishermen told them that the night before, one of their companions had fallen into the water and the others had seen him being taken by a crocodile.

It transpired that two of the rescued fishermen had connections with the terrorists and had been arrested with their AK47's when they tried to use them to poach game on one of the nearby ranches. They had been given basic training on the use of the firearms and sent to spy on the movements of farmers. The man who had trained them and given them their orders was called 'Mamba'.

"Tom I am about to have a baby, and here you are rushing around helping to rescue people from trees in swollen rivers. They shouldn't be there in the first place. What happens if I go into labour while you are on one of your rescue missions?" Julia wanted to know.

"You are quite right. I will tell Phil that because of your condition, I will not be available for any more rescue operations. He will just have to find someone else to help him. He can always borrow the boat. Let's hope that the river subsides before you decide to go into labour," Tom said.

A week later, and after the river had dropped, Julia gave birth to another boy. They named him Kyle as he had been conceived while they were on a weekend break at Lake Kyle. Stuart, who was now two years old, was fascinated by his new brother and had to be watched the whole time as he was eager to involve Kyle in his games and to share his toys with him. Tom was very proud of his little family.

The salary and working conditions were good, but there was no profit-based bonus like there had been in the tobacco industry. They were, however, paid a thirteenth cheque at Christmas time. With these financial constraints, the plan to buy a farm had to be put on the back burner until the settler farm scheme was announced.

****

Chapter 12

Life was treating Lucas Mpofu very well. He had grown up in the Chiweshi Tribal Trust area in the northeast of Rhodesia and he was educated at the Secondary School in Umvukwes. Umvukwes was a commercial farming area with a large number of white farmers running big productive farms, each with at least 100 farm workers.

The farms were all self-contained communities with a clinic and school for the families of the workers, all of whom were housed on the farms. His parents lived on a farm in the district, where his father worked as the farm foreman. They were provided with a good house, he was paid well, and the children's education was paid for by the farm owner.

As he neared the end of his schooling, Lucas set his mind on joining the police force. Policemen seemed to have good lives and were respected members of the community. When he left school, his father insisted that he work on the farm until he reached the age of twenty. Then he would be eligible to apply to join the police. Being a bright youngster, literate and able to speak English, he was soon given the job of recording task work on the farm. He enjoyed this work as it put him in a position of responsibility with a slightly better wage than the average labourer.

Two years later Lucas joined the police force, and after completing six months of training, he was posted to the Harare Police Station in the township south of Salisbury. Within a couple of months, he was moved to Stodart, one of the substations of Harare and right in the middle of the location.

Constable Mpofu was enjoying his life. He wore a smart uniform, he had good living quarters, and he had a bicycle which he rode to and from his quarters every day. He also used it to carry out patrols and enquiries in the area. He had arguably one of the best jobs a young black man could have in the country.

Patrol Officer Tom Owen was posted to Stodart shortly after Lucas. They met each other in the Charge Office at Harare a couple of times. He was a tall young man who appeared to be a reasonable sort of person and who got on well with his peers. The Station Sergeant selected Lucas to work with Tom as his assistant. This meant they would work together at all times when on duty. Lucas was pleased with this promotion from the humdrum of Charge Office duties. He had a feeling that they were going to get on well together.

Lucas worked very well with Tom, and they became a formidable team, well known and respected by the residents in the area where they worked and policed. When there were riots, the crowds preferred pushing their way past a whole squad of 'Riot Stand By', made up of policemen from other areas, on one side of the road, then Tom and Lucas on the other.

After he got married, Tom transferred to Rhodesville, a Police Station in the eastern suburbs of Salisbury. They had worked together for two years.

"We have been a good team, you and I," Tom said on the eve of his departure to Rhodesville. "Why don't you try to get a transfer to Rhodesville or Highlands?"

"Yes, we have worked well together. I am sorry that you are moving. I will try to get a transfer as soon as I can," Lucas said.

"That will be good. I am sure that we will see each other again soon in any case. We still have cases to attend in court together," Tom said

"Yes I will see you in court when our cases are heard, and I too am sure that we will see one another again in time to come. Good luck and go well," Lucas said.

"And you stay well my friend," Tom said shaking Lucas' hand.

Tom left the police force six months later and went to work on a tobacco farm in the Goromonzi area. Lucas knew that he had always wanted to return to his life of farming and was not surprised to see him go. He was different to the other white policeman, and he understood the ways of the black people. They lost touch soon after that.

With the political situation in the country getting worse and worse, Lucas was worried about the future. He did not want to see relations in the country deteriorate like those to the north. He was happy with the way the country was run by the current government and was encouraged by the fact that the Prime Minister wanted to include responsible black people in the running of the country. The British Government did not agree with him and after a lot of failed discussions and negotiations, Ian Smith declared independence from Britain on 11th November 1965.

The following year, after passing his examinations, Lucas was promoted to Sergeant and transferred to Bikita police station in Victoria Province. Bikita, a small settlement in the hills above the Lowveld to the east of Fort Victoria, consisted of the Police Station, the District Commissioners Offices, a clinic, the school and a few trading stores. He was pleased to be back in a rural area because he had grown up on a farm he was much happier carrying out farm and Tribal Trust patrols than he had been working in the city.

With his promotion, he was earning a much better salary with additional benefits and perks. He had been to Police Driving School and now had a motor vehicle and motorcycle licenses. Most of the patrols he carried out were either in the station Land Rover or on the motorcycle. His bicycle days were over.

Insurgents were becoming a real problem in the country. It became necessary for all members of the Police Force to perform border duties in the worst affected areas. Being a staunch supporter of the government and deciding that he wanted to be of greater service to his country; Lucas volunteered to join the Police Anti-Terrorist Unit and was sent away on a course to learn about anti-terrorist operations.

On his return, he was ready to join a PATU unit. This would give him a more active role in the fight against the terrorists. With only a few commercial farmers in the Bikita district, and most of the area consisting of Tribal Trust land, there were no PATU units there, and he was used to make up numbers in other units in the Victoria Province when they were short. (PATU units were generally made up of white farmers with the odd black policeman.)

After spending a year at Bikita, Lucas heard of a vacancy for a Sergeant at the Triangle Police Station. It would be a step in the right direction for him as it was a much bigger station than Bikita and would help with further promotion. He would also be able to join a PATU unit there as he knew there were some units in the Lowveld.

Although he had never been to this part of the country, he had heard a lot about it, and so decided to apply for the position. His application was successful, and within three weeks he moved to Triangle.

Once Lucas had settled into his new station, he organized his shifts and then checked the list of farmers living in and around Triangle. He would be carrying out an orientation patrol in a few days' time and needed to know who was where in his area.

It came as a complete surprise to him to see Tom Owen's name on the list. He was a Section Manager on one of the sugar cane sections on the sugar estates. Lucas had assumed that Tom was still in the Highveld on a tobacco farm.

As soon as he was able to, Lucas made a telephone call hoping it was the same Tom Owen he had worked with in Harare.

"This is Tom Owen. Can I help you?" Tom said answering the call. Lucas was delighted to hear his voice on the other end of the line. It had been five years since they had seen each other.

"Good morning Sir. It is Lucas Mpofu. We used to work together at Stodart."

"Lucas! Hell, it is good to hear from you. Where are you now?"

"I have recently been posted here to Triangle. I am looking forward to seeing you," Lucas replied. They arranged to meet the following day.

****

Chapter 13

The Rhodesian Bush War was escalating in the northern parts of the country. Since his arrival in the Lowveld, Tom had not been called out on PATU operations and had only been used for other police reserve duties. All men under 50 years of age had to complete four two-week call-up stints in the Security Services every year.

He had only been involved in the guarding gangs of labourers who were erecting a security fence along the northeastern border of the country. This was an area where illegal border crossings by insurgents were rife, and so it was a double fence with each component standing 30 paces apart and ten foot high.

The area in between the two fences was cleared, and anti-personnel landmines were laid. By the time it was completed, the fence must have been 320 miles long. The highlight of each day was to race back to base camp to get the first cold beer; each man was rationed with only two beers a day.

A favourite game played at night in the camps at Mukumbura and Nyamapanda was 'Bezant'. This was a game similar to baseball, only it played with a strong stick and empty Bezant orange juice can. All players were naked and could be hurt quite badly. Best played when totally inebriated; these games were quite often interrupted when the camp came under mortar fire. Men sober up very quickly when bombs start exploding around them.

Like most other young men, Tom found this duty extremely boring and looked forward to the day when he would once again be used for follow up and anti-terrorist patrols.

Tom had been working on Mpapa for two years when he was promoted and moved from the diversified farm to a sugar cane section on the estate. This was a step in the right direction as it would enable him to earn a reasonable profit-based bonus. He was pleased with the move and the opportunity it presented.

Phil was transferred to Fort Victoria to take over the training of all Police Reservists in the province. Tom was to see him when passing through that town and when he came to the Lowveld on training weekends.

On his first morning, he took his horse from the groom, mounted up and trotted off to organize the workers in the fields. It was still dark, and as he rode, he heard the sound of footsteps padding on the road behind him. He increased the pace of his mount, hoping to leave his follower behind, but the footsteps also increased their pace, keeping up with Tom. Twenty minutes later he arrived at the work front and there standing beside him with his hand outstretched, was his groom, gasping for breath.

"What are you doing Phineas?" he asked the groom.

"I have come to hold your horse Ishe (sir)," Phineas replied.

"Can't one of the other workers do it for me?" Tom was incredulous.

"No Ishe. It is my job, and I am trained by the other Section Manager to follow behind to hold the horse when you walk in the fields."

"So you will follow me all day to hold my horse every time I get off?"

"Yes, Ishe."

"Phineas you will go back to the stables now and do your work there. I will not need you to hold my horse in the fields thank you."

It didn't seem such a good idea to have a stable hand running after him all day just to hold his horse every time he stopped. From then on, Tom used his motorcycle in the early mornings and only used horses when he was riding around the section checking the day's work.

Mastering the art of burning the sugar cane fields before harvesting presented some interesting and sometimes frightening experiences. It was very easy for a fire to jump the break, surround the workers and engulf them in smoke and fifty to one hundred foot flames. Sprinting came easily on these occasions.

As they now lived much closer to the club, Tom and Julia were able to start playing sport and became more involved in the community. Tom played rugby for the Lowveld team, and Julia enjoyed tennis and squash. They both played golf almost every Sunday. A small game park on the estate stocked with a variety of animals provided them with enjoyable game-viewing drives, which the boys loved.

Terrorist attacks on farms were becoming a regular occurrence. Following the coup in Portugal, Portuguese control of Mozambique collapsed, and control of the country was taken over by Frelimo forces.

The Portuguese, no longer in control, quickly fled and the new government was quick to assist the forces invading Rhodesia. This immediately increased terrorist activity in the south-east of the country.

The men in the Lowveld would no longer be carrying out duties in the north-east and the north of the country but were to protect their own area. The national call-up commitments were increased to two weeks duty every three months. Tom called for volunteers to join him in forming a new PATU unit. He approached four members of the local Police Reserve who all agreed to join him. They were 'seasoned' men who had been involved in previous skirmishes with the terrorists.

John had been in Tom's first PATU unit, and they had been together when they tracked and ambushed the terrorists that had attacked the Fuller's farm. He had accepted a position with a local rancher to start big game safari's in the Lowveld. Gary was the manager of the local Ford tractor and implements branch, Terry was a local cattle rancher and Nick, like Tom, was a sugarcane grower from the neighbouring estate.

Out of the blue, Tom received a phone call from Lucas Mpofu, his old assistant from his time in the police force. He had been promoted and was now stationed at Triangle police station. Tom was delighted to hear from him, and they arranged to meet the following day. He looked forward to seeing his old sidekick again.

The next day Tom went into the village and stopped at the police station. Lucas was on duty in the charge office; he was now the station sergeant. They sat outside in the shade of a flamboyant tree and caught up on each other's news.

"I see that you are a PATU Section Leader. I am also a member of PATU and have had the necessary training," Lucas said.

"Are you a member of a stick?" Tom asked.

"Not as yet. Have you got a place in your stick for me?"

"There is indeed. I will arrange for you to meet the other members as soon as possible."

Tom called a meeting at the police mess with the members of his section to introduce them to Lucas. Knowing him as he did, Tom was sure that he would be a valuable member of the unit. It was agreed that Lucas would join them on their next patrol. After the meeting, they adjourned to the bar to discuss matters over a couple of beers. The mess was always the most difficult place to get away from; the beer was cheap and the company entertaining.

Tom was pleased that they now had a trusted interpreter. A black policeman would be very useful in the bush; Lucas would be an asset to the Section. 'Tango One' PATU stick now had six members, enabling one member to be rested, and left behind each time they went into the bush. After a few training exercises working as a unit, they were ready.

****

Chapter 14

The Frelimo forces, having fought a long hard campaign to gain control of Mozambique, were keen to assist their neighbors to do likewise in Rhodesia giving the Zanu soldiers all the help they could. With them in control of Mozambique, movement around the border and into Rhodesia became a lot easier.

Because of his early blunder, it had taken two long years for Mamba to be promoted to a sector leader and moved to the south where he was to lead ground operations into the Lowveld from Mozambique. He had operated in that area for a short time when he was busy establishing supply lines and recruiting locals to spy on the whites, and so he knew what to expect; it was an exciting development for him.

He traveled by road, with other freedom fighters, from the camp at Catandica to Espungabera where they spent the night in a large military camp outside the town. The following day they moved on to Massangena, Machaila and finally to Chicualacuala.

As the main camp at Chicualacuala was eighty miles from the border, it meant that Mamba would have to set up a forward camp much closer to the fence, opposite the Gona-re-Zhou (Place of Elephants) Game Conservation Area in the Southeast of Rhodesia.

Apart from the Rangers Camp, nobody lived in the game reserve, so this provided him with easy entry and little chance of detection. The only potential problem was encounters with lions and other big game. South of the reserve, all along the north bank of the Limpopo River, the area was sparsely populated and would provide an ideal springboard for their operations.

ZANU forces were gathering in the camp, preparing for a big push into the southern section of Rhodesia. The Freedom Fighters used the Mozambique troop train to travel from Maputo after arriving by ship from the Tanzanian training camps. The border was closed and the trains no longer running to Rhodesia were now only used to transport troops and supplies.

Once routes had been established, they were to infiltrate into the country via Crooks Corner, at the junction of the borders between Rhodesia, South Africa and Mozambique on the Limpopo River.

Mamba knew that it was an area which had, as yet, not been targeted by Freedom Fighters. From initial scouting reports, it seemed that the Rhodesian Security Forces were not present in the area. It was imperative that routes be established as soon as possible before it became known that the area was being used as an entry point. The prospect of attacking isolated ranchers and sugar farmers made him anxious to get started.

Speed being essential, Mamba selected his group of twenty men from the 300 who were in the camp. Their training, in groups of five, started the following day, and a week later they were ready to move closer to the border. From there they would launch their sorties into Rhodesia. A Frelimo troop carrier was made available to transport them with their equipment, extra stocks of landmines, mortar bomb launchers, and bombs, RPG rocket launchers, ammunition, and food.

A camp was set up on the banks of the Limpopo River, just to the east of Crooks Corner. The five additional men who accompanied them would be left to guard the camp, and to liaise with the base camp. Once their camp was set up, Mamba sent small groups of two and three men into Rhodesia to check the 'lay of the land', and make contact with sympathizers who would be willing to help them with food and information.

Within a week these scouting men returned in dribs and drabs, to report that all had gone according to plan, with people in some of the villages willing to assist. The two men who had checked the paths on either side of the border fence from the Naunetsi River to the Limpopo River had seen no sign of security-force movement.

They were ready to move four units of five men each into Rhodesia. Mamba instructed the leaders of each group that they should all enter the country together and then split up into their groups at Sengwe; with each proceeding to their previously selected targets.

****

Chapter 15

The men were spending more and more time away from home. National Service commitments were again increased with men up to the age of 60 now being expected to carry out duties. Many of the women volunteered to help operate the radios and assist with catering at command centers around the country. Husbands and fathers went off into the bush for long periods at a time and sometimes never returned home.

In Salisbury some men on the way to the 'Sharp End,' with the possibility of never returning, went for their last night of clubbing at 'Grab a Granny' where they met up with women, some of them married to men away on military duty. The security situation in the country put a huge strain on the family unit, and the divorce rate was rising rapidly in the country.

When Tom was out on patrol, his family, for their safety, spent nights at the Country Club where accommodation was laid on for them. In the mornings, after the roads had been checked for landmines and ambushes, they would go back to the farm.

Although Julia had her hands full with her two young boys growing up when Tom was away in the bush she was lonely and decided that she would assist the war effort. She volunteered to help as a radio operator at the operations command center based near the village. On the days when she was on duty, the children were left with other children at the Country Club and could still attend school, which was adjacent to the club.

Julia enjoyed her role as it made her feel useful and she was able to keep abreast of the war situation in the country. Before joining the forces, she felt as if she and Tom were being torn apart, but now she was able to be involved with him and keep in touch with his activities. The day before Tom departed on stints in the bush, when he was packing his kit, he always became quiet.

Although he never said anything, she knew that he was nervous and worried. She felt the same as she never knew whether she would see him alive again or whether he was going to be wounded. Once he was in uniform and she dropped him off with the rest of the stick, he changed and seemed to relax as he cheerfully set about organizing the unit. He was confident and comfortable with his men.

....

Knowing that his family was safe while he was away on patrol was a great relief for Tom, and he was proud of his wife for getting involved. It was comforting to know that she was at the other end of the radio.

Apart from emergency call outs, the unit was now spending two weeks every two months in the bush and had become a very well-organized and efficient fighting unit. They had been on some patrols, and a few call-out operations and each member knew exactly what his role was within the unit. They learned to trust each other implicitly. With the need to be as invisible as possible in the bush, they grew beards to break the sharp outline of their faces, and their clothing was basic and tatty.

The stick was deployed to the South Eastern corner of the country where insurgents were suspected of entering from Mozambique.

"We have had some reports from game guards, at Malapati Game Reserve, that insurgents are entering Rhodesia from Mozambique at Crooks Corner. I need you chaps to get down there and investigate these allegations." Inspector Seward told them at the briefing.

"What approach must we use, and what must we do if we suspect anyone of being a terrorist or a sympathizer?" asked Tom.

"Keep an eye on them, find out as much as you can, and report back to us. There is an RLI troop being moved into the area from the west within the next couple of days. It will be beneficial for them to know what to expect when they get there. My gut feeling tells me that these reports are true, so you must be vigilant at all times. I have also been in touch with South African Parks Department in the Kruger National Park who have also heard that illegal crossings are being made at Crooks Corner. It's where the boundaries of Rhodesia, South Africa, and Mozambique meet on the Limpopo River. A Mission Station was established there during the early slave-trading times but was later destroyed. In more recent times it has been used as a hide-out for fugitives and ivory poachers," Inspector Seward said, concluding the briefing.

Tom and his men were dropped off just south of Malapati Game Reserve, and at noon they set off along the banks of the Naunetsi River, heading south-east in the direction of the Mozambique border.

The vegetation was sparse along the river, with the only shade and relief from the blistering heat, coming from the dark green foliage of the massive wild fig trees, whose ripe yellow fruit hung like bunches of grapes from the branches.

To begin with, the team made good time, covering about 10 miles before setting up camp for the night. Although it was not a likely area for terrorists to be passing through, they still took precautions; picking their spot carefully to ensure they had plenty of cover. With water on hand from the nearby river, they were quite comfortable.

The following morning they moved through a Mopani forest then into an area of low scrub. Every now and again they would disturb a bush shrike that would give a loud shriek as it fluttered out of their way. The river was still flowing in the direction they wanted to go, so they decided to continue following its course towards the border. As they progressed, they crossed some game trails and pathways leading to and from the river.

All at once John stopped and gave the 'down' signal with his arm. They all stopped and crouched low, facing outwards as he slowly moved forward to examine the ground. He signaled for Tom to join him. They had come across a fairly well-used path with tracks in the dust leading to the west, which appeared to have been made by only one person. On examining the spoor card Tom carried, it seemed as if the tracks matched those of insurgents and were not more than a day old. It seemed odd for there to be only one set of tracks, so they decided to sweep the whole area, searching for signs of other movements.

The map showed no significant pathways, nor were there any villages within three miles of their present position. Exploring in the direction from where the tracks came led them back to the river and a rocky crossing. Further on, the path made its way to the border fence about a mile away. Someone had crossed from Mozambique into Rhodesia illegally and was up to no good.

Careful examination of the map revealed that Crooks Corner was only fifteen miles distant and that there was a fairly large settlement close to the border. It was the direction in which the tracks were leading them; they were now heading away from the Naunetsi River towards the Limpopo River.

By mid-afternoon the scrub had thinned out, becoming less dense with the vista changing to open grassland with only a few Marula trees and one or two Leadwood and Sausage Trees offering little or no cover. The chance of being spotted from some distance away made them all a little uncomfortable. Using what cover they could find, they crisscrossed the path frequently.

Tom called a halt every hour to rest and to study the terrain ahead. The only movement they had seen was an army of large black fighting 'Matabele Ants,' thousands strong and each over an inch long, as they marched off into battle.

It had been hot and cloudless all day with no wind to cool them down. At last, as the sun started to sink towards the horizon, a slight breeze picked up, bringing great relief to their weary bodies. Moving some distance off the path, they found cover along the bank of a small stream where they squatted down to eat a meal. After sunset just as it got dark, look out times were set, and they 'bomb shelled' (spread out) to get some rest.

They were on the move again at first light. The weather had changed during the night, and it was a lot cooler now, with a stiff breeze bringing in moist air from the south-west. It was overcast, and the low heavy clouds promised rain. If they were to find out whose tracks they were following, they would have to hurry before the rain washed the signs away. An hour later they came across a small rise topped by an untidy group of four huts with a small grain storage hut.

About thirty paces to the left of the huts was a large Marula tree with three or four logs placed in a circle beneath it. To the right, there was a small cattle kraal bordered by with a few paw-paw trees and between the kraal and the huts was a group of five or six Mango trees with a few chickens scratching busily around underneath. Two scrawny brindle dogs sniffed around looking for scraps, and a baby sat on a grass mat in the middle of the clearing in between the huts, while a woman pounded grain in an oversized mortar with a pole. Another woman was bent over, sweeping outside one of the huts with a grass broom.

The 'stick' sat and silently watched for half an hour before Tom decided they would have to take a chance and approach the huts openly without trying to conceal their presence. There had been no sign of any other tracks leading to this settlement, and he felt quite sure that the occupants had nothing to hide.

They were about to break cover and approach the huts, when another woman appeared walking along a pathway from the east, carrying a container on her head. Tom knew that there was a stream about 200 paces away in that direction, so he presumed that she had been collecting water and washing clothes and utensils.

As they approached, they saw another path leading away from the huts in a southerly direction. John pointed out that the tracks they were busy following continued along that path. They would get back on the trail after speaking to the two women. Lucas went forward to greet them and after the ritual handshaking and salutations, questioned them about strangers and movement of people in the area.

"Where are your menfolk?" Lucas asked them once the lengthy greetings were completed.

"My husband has gone with my son to work," the older of the two replied.

"Where is it that they work, Mother?" he asked her respectfully.

"They work on the mines at Egoli (Johannesburg) in South Africa."

"When will they be returning? How long have they been away?"

"They went away at the beginning of the year. They will only return in December when they have finished their contract."

"Have you seen any strangers passing this way in recent days?"

"No. I have not seen any strangers, but I have heard that there are ngandanga's passing near here from Mozambique," the old woman informed them.

The child had started to cry prompting its mother to pick it up. Tucking it under her arm, she stuffed her sagging breast into its mouth and wandered over to join them. Lucas greeted her in the same manner that he had greeted the older woman then questioned her asking if she had seen any strangers. She agreed with the older woman; she had also heard that men were entering the country from Mozambique.

"I have heard that they demand food from the villagers along the river," she said pointing in the direction of the Limpopo River.

"*Tatenda Mama.*" (Thank you, mother) Lucas bade them farewell as they turned to leave. The women both seemed relieved to see them go.

With no further information forthcoming, the men moved back to the path and continued following the tracks to the south. The wind had picked up bringing the rain closer. Estimating that they only had an hour at the most to find out where the tracks led to, they pressed on as fast as they dared. It was open grassland so there was no need to stick to their normal formation and they walked along the path in single file about five paces apart.

As the first drops fell out of the low swollen clouds onto the hot, dry, dusty land, it gave off a good earthy smell. At first, the rain was just a light drizzle, but enough to make them don their shower-proof ponchos. The path led them up a small hill, and as they crested the rise, they could see the wide sandy Limpopo River about half a mile away.

Even from that distance through the light rain, the wide, sandy riverbed was visible. Blue-green reeds along either bank hugged the trunks of Wild Fig and Fever trees, that grew amongst them and presented such unexpected beauty that Tom was compelled to stop for just a moment and take it all in.

He wished he could share these moments with Julia; show her this postcard picture and this perfection before him. For an instant, he feared that their lives were pulling apart. There was so much she would never know, and even if he told her, she would never understand. Tom looked at these men around him and realized they knew parts of him his wife would never see.

The intensity of the rain was increasing, and so they hurried along looking for a place to shelter. There was no point in trying to continue the tracking; all sign of the spoor was already obliterated. A large Wild Fig tree provided them with the shelter they were looking for, and they settled down covering themselves as best as they could with their ponchos. They had good visibility all around and were well off the path leading along the river, which they would keep an eye on still.

The rain came down harder, but with the help of a few large palm leaves, they were able to construct a makeshift shelter and managed to stay reasonably dry. As it looked as if they would be there for some time, they made themselves a meal. Two men stayed on watch at all times.

"That sod we've been following could be a scout for a larger group. We must keep our bloody eyes skinned. There might be a damned big group following a day or two behind the bugger," Tom expressed his thoughts to the others.

"Ja, I agree. Who else would be coming from inside Mozambique wearing good boots? He must be a gook come to have a look see," John agreed.

"I'm sure those women back there have not told us the truth. If there is a route into the country through here, they'll know about it. They fear for their lives and will not tell us everything," Lucas added, sucking on a Marula berry he had picked up.

"We'd better let HQ know what we are doing; we are scheduled to call in at four," said Nick the radio man.

"Yeah, and tell them to drop us some warm kit, while you are at it. A bottle of brandy would go down well right now," said Gary. As the medic, he was always the most practical. "I am wet and freezing my arse off," he complained.

They weren't carrying a change of clothing, and so would have to dry out in the sun; when it came out again. The rain had eased off and seemed to be clearing when they made their call to base at four. The aerial was strung between two branches, and communication was established. After giving their location in code, and bringing HQ up to date with the progress of their patrol, they were instructed to stay where they were and to monitor all movements in their immediate vicinity.

As it was too late to move and they were reluctant to leave the shelter of the big tree, they decided to find a more suitable spot in the morning. Although it didn't rain again, they had a cold, wet and uncomfortable night.

By the morning, the clouds had disappeared, and the sun started to peer out over the low hills in the east. As the first rays of sunlight touched the trees and the grassland around them, the landscape lit up with a warm orange glow. The trees looked as if they had been washed and with the rain still on the bright green leaves; they glistened like jewels in the sun.

As the warmth from the sun began to dry everything, little wisps of steam rose from the ground, and from the tufts of light brown pampas grass. The birds began to sing their happy chorus as they flittered around looking for food. Tom had always enjoyed the 'after rain' feel of Africa.

John and Nick went off to scout around and to ensure that they had not been seen in the night. They checked the path for any movement they might have missed and returned to report the path was clear. They had seen a small koppie with large granite rocks and trees offering good cover, overlooking the path about a mile further to the west. It was a possible observation position.

A warm meal, made from 'bully beef' and biscuits, was prepared in a mess tin over a small burner and accompanied by a hot mug of tea. Then after eating they rolled their wet sleeping bags up with their ponchos and were ready to move. They would dry their sleeping bags out once they reached a suitable place.

It took them some time to reach the koppie; slowed by the need to cover their tracks in the moist surface of the soil. Arriving at the spot John and Nick had found, they worked their way up to the crest of the hill. The koppie was surrounded by thorn trees and thorn scrub, with a few Mopani trees near the base of the hill. A large Wild Olive grew alongside a huge pair of granite boulders that leaned against each other.

It was perfect for their purpose, and they were able to make themselves quite comfortable. The cover was abundant with shelter and shade under the base of the rocks offering good all round views of the surrounding area. Satisfied that they had covered their tracks and they were well concealed from the path below, they settled down to their task of watching all movement in the area.

Tom had a good look around. Their position was well above the path, and from there he could easily see the Limpopo River. It was about half a mile wide, well beyond the path and 500 paces to the south. He could see the wide sandy riverbed disappearing about 2 miles upstream to the west, and 3 miles downstream to the south-east. Through his binoculars, Tom noted that the weaver birds had built their nests low down in Fever trees; a sure sign that it was going to be a dry summer. When they build high in the trees, it meant floods.

They were about a mile from the Mozambique border at Crooks Corner. The path below them passed under the trees as it wound its way to the west. Large clumps of 'Lala' palm bushes were scattered about in the open areas. Watching anyone walking along the path would be easy.

By the time they had settled down, organized themselves, and set their watch times, the sun was at its zenith. A few puffy clouds still drifted lazily across the blue sky. They spread their sleeping bags out under the sun to dry off and moved around freely, confident that they would not be spotted from the path below, and that their presence would not be compromised.

Time passed slowly as it always did when carrying out an OP (observation post). They had nothing to do and nothing to read except the map, the spoor card, and the patrol notebook.

Tom, suspecting that they might be there for a few days, suggested that they record all species of birds and game that they spotted while they were not on the move. John, who was the expert, was to identify the species, then teach them all a bit about each bird they spotted.

Lucas produced a pack of cards which also passed the time, and was a welcome distraction.

John, always making a plan to provide fresh meat, made a trap to try and snare a Francolin or even a Guinea Fowl. Using a few grains of corn he had picked up at the kraal, he placed them under a large flat rock, propped it up by a small stick attached to a six-foot-long piece of string he held in his hand, then he waited patiently.

With their sleeping bags spread open all the time, they had to constantly check to make sure scorpions didn't crawl inside them. Spiders and snakes could also be a nuisance and a danger.

The only movement they saw over the first few days, apart from birds, was the appearance of a small brown duiker which walked slowly and daintily among the trees, stopping now and again to nibble on some juicy young shoots. The young ram stood about 18 inches high with its small straight horns protruding from the top of his head.

Any trained insurgent would know that it was not a good idea to move around shortly after the rain, as tracks left behind would be clearly visible, very easy to follow and almost impossible to erase, so the chance of seeing anyone in the first day was pretty slim. With this in mind, the men in the stick had ample time to study the vista, noting any feature that might be of interest or useful to later operations.

The highlight of the day was the radio communication with HQ. Using the code of the day, they gave their position and the 'Sitrep' (Situation Report) asking for an update on any reported activity in their sector. Nothing had changed from the previous day. Late in the afternoon, they enjoyed a meal of Guinea Fowl which John had proudly prepared.

The days dragged by with little or nothing to report. Four days after taking up their position on the hilltop near Crooks Corner, and just as they were beginning to think that they were in the wrong position to monitor any movement, they were rewarded.

Two hours after sunrise the sudden hush of the cicadas warned them that something was on the move. Gary, who was on duty at the time, spotted someone approaching along the path from the direction of Mozambique. Quickly they turned their attention to the path and watched.

After a short while, a man came into view, walking slowly as he carefully studied the ground and the surrounding area ahead of him. He was dressed in olive green fatigues and carried an AK47 rifle at the ready. There was no doubt that he was an insurgent.

****

Chapter 16

Making use of the information his men had given him, Mamba decided that it was safe to move in the daytime and he and his group of freedom fighters set off on their mission. Four days after the rain they crossed the border at first light and then proceeded along a path leading from the border towards Sengwe in the west.

After entering the country, Mamba had one of his men go ahead as a scout, then followed some distance behind with the rest of the big group spread out in line behind him. There was no sign of tracks or that anyone had moved along the path since the rain.

A mile into the country, the path passed between a small hill and the Limpopo River, but before moving into the open ground and approaching the base of the hill, Mamba stopped and carefully examined what lay ahead - he was sure that if they were going to be ambushed, the attack would come from there.

....

With their nerves jingling, Tom and his men waited and watched to see if there were others with the lone insurgent. A few minutes later, when he was almost opposite their position, a second man appeared and stopped briefly to look in their direction before moving on. He was a tall, well-built man wearing dark glasses and dressed in the same uniform as the first man. He wore a pistol in a holster on his hip, carried an AK47 slung over his shoulder, and walked with an air of authority.

Close behind him, eight more insurgents followed with another ten two minutes later. They all walked along the path in single file and about five paces apart. Tom knew that there were no others when he saw the last man dragging a small branch behind him to sweep away their tracks. Apart from the first two men, all carried packs on the backs as well as AK47 rifles.

Nervous tension quickly replaced boredom. If they had been seen, the insurgents could easily surround them and attack their position. As they watched, the group seemed to pick up speed and within minutes, disappeared along the path to the west.

"Shit, that's a bloody big bunch of the bastards. I reckon the second man is the leader of the group," Tom whispered to others. "We must wait for a while to make sure that there aren't anymore following. Keep watching, all around our position, and don't move until I give the all clear."

Silently and nervously they waited and watched as the minutes ticked past. Ten minutes later, when they were sure there were no others tagging along behind the main group, or that they were not about to be attacked, Tom broke the silence.

"Get on the radio and report this mob. Ask for instructions. Must we follow or engage them when we can?" he said, addressing Nick.

"Will do," said Nick.

"John, take Lucas with you and have a scout around further along the path to make sure they haven't doubled back. They might have spotted us or got wind of us being here," Tom quickly gave orders.

With a crackle of static and the volume turned low, Nick made contact with HQ

"Go ahead Tango One. Over," a female voice responded.

"Chiredzi this is Tango One. You have our position. We have just observed a group of twenty insurgents entering from Mozambique. They are heading in a westerly direction. Over."

"Copied that. What are your intentions? Over."

"Request permission to follow and engage. Over."

"Stand by Tango One." After a short pause, the operator came back on the air.

"Tango One, this is Chiredzi. You are not, I repeat not, to follow the insurgents. You are to stay in your present position and continue monitoring. There is a unit from the RLI fire force moving into position to engage the insurgents. Do you copy? Over."

"Copied. We are to remain in our present position. Over."

"Affirmative Tango One. Out."

It was the right call. The group of terrorists was far too big for their stick of five to engage. They would not be able to get ahead of them in time to set an ambush as they were moving far too quickly. Although disappointed at not being in for the kill, they were relieved that the army had been deployed.

....

Seeing and hearing nothing out of the ordinary, Mamba and his operatives continued uneasily along the path. Crossing the open area before passing below the hill was unnerving; they had just got into the country and Mamba did not want his first major operation to be compromised by carelessness. With a sigh of relief, they were soon past the hill and into denser cover. It would not have been good to walk into an ambush only a mile from the border.

Calling a halt half an hour later, Mamba gave his final instructions for the mission.

"I am taking my four men and proceeding north-west to attack targets in that area. The rest of you will continue to the west before making your way to the target areas splitting up into your groups before reaching Sengwe. I have already discussed this with you. Are there any questions?"

"Will we meet up with you again before returning to Mozambique or must we return as soon as we have accomplished our mission?" Sipho asked.

"No. Each group must make their way back to base camp as soon as you have succeeded. That way there will be less chance of being apprehended," Mamba said. "Is there anything else?"

They all shook their heads except the commissar who just glared at him.

"Okay. Now get moving. I will see you all back in camp in about ten days." Mamba and his four walked away leaving the others to continue along the path.

Splitting them into smaller groups was not well accepted by the political commissar, who would have preferred to have them stay together so that he could keep an eye on them all. He maintained that their duty was to indoctrinate the people, and not to enter into contact situations with the enemy.

Mamba, who had been trained as a soldier, preferred to have his men operate in smaller groups. They could cover a far larger area, creating widespread havoc with far less chance of capture, or of being killed. The political education he would leave to the commissar. Mamba had clashed with him on several occasions until he had to physically threaten the man. He now went along with most of Mamba's decisions but made his feelings known from time to time to save face. Mamba's philosophy was to attack and terrorize first, then convert and re-educate afterward.

Making off on a path leading in the direction of Malapati Game Reserve they were soon well away from the others. He had selected two main targets for his attacks, Chikombedzi and Malapati; both isolated areas that would provide him with sufficient targets to cause mayhem. Between them, they carried three landmines that were to be laid in the roads to cover their retreat. These they would stash somewhere en route.

Mamba set a course that should take them to the vicinity of Chikombedzi. Moving at a fast walk, they were soon a long way from the rest of the group who, by mid-afternoon, would split up into three groups with each heading towards their allocated areas.

After splitting up, the other three groups were to head west towards Chipise and Matibi, where they would launch attacks on ranchers and settlements in those areas. They had the political man with them.

He was pleased with the first phase of the operation. They would all meet back at their camp in Mozambique in ten days. Keeping up a fast pace, Mamba and his unit made good ground and by sunset had covered about 20 miles. They camped that night on the banks of the Nuanetsi River where they stashed their landmines and two of their rocket grenades.

Crossing the river at first light the following day, they kept up the blistering pace of the previous day, arriving at the dam on the outskirts of Chikombedzi by late afternoon. Finding a suitable hiding place in the thick riverine forest along the stream feeding the dam, they settled down to rest and planned their attack on the Mission Station, the school, and the Hospital in the village.

. . . .

Headquarters informed Tom during their afternoon 'sitrep' that the Army had successfully engaged the insurgents. Only fifteen of the original group was engaged and accounted for; the other five must have broken away. The stick was instructed to remain vigilant as it was expected they might be heading back to the border.

The following day, after having seen no sign of other insurgents - or the five who had escaped - the stick was ordered back to the Malapati Game Reserve where they would be picked up. Clearing up the area they had been camped in for the past five days, and making sure they left no sign of them having been there, the stick headed north to their pick up point.

A day later they were collected by helicopter and flown back to Chiredzi for debriefing. It had been a fruitful patrol, and on their return, they were informed that five of the terrorists had escaped, two had been injured and captured with the remainder being killed. Two members of the RLI platoon were slightly injured in the skirmish. Follow up on the escapees was being carried out by the army.

The army trackers found the spoor of the five terrorists who had broken away from the main group, but they had lost the trail near the Naunetsi River.

....

The day after arriving at Chikombedzi, Mamba went with two of the men on a recce of the settlement. They wandered around individually, checking the layout of the hospital, the school, and the mission station. Mamba, who had removed his fatigue jacket, purchased a few cool drinks and some cigarettes at the local store.

Some young women were walking around and Mamba, who had not been with a woman for some time, had difficulty controlling his lust. Later on, each of his men took turns to buy refreshments and canned food. Having changed their uniforms for old clothes, they did not raise any suspicion with the local inhabitants. Taking turns to go wandering, they left their weapons and equipment to be guarded by two of the men in their makeshift camp. There was no sign of military presence anywhere.

In the afternoon, Mamba, who had been struggling to contain his urges, went in search of a victim. Leaving the other four men in their camp, he went on a final reconnaissance of the village. He set off in search of a woman, and with the help of some sweets and a cold drink, he soon found a willing participant.

Together they went off to a dense thicket about 300 paces from the school where they would not be seen or heard. An hour later, after having raped the girl and then cutting her throat to ensure her silence, he went back to join his men – 'Nothing to report' he said.

Mamba had chosen to attack this village as the inhabitants were known to support the government, and had refused to participate in helping the Freedom Fighters. They needed to be taught a lesson. The object of their mission was to create mayhem and fear while killing as many as possible. The main targets were those people working in the school and the hospital. The Missionary Station was to be left alone as most of the missionaries in the country were known to harbor and assist insurgents.

Mamba was disappointed that he did not see any white people as he wandered around the village. The settlement was spread out with the buildings spread far apart. Each of his men would have specific targets for their carefully-timed attack. After breaking off the attack, they would regroup back at their camp, before making their escape.

The first thing to be done before the attack was to cut the overhead telephone lines. It was to be a daring daylight attack, but isolated as this location was, Mamba felt confident that they would have at least 18 hours head start on any government forces.

Before first light the next morning, they cut the telephone line on the outskirts of the town. Taking up their allocated positions, they each observed their sectors. Mamba was opposite the main entrance to the hospital with one man out to the left, and one to the right each covering side and rear entrances. The other two men were positioned to attack the school.

An hour later and just as the sun was rising, children started to emerge from the houses and the inhabitants set about their business for the day. Mamba, with a short burst of automatic fire, signaled the start of the attack. Two women ran to the front entrance of the hospital to investigate and were immediately cut down by a burst from Mamba's AK47 rifle. The man on his right fired a rocket into the kitchen, which exploded.

People ran screaming, trying desperately to take cover from bullets. Dogs rushed around barking, chickens cackled wildly, and women were shouting to their children who were running around, screaming and crying as they tried desperately to find somewhere to hide. Some of the younger children stood frozen with fear in the middle of the road.

It was total pandemonium. Mamba could hear the gunfire of the other two who were attacking the school. After he had expended two magazines of ammunition, he broke off the attack and walked into the open. Dead bodies and the injured lay intertwined across the road – the only way to distinguish between them was the deep moans that those in pain made. Now and then Mamba would lift his rifle and fire at a random sufferer; a mercy killing he thought.

All in all, he was pleased with the result but did not have too much time to admire their handiwork. They needed to maximize on the time remaining if they were to make it to the border unhindered.

Mamba estimated that it would take at least two hours to get a message to the Security Forces, another two hours before they arrived on the scene, an hour to find their tracks and be on their trail. By that time they must have been 15 to 20 miles away from Chikombedzi. He intended to attack the camp at Malapati Game Reserve that night, before making for the border. The forces would have been on the alert, and by the next day, they would not be able to get near the camp.

Collecting their landmines as they passed their old campsite, the insurgents arrived in the vicinity of the Malapati camp just as it was getting dark. Carefully they laid the two landmines in the approach road. Covering them with soil and cow dung, they hurried on to get into a position where they could attack the Game Camp.

They were a little nervous, suspecting that the Manager might well have been alerted by radio to the Chikombedzi killings, and so Mamba decided that there was not sufficient time to make a planned attack. It would have to be a 'hit and run'. Waiting until it was completely dark; the group spread out and quietly crept up towards the Ranger's house.

From outside the surrounding game fence, they launched the two rockets into the house which exploded with a loud 'woomp' and lit up the night. The exploding rockets were followed by long bursts of automatic fire which sprayed bullets at the house and surrounding buildings. Hoping that any surviving occupants would keep their heads down for a few minutes, they took off into the bush as fast as they could. Behind them, as they retreated, they heard the odd gunshot and dogs barking.

Making due east from Malapati, they walked fast for three hours, before turning due south and heading for Crooks Corner. It was dark, and the thick bush made their progress very slow. They were in the Game Reserve and had to look out for wild animals in the dark, and were also very aware that leopards hunted at night. At one time they almost walked into a small herd of buffalo standing quietly in the night.

After the long, hard walk from Chikombedzi, followed by their attack on Malapati, they were exhausted, and at sunrise stopped on the banks of the Nuanetsi River to rest, and eat the last of their rations. Although there was no sign of pursuit, Mamba knew it would not be too long. At first light, the enemy would be following their trail from Malapati. But they needed the rest. He sat on the ground, leaning against the trunk of a Wild Fig tree and congratulated himself on the success of his mission. It would show his superiors that he was a great leader and tactician.

Where they stopped to rest was well away from any roads so they could not see or hear vehicles that might have been transporting troops to block their escape. Nevertheless, Mamba decided it would be safer to follow the river across the border and back into Mozambique. By nightfall, they were safe across the border and stopped to sleep. They arrived back in their forward camp by mid-morning the next day. It had been six days since they left.

....

The captured insurgent disclosed that their leader, one of the five who had escaped, went by the name of 'Mamba.' This was the second time Tom had crossed paths with this man. The first time had been in the Mrewa area. A day later it was reported that 23 women and children had been killed in an attack on the school and hospital in Chikombedzi.

A young woman was found dead lying in a thicket of scrub not far from the school. She was naked with her throat cut and she appeared to have been raped.

That same night the main camp in Malapati was attacked, but no one was injured. Earlier that day Tom and his stick had been airlifted from the camp. The following day they heard that a Land Rover carrying five soldiers that were following up on the attacks had been blown up when it hit a landmine. Thanks to their vehicle having been mine-proofed, the soldiers were lucky to escape without injury.

....

On his return to the camp, Mamba learned from the news over the radio, that the other three units had been ambushed and all killed on the first day; only two hours after he had left with his group. He had congratulated himself too soon and was furious. How could they have walked into an ambush so easily? On the upside, at least he was now rid of that infernal political commissar.

"The stinking Makiwa's were waiting for us. They knew we were coming," Mamba said angrily. "They must have been watching us from the top of that small gomo (hill) just after we crossed into the country and set an ambush," he concluded.

The bitterness he felt was made easier when the news broke on the Rhodesian Broadcasting Service, that he and his group had been responsible for the killing of 23 women and children in Chikombedzi. The landmines they had planted were set off the day before their return to camp, with no reported deaths and no killings at Malapati.

It would have been a lot better if he had killed the white Manager and his family at Malapati, but there had not been time. Next time he would know better.

They would not be able to enter Rhodesia via Crooks Corner for a while with the security forces now alerted to their presence in the area. The next operations into the country would have to be launched from further north and would be towards the Chiredzi and Triangle areas.

Mamba decided to move his base to Mavue, 170 miles north. Once again with the help of the Frelimo transport, they settled into their new camp within a week, with a stock of food and ammunition. He had also selected 15 new soldiers to replace those who had been killed at Sengwe.

****

Chapter 17

Reports of incidents and attacks on farms were now a daily occurrence and becoming more widespread along the perimeter of Rhodesia, except the south and south-west. It became more and more necessary for everyone to be vigilant and report any suspicious characters or movements.

Extra training was introduced for men on active duty. The need for Tom and his unit to become more familiar with the areas where they were likely to be called on to patrol or carry out follow up operations, was vital to their success and survival.

With this in mind, Tom volunteered to fly as an observer with his friend Fred when he was carrying out 'Telstar' flights to relay messages from ground forces to command centers. It gave Tom a good opportunity to study the terrain in remote areas from the air and make a note of water holes and other points of interest that might be useful to the stick. During these flights, Fred, who was a qualified instructor, taught Tom how to fly a light aircraft.

With the Bush War hotting up, military commitments were once again increased. Most of the sporting activities were suspended in all rural areas as it was dangerous to travel on the roads at night for any great distance. All rugby and fishing tournaments were stopped as it was impossible to travel to away matches, or to protect visiting sportsmen. Travel by car in and out of the Lowveld could only be made in convoy.

Mamba and his band of merry men were making life very difficult. The incursions into the south-east of the country all seemed to be under his leadership and, by all accounts, he was totally ruthless. Nobody knew his true identity, but he and Tom had crossed paths on three occasions. In all probability, there would be other encounters in the not too distant future. Tom would have to try to out-think his enemy.

At long last, the Minister of Agriculture announced the Settler Farm Scheme for the Lowveld. It had taken five years from the time Tom had first heard of the possibility of this scheme. He was one of the first applicants but was still waiting for the selection of successful farmers to be announced. His chances were good, and now finally it seemed as if he was on the verge of achieving his dream.

There was a brutal attack on tourists in Victoria Falls, in the middle of the day, with two young Canadian women being killed. It was an unprovoked attack on them and had come from the Zambian side of the river. A good friend of Tom's, who had shared a barrack room with him when they were in police training together, was the Member-in-Charge of the Victoria Falls Police Station and led the rescue party down into the gorge to recover their bodies.

At the time of the attack, the group was all wearing tourist type clothing, and the girls were wearing colorful dresses. The Zambezi River at that point is narrow, and the water flows rapidly through the gorge. It is impossible to swim across the river anywhere near there. The Zambian authorities claimed that they thought the party was about to sabotage their power station.

Around the same time, all the members of a South African Police Unit on patrol in the Victoria Falls area were shot and killed by terrorists. Nearing the end of their patrol, they stopped opposite Kandahar Island, about a mile upstream from the falls, to refresh themselves in the river. All were killed in the attack, and one of their bodies was never found. Kandahar Island was used by pleasure boats from Victoria Falls as a stopover two or three times a day.

An elderly man was killed in a landmine explosion at Mana Pools on the Zambezi River, and firing from across the Zambezi River resulted in two fishermen being killed in their boat. These were all unprovoked civilian attacks.

A ranch manager from Nuanetsi was attacked and killed while dipping his cattle. A telephone technician was kidnapped while checking the lines. His abandoned vehicle was found where he had been working, and his naked dismembered body located two days later by a cattle herdsman.

In retaliation, a training camp and military base for terrorists on a farm in Zambia was destroyed by the Rhodesian Air Force and a platoon of SAS soldiers. 'Green Leader,' in a Hawker Hunter circling the Lusaka Air Force Base prevented any aircraft from taking off. This mission was a total success and a massive morale booster for all Rhodesians.

As a result of these attacks Tom started carrying a small .32 automatic pistol when he went into the bush; if he was going to be captured and cut to pieces, he would rather take his own life. Whether he would have the courage to use it, if the time came, was another matter. But it was comforting to have.

．．．．．．．．．．．．．．．

After there had been several gruesome murders in the Lowveld, obviously committed by terrorists, Julia noticed that Tom started carrying his pistol when he went on patrol.

"Why are you taking your pistol with you into the bush?" Julia quizzed him.

"There are times when I think it might be handy to have with me as a backup," was all Tom said.

"Well you know best, but I still think it's a bit silly. As it is you have to have your FN with you all the time, even when we are at the summer house in the garden. I know it is for our protection, but sometimes it seems a bit much," Julia said having the last word although she knew that it was necessary to take the precaution and be armed at all times.

It worried her to think that he might be taking it to use on himself if captured. But she was confident in his ability and had faith in the rest of Tom's stick, and so she accepted that it made him feel more comfortable.

Julia was a good wife and mother. The three men in her life kept her busy and with Tom away in the bush so often, the responsibility of parenthood rested more and more on her. She did radio duty four days a week but was with the boys in the evenings. Like all the other young families in the farming community, they learned to cope and adjust their lives according to the situation.

When Tom was away on patrol, she worried herself sick and lay awake at night wondering where he was and how he was managing. The conditions under which they had to survive in the bush were not easy. When he came home after two weeks, she was always so excited and relieved. He would spend time playing with the boys and telling them stories of what he had seen in the bush, wildlife, scenery, and rivers, but never the horrors of war.

Stuart was now six and Kyle four years of age. They were both growing up so quickly and, apart from the odd squabble, got on well together. At an early age, they were taught how to load magazines for their father's rifle, and that obedience was most important. Although they knew about terrorists and the war, they were blissfully unaware of the seriousness of the unfolding drama taking place around them.

....

Security forces were carrying out 'Hot Pursuit' operations into neighboring countries and destroying large well-established terrorist base camps. In Mozambique the Rhodesian Forces had taken control of large areas in the north, keeping the insurgents at bay.

Political talks, instigated by the western nations, came with the proviso that the Rhodesians withdrew from their forward positions in Mozambique. This was agreed to, but no sooner had they withdrawn than the insurgent forces, moved forward into the vacated positions. The subsequent retaliation by the Rhodesians was blamed for the breakdown of the talks. This scenario was repeated every time talks got underway, with the lost ground having to be re-taken time and again.

Tom and his stick, 'Tango One', were on patrol in the vicinity of Vila Salazar on one such occasion. They were set to destroy a machine gun position in Mozambique that was making life difficult and dangerous in the Vila Salazar Police Station. Every day the Frelimo gunners would fire a burst at the water tanks, filling them with holes. Every night, members of the police would shin up to the water tanks and plug the holes with bits of wood. It became a daily 'game'.

When Tom requested permission to cross the border and destroy the machine gun post, he was ordered to withdraw because the political discussions were at a delicate stage. To launch an attack on a neighboring country was out of the question.

The American Head of Foreign Affairs, Henry Kissinger, managed to persuade the South African Foreign Affairs Minister, Pik Botha, to stop assisting Rhodesia. With the threat of embargoes against their own country, the South African Government agreed to terminate the supply of arms, ammunition, fuel, and vehicles. Rhodesia would now have to 'go it alone.'

This was serious for all the armed forces, and the men in PATU were restricted to carrying only two magazines of ammunition and one hand grenade instead of the normal four magazines and two hand grenades. It made their load much lighter but left them feeling uneasy. Two magazines could easily be used up in one ambush. The incursions were on the increase with military supplies for Rhodesian Security

Forces becoming limited. The insurgents who were being supplied by both the Eastern block and the Western Nations had unlimited supplies of arms and ammunition.

The news was very disturbing for Tom, who was always concerned for the safety of his family while he was away on military duty. He knew that they were well cared for, but the terrorists were becoming more and more aggressive and blatant in their attacks on 'Soft Targets.' For security reasons, when Tom was away in the bush, Julia was not called on for radio duties at JOC (Joint Operations Command center). It might compromise a situation if a wife was involved on the radio network when her husband was in a dangerous situation.

The owner of Bangala Ranch was attacked and shot to death at the front gate to his home. His wife and children, who were standing on the veranda, saw him open the gate and then watched in horror as three terrorists appeared from the bushes alongside the road and gunned him down. After the attack, the terrorists fled back into the bush.

Tom and his unit were called out to carry out follow up operations. The tracks lead them into the Mtilikwe Tribal Trust area where terrorists were reported to be intimidating the locals and carrying out attacks on the nearby ranchers. After making an attack, it was relatively easy to escape into the Tribal Trust Land and after hiding their arms, blend in with the inhabitants and just disappear.

A few days after the murder, 'Tango One' caught up with the terrorists and pinned them down in a small rocky koppie. The koppie was surrounded by open ground making it impossible to flush them out. Needing assistance, Tom called JOC requesting an air strike. The strike was agreed, and after confirming their position and that of the terrorists, they took shelter where they could observe the koppie while being safe from debris and shrapnel sent flying by the attack. Then they turned their caps inside out making them visible from the air. (Bright reflective orange patches were sewn inside their caps for this very purpose)

Thirty minutes after calling for the strike, a Hawker Hunter from the Rhodesian Air Force swooped low over their heads and blasted the koppie with rocket and gunfire before disappearing. The blast from the jet engine and the explosions from the rockets were deafening. Before the dust settled, they quickly stormed the koppie to find all four terrorists had been killed with severed arms and legs lying around the dead bodies. It was a mess. Helicopters arrived to clear the scene and transported them and the dead bodies back to base.

After the murder on Bangala Ranch, the family was taken to South Africa, and Tom was given the task of managing the ranch as well as his Section. This meant that he had to travel the round trip of 40 miles to the ranch and back every second day through dangerous territory on his own. The old man had developed the irrigated portion of his ranch from uninhabited scrubland in the early part of the century.

He had built a weir across the river and designed and made a hydroelectric plant that generated sufficient power to irrigate 500 acres of sugar cane, the workshop, the homestead, and the manager's residence. It was an amazing achievement and is still fully functional. Tom was green with envy; the farm would have suited him very well indeed. A month later the family appointed a manager, and Tom handed the management of the ranch over to him.

The following year, the Minister of Agriculture announced that due to the security situation in the country, the Land Settlement Scheme in the Lowveld was being put on hold until 'Stability returned.' Those who were to be allocated farms would be advised in due course and they would be notified which farms were available when the time was right. As far as Tom was concerned and with the way things were going in the country, it might be a long wait.

It was a bitter disappointment, and the second time Tom had been forced to put his plans onto the 'back burner.' Although reluctant to admit it, he had to agree with the decision; it was a bad time to move onto a new farm in an operational area, and still carry out his military commitments. It would have exposed his family to the additional dangers. The nation was confident that the war against the insurgents would be won, but it was going to take longer than expected. Only then could he and Julia they think of moving forward with their plans.

****

Chapter 18

Maria was in love with a wonderful man who she was working for in Triangle. She had been recruited by Triangle Sugar Estates in the Lowveld as an area nurse and health officer for five of the sugar cane sections. When she reported to the senior manager on his section, she knew straight away that they would get on well, and not long after she fell in love with him.

Maria had felt no emotions for anyone since that dreadful day at the Mission school six years earlier, and she did not think that she would ever be able to fall in love and live a normal life, so her feelings surprised.

She was a good-looking, fully-developed happy young girl with long dark hair and light olive skin. She had an outgoing personality and as a result, had a lot of friends. She had loved school and had been a keen pupil. During the week Maria stayed with friends at the Mission near Zimbabwe Ruins, with ten other white children, and went to school in Fort Victoria by mini-bus every day. Her home was too far away for her to travel from there every day, and there were no boarding facilities at the school.

Most weekends she was given a lift home where she helped her mother in her shop in Chibi, where she had grown up. On other weekends she stayed at the Mission with her friend Mavis. Although she had been brought up speaking English, she also spoke Portuguese and learned to speak Shona fluently. Her parents were both Portuguese from Mozambique where she had been born.

When they moved to Rhodesia from Mozambique, to get away from the civil war there, her father bought a workshop with a filling station and a shop in Chibi, a small town south of Fort Victoria, on the main road to South Africa.

Not long after arriving in Chibi Ian Smith's government broke away from Britain and sanctions were imposed against the country. As a result, there was a shortage of fuel, and her father was forced to close the filling station and go to work in Bulawayo, leaving her mother to run the shop. He only came home every third month for a long weekend to visit her and her mother. Theirs was a strange relationship.

The only thing that Maria had not liked at the mission when she was there was the bullying of the smaller and weaker children by some of the older boys. One boy in particular who she came to despise was a large fellow called Titus. He was much bigger and older than the others and was disobedient. He was a law unto himself, and the teachers did nothing to control him.

One day she came across him and his little gang beating up a much smaller boy. Although it was not her place to do so and she was not meant to have anything to do with the blacks in the school, Maria stood up to him and made him stop, belittling him in front of his followers.

There was a lovely quiet spot amongst some large boulders with a mango tree where she and Mavis could get away from everyone to study together in the shade of the mango tree. Nobody disturbed them there - it was peaceful and some distance from the Mission. They went there most afternoons after getting back from school.

Maria and Mavis were sitting under the mango tree one beautiful Friday afternoon, studying quietly, when suddenly they found themselves surrounded by Titus and four of his gang members. Before they could shout for help, they were grabbed by the arms and gagged. Mavis was dragged off behind the boulders by two of the boys, while two others pushed Maria to the ground and held her there. She struggled wildly but could not break free.

"You think you are so clever? Well I am a Mamba, and I am going to teach you a lesson, you white bitch," Titus sneered at her.

"Hold her still," he ordered his two cronies.

Then Titus raped her while his two sidekicks held her down on the ground. The awful stench of his sweating smelly body on top of her was overpowering. She felt as if she would die from the terrible invasion and pain of this assault on her.

Leaving her lying on the ground crying, the boys disappeared around the boulders. As she lay there sobbing, unable to move, she wondered what she had done to deserve this attack. Mavis appeared from around the other side of the rocks with her eyes wide in horror from their ordeal: she had been molested but not raped.

After tidying themselves up as best they could, they made their way back to Mavis' home. Swearing Mavis to secrecy, Maria did not report the rape to anyone or the police; she did not even tell her mother. She felt too ashamed and did not want to be exposed to any further humiliation. For a white girl to be raped by a black man would ruin her life forever. She only hoped that she did not fall pregnant.

The five boys involved in the assault all disappeared and never came back to school. Maria swore that one day she would get her revenge on the animal that had raped and degraded her in that way. She did not think that she would ever want to go out with any man, ever. The thought of a man touching her made her ill.

Luckily Maria did not fall pregnant, but something had changed deep inside her. She was no longer the happy, cheerful girl she had been. The teachers at school could not understand and constantly questioned her, but she could not bring herself to tell them. She just wanted her school days to end so that she could move on.

After leaving school, Maria spent a year at home helping her mother in the shop, before being admitted to the training establishment for nurses in Bulawayo. She had wanted to be a nurse for as long as she could remember and so finally something brought her a spark of joy. She went to stay with her father and for the next two years trained in the hospital.

Once graduated, she got a job in the Bulawayo General Hospital as a nurse. Two years later the Matron from Triangle Hospital recruited her to work in the Lowveld. Maria was tired of being pestered by young men wanting to take her out. She had no interest in them. She had not been involved with anyone and was still suffering from the effects of the attack.

She accepted the offer and was glad to return to that part of the country. It was a lot closer to her home than Bulawayo, and the work sounded interesting. Maria arrived in Triangle and reported to the Matron at the hospital. She was given a room in the nurses' home and reported for work the following day.

Two weeks later she was sent out to be interviewed by one of the Area Managers whose area was looking for a Field Nurse and Health Officer. The interview went well, and the next day she moved into her own house on his section. She was pleased with the way her life seemed to be coming together at last. She reported to Tom Owen the following morning to discuss her duties with him.

Maria was the first Health Officer for the area, and she was kept busy, getting all the hygiene and welfare organized on the five sections. She was put in charge of all the section health workers and started woman's clubs, held daily baby clinics, saw to the dispensing of malaria tablets, treated all minor injuries, monitored the cleanliness of the kitchen areas and inspected the toilets and washrooms daily. Under her supervision, the compounds began to improve rapidly.

Tom was happy with her work, and they would meet on a weekly basis to discuss progress and problem areas. She looked forward to these meetings with him. He was like a tonic, and she could feel that, at last, she was starting to heal. She loved being near him, and when she sat next to him examining her register, it excited her. There was, however, a major problem; he was happily married with children. She would have to be satisfied with just being close to him.

Every now and again, Tom would be called on to carry out duties in the 'Bush War', which was raging in the country. Maria never knew where he went or when he was going. He just disappeared for up to two weeks at a time. She knew that he was doing dangerous work and worried the whole time he was away. Whenever he reappeared, it took a massive effort to stop herself throwing her arms around his neck, but a thankful side effect of the Mamba incident was that now she was well practiced at hiding her emotions her feelings.

Maria was not interested in politics and was happy with the way things were in the country. Why should they follow in the footsteps of other countries to the north? It seemed to her that everything was collapsing where there had been drastic changes.

One day, when Maria was in a meeting with Tom in his office, a police Sergeant arrived and was ushered in by the clerk. Tom greeted him happily and introduced him to her. He was a good looking black man with a nice smile. Tom explained to her that they had known each other for years and had worked together in the police force in Salisbury. His name was Lucas Mpofu, and he was stationed at Triangle Police Station.

Maria never let it be known that she was fluent in the Shona language - she felt it might be useful and help with her duties to hear what the people were saying - when they thought she could not understand them. During the course of her duties, as Maria patrolled around the compounds, she heard some of the men and women discussing the 'War' situation. They talked about the problems their families were facing in the Tribal Trust areas where the workers had their traditional homes. Many of them had family or friends who had been tortured, and some killed by the so-called 'Freedom Fighters,' and they worried about the safety of those they loved.

Maria decided that it would be a good idea to note what was said without them knowing. There might be information that would be useful to Tom when he went into the 'Bush.' It was important to her that nothing happened to him.

As time went by Maria got closer to Tom who sometimes told her in advance when he would be going away. He asked her to keep an eye on his family and to make sure they were looked after while he was gone. Tom loved his family and Maria had got to know his wife and two boys pretty well.

Julia was a lovely woman and, even though Maria was jealous of her for being married to Tom, they became good friends and spent a lot of time together – especially when Tom was away on military duties. Plucking up the courage during one of the meetings with Tom, she decided to let him know what she was doing.

"I don't know where you will go next time you are away, but if I hear anything in the compounds while I am on my rounds that might be of interest to you, I will tell you," Maria said to Tom putting her hand on his.

"Thank you, Maria. That will be most useful. But you must not put yourself in any danger. You know what people can do if they think you are betraying them," he responded squeezing her hand.

"I will take care," she assured him with a gentle smile.

From then on Maria reported everything that she heard regarding the terrorist movements in the Tribal areas to Tom. She was excited by this personal contact she had with Tom and that they were now sharing a secret, made it all the more exciting. She dreamt of what their growing intimacy might grow into and had come to accept that they would have to keep their relationship undercover if there was ever going to be one. True love made one accept such limits and take the little one could. Besides, she would never do anything to hurt her friend, Julia.

****

Chapter 19

Mavue was a typical Portuguese outpost town on the border of Rhodesia and Mozambique. The town was situated on top of a hill overlooking the junction of the Sabi and the Lundi Rivers and boasted the Chef de Post's (Mayor) residence and office, a few dozen brick houses, a bottle store, a couple of small shops and on the outskirts, a small military camp.

The main feature of the town was an enormous Baobab tree in its center where the whole town gathered to eat and drink. Chickens and dogs wandered around and scavenged for food in the filthy run down streets. About 200 soldiers were housed in the Frelimo camp where Mamba and his men were allocated tented accommodation.

Once again entry and exit routes needed to be established for the Freedom Fighters who would be penetrating the Eastern Lowveld. Mamba was charged with the job, and he was to ensure that the local inhabitants co-operated with them and did not report their activities to the Security Forces.

After two short exploratory ventures along the Sabi River to the north, he decided to launch attacks on farmers in the Chiredzi district. The purpose would be to intimidate the workers. He had discovered a large island in the middle of the Sabi River which would be an ideal place to set up a base for operations in that area. The surrounding area was dry with little grass on the eastern bank, but there was ample good cover in the Gona-re-Zhou game conservation area to the west.

The island offered them a good position from which to reach targets quickly, and return safely for re-supply. The main danger was wild animals, crocodiles in the river and patrolling game rangers; so they would have to avoid using paths and roads. The summer rains had finished, and it was moving into the winter months with little chance of the river flooding at that time of the year.

Mamba planned for two units to go in and set up camp on the island, taking with them a substantial supply of arms and ammunition, which would have to last for three or four months of operations. Each unit would set off two days apart. He would then follow with his four men two days later, leaving a unit of five men and the new commissar to wait for three weeks before joining them with further supplies.

Radio broadcasts from Rhodesia announced that groups of insurgents had been tracked down, and so their first task on the island would be to develop anti-tracking methods to avoid being easily followed.

....

By the time 'Tango One' reached its destination, the sun was well down near the western horizon. They had been making for the highest point on Gombe hill, overlooking the Sabi River and it had been a long slow trudge through heavy thorn scrub with patches of Mopani forest. The tall buffalo grass had assegai-like seeds that scratched and stabbed their legs. A small herd of impala pranced out of their way, startling a hornbill that had been busy eating grubs on an old dead tree stump.

Nearing their destination, a Honey Guide bird flittered in front of them, trying to persuade someone to follow it to the prize bee's nest it had found. Deciding that it might be a good idea to have a little added nutrition n their diet, a rest stop was called while John and Lucas followed the bird. They returned with two large dripping combs. After rewarding their guide with the grubs, they pressed on to their destination.

The team's mission was to observe and monitor that section of the river, paying particular attention to a large island in the middle. The island was an ideal place for the insurgents to set up a staging base, and there had been reports that they might be operating in the area. The vista to the east of the river was crisscrossed by paths and roads, and there were plenty of villages where food was readily available.

The position at the top of Gombe Hill was perfect. It was high above the river and overlooked the island with the river flowed strongly on either side of it. From their position on top of the hill, they could see all the way to the Tribal Trust land on the eastern bank. Its landscape scattered with ancient Baobabs and the overgrazed desolate terrain stood in stark contrast to the lush ranch land on the west.

Water was always a problem on patrol. It was impossible to carry sufficient supply for even a five-day patrol, let alone a two week one. Whenever the opportunity arose, it was essential to make sure that the water bottles were filled. Where there were Giant Euphorbia or cactus trees, emergency water could be drained from the branches. Here they had both a river below them and some cactus trees on the hillside.

Although it was July the day had been hot, as is usual in the Lowveld, even in winter. It would cool down rapidly as soon as the sunset. The five men were tired and their arms and legs stung with scratches. Well-concealed from below, but with a good view of the island, they settled down and reported to HQ. A cup of tea and a bite to eat before it got too dark made them all feel refreshed.

As the orange orb of the sun disappeared behind the hill, the temperature started to drop, and they pulled on the pantyhose they used to keep their legs warm in winter. Then setting the watches, they climbed into their sleeping bags.

From where he lay, Tom had a good view of the island, and from time to time he was able to check for any sign of movement or even the flickering of light from a fire. The call of a nightjar now and then, in the still night air, seemed to emphasize how cold it was.

. . . .

With their destination only a day's march away, the advance party of freedom fighters set off from Mavue and, once across the border, they split up, each making their way to the island in the middle of the Sabi River.

The going was easy, but to make sure they not to be seen, they avoided any settlement or kraal and kept to the hard ground wherever possible. Mamba's directions were good, and by the end of the day, they had crossed the river to the island where they set up camp.

The next two days were spent getting settled into the campsite, watching the river banks for any movement by locals and waiting for the rest of the group. The second lot arrived on schedule and pitched their makeshift shelters under the trees, where they were well hidden from view along the river banks.

Early the next morning, a member of the second group, without thinking, put a green twig on the fire in the middle of the clearing. It created smoke, and he was rebuked by the leader of the first group for being so careless. Towards midday, the same man tossed what he thought was a dry branch onto the fire. It was still wet, and a puff of blue smoke rose into the air. Again the leader of the first group berated him for being 'stupid.' Not taking kindly to this second but more insulting reprimand, he stalked off with two of his companions to the waters' edge to wash and cool down.

At daybreak just before sunrise the following morning, Tom was struggling to see through the early morning mist, when he thought he saw something move. Unsure of what he had seen, he sat up and woke the others. John, with his trained hunter's eye, was quick to point out a thin wisp of smoke rising in the cold early morning light. It was coming from a thick clump of acacia trees very close to the Fig Tree. Someone was on the island and had made a fire to get warm. They would have to watch very carefully. And so Tom put two men at a time on duty with overlapping shifts.

"I don't think any local fisherman would camp down there when he can easily go home at night. In any case, if it was a fisherman, I am sure we would have seen smoke and movement yesterday or last night," Tom concluded.

"I think there must be gooks down there under that fig tree," John said.

"I agree with you. I wonder how many there are?" said Terry.

"I think there are only a few," said Lucas "If there were many of them, we would have seen some sign of them moving around."

"They could have sneaked onto the island during the night or very early this morning," said Tony.

"Well, we know there is at least one person down there. We need to be extra vigilant and keep our eyes open for anyone approaching the river from any direction or leaving the island. As soon as we have something definite to report we will call HQ."

As the sun climbed into the clear blue sky and the dew dried off their sleeping bags, they moved their kit under the shade of a large Baobab about twenty paces back from their observation spot. Only the two men on watch stayed where they were; moving only when they changed over. Each man did a two-hour stint, and with overlapping changes every hour, it ensured there were always fresh eyes on watch.

By mid-morning the sun was blazing down on them, and they were all drenched in sweat. The men on lookout duty lay under the semi-shade of small thorn bushes, their faces covered with camouflaged face veils. However, the Mopani bees still managed to penetrate and found their way into their nostrils and the corners of their eyes to suck up the moisture. They tickled, making it almost impossible to keep still and not brush the pests away.

Tom, sitting on his sleeping bag and leaning against the trunk of the Baobab, wondered if two hours was not too long. As he sat there, he watched a brown and white crested hoopoe tapping on the trunk of a flat-crowned acacia with its beak, inviting insects to pop out of hiding so that it could feast.

Nick and Lucas were on watch duty when Tom saw Lucas beckoning. Getting up quickly, he went to where they were lying. Three men wearing what looked like green fatigues sat on the bank of the river. They were in a huddle and seemed to be having a discussion with arms waving around and pointing back to the spot where the stick had seen the smoke hours earlier. Something seemed to be bothering them. Was this a staging post, or was it an arms cache; or were they waiting for reinforcements to arrive? One thing was certain – the men were insurgents.

The three men got up and disappeared back into the undergrowth, in the direction of the big wild fig tree. Tom was certain that something was going to happen fairly soon. Nick moved quickly to the radio.

"Chiredzi this is Tango One. Over," he called.

"Go ahead Tango One," the response from the controller was rapid.

"We have sighted insurgents at the location we are observing. Over."

"Tango One. What numbers. Over."

"Three, possibly more. Over."

"Roger that. Stand by your radio. We will advise you later. Over."

"Roger. Wilco. Out," Nick replied switching the radio to stand-by with the volume turned low.

Half an hour later, the radio came to life. "Tango One this is Chiredzi. You are to keep the insurgents under observation. We have a backup unit on its way to your location. They will be there early tomorrow morning. Notify us immediately if there is any change in the situation. Over."

"Chiredzi. Tango One. Roger that. Will be in contact early tomorrow. Over."

For some time they saw no further movement on the island. They suspected that the insurgents would either move off soon or for others to join them. They would not take the risk of camping on the island indefinitely. As it was, they had been there at least two days, and there were already signs of unrest.

Just before sunset, Gary, who was on watch, beckoned urgently to Tom. They watched as three men, also wearing what appeared to be green fatigues, stopped on the far bank of the river, removed their boots then waded over to the Island. They disappeared into the trees where they had seen the smoke early.

Half an hour later, they observed another two men cross the river to the island. Tom, watching through his binoculars, saw that one of them was wearing dark glasses. He seemed familiar and seemed to be looking straight up at him. This meant that now there were at least eight men on the island.

"It looks like they are planning a big hit somewhere," Gary said.

"The only thing we can do from up here is to wait and watch. What worries me is how many more will cross over tonight when we can't bloody well see. It will be dark in an hour, then who knows how many more will arrive or how many will leave during the night. I wish we knew what their intentions were and where they are heading. We might even be able to hear something if it is still with no wind tonight." Tom responded. They all knew how well voices carried on a cold night.

. . . .

Late that afternoon three of Mamba's unit arrived in the camp followed a little while later by Mamba himself with the last man. All fifteen men were now camped on the island, ready to move off on various missions.

On the approach to the island, Mamba carefully studied the high Gombe hill on the opposite side of the river. It would make an excellent lookout position with a clear view of the river, the island, and the surrounding area. He would climb to the top the following day to check it out.

On his arrival at the camp, Mamba sensed tension among the group, with one man looking surly, and sitting apart from the rest.

"What is the problem here? Why have you been arguing with each other?" he asked.

"It is Sando. He was being stupid and put some green branches on the fire making smoke," Jeremiah said.

"I am sorry Comrade Mamba. I did not think when I made a mistake," Sando said.

"You are an idiot. You know that if there is smoke someone will know we are here," Mamba said turning on the offending man and slapping him hard across the face.

"If you ever make another mistake like that I will cut your throat and throw you to the crocodiles," Mamba warned him in a vicious whisper. "I am not pleased with you and will deal with you later. Now clean your weapon and think about your mission," Mamba said turning away.

He was furious that the man had possibly compromised their position with his carelessness. Before nightfall Mamba held a briefing with the leaders of the other two units discussing their intended target areas. Jeremiah and his unit were to make their way to Chisumbanje to educate the people in that area and attack whatever targets they could find. Mfana's unit would attack a farmer in Mkwasine area and Mamba, with the most experience, would attack a target near Chiredzi. They would all meet back on the island in about seven days.

Surplus food supplies and ammunition were wrapped in a piece of canvas and tucked into a hollow beneath the Fig Tree under which they were camped. Mamba's unit would move out early the following morning, checking the hill before moving on. The other two units would move out later in the day.

An hour before daybreak the next morning, Mamba and his four men crossed the river to the west. Once off the island, they waited for it to get light before continuing towards the base of the hill. As the climb to the summit on the side adjacent to the river was too steep to negotiate, he decided to move around to the opposite side where the going would be a lot easier.

He had sensed friction between the two other units on his arrival the previous evening and wanted to spend the day observing the camp from the top of the hill. He was not sure that his orders were going to be followed. If not he would return to the island and deal with them severely.

················

As expected, it was another bitterly cold night with only a slight breeze rustling the leaves now and then. Despite their concentration and straining their ears, the only thing they heard from the terrorist camp below was an occasional murmur of voices, and the sound of the water in the river bubbling and splashing over the rocks.

In the early dawn light, just before sunrise, there were signs of activity again. John and Tom who were on watch, once again saw a faint wisp of smoke rising slowly from near the fig tree below the mist over the river. The smoke did not dissipate into the air but hung around just above the trees, trapped by the cold morning air. The insurgents were still down there at their camp.

Making sure that they could not be heard, Tom and Nick retreated to the Baobab to report to HQ. Tom was instructed to maintain a watch on the terrorist position. The army unit was on its way to their location and was expected within the hour. 'Tango One' was to establish communication with them and to guide them to the target area.

"Nick, you'd better maintain radio watch here. Call me as soon as you hear from the cavalry," said Tom leaving him to rejoin the other three who were all keeping watch. The smoke had gone, and nothing moved.

"I hope the army boys get here before the bastards move out," Tom said.

"What do we do if they move before the cavalry arrives?" asked John.

"Good question," Tom replied. "The chances are they will split up. If we try to follow, we will get caught between them and the army. We will have to wait and see what happens. We might have to pin them down on the island with fire from up here to stop them getting away. If they do make a break for it, we will join the army blokes and help to follow up and catch the sods."

....

Just as they were nearing the western base of the hill, Mamba heard the sound of a vehicle approaching. Quickly taking cover behind an outcrop of boulders 30 paces from the track they had just crossed, he looked back in the direction from which the sound had come. It was quiet; the engine had either been switched off, or the vehicle had moved out of earshot.

They waited nervously, adrenaline pumping through their veins and sharpening their senses. Mamba heard a faint clink of metal on metal followed by the sound of subdued voices and the hiss of static from a radio. They dared not move for fear of being spotted. How had they been compromised?

Suddenly, through the Mopani trees, they saw white soldiers in camouflage uniforms running along the track, towards the river only 100 paces away, confirming his fears. The Security Forces knew of their presence on the island and were mounting an attack.

There was nothing he could do to warn his men, or to help them in any way. Mamba's unit had to get away fast before their tracks were found, and they were hunted down like wild animals. That idiot who had put green twigs on the fire making smoke must have given up their position. If the security forces didn't kill him, he would do so himself.

....

Half an hour after the communication with control, the troops arrived. Tom expressed the need to have men approach from the west bank as well as from upstream to ensure all the occupants were caught in the net without them firing on their own men. They agreed on the plan of attack, and Tom and Nick returned to the lookout post to direct operations from there.

Soon they saw a group of ten soldiers gingerly entering the cold water of the river about fifty paces upstream, and start to wade their way down in a battle line. Once they were twenty paces from their target, the second group of ten soldiers made their approach from slightly downstream of the terrorist camp. Suddenly the alarm was raised by an insurgent, who saw the troops approaching as he was about to collect water from the river.

Firing on the move, the men from the upstream splashed their way quickly onto the island and began to sweep the north and east side. The soldiers from the western approach swept straight across to the east swinging to the south.

Mayhem broke out on the island with terrorists running in all directions trying to escape and return fire at the same time. Two men tried to escape from the south-east of the island, but were spotted by Tom and his men up on the hill, and were fired upon. Realizing they had no chance of escape they quickly threw their weapons in the water and stood in the river with their arms above their heads.

It was over in about fifteen minutes, with the troops turning around at the southern end then sweeping back to the north. The two in the water were led away to the west bank. From the top of the hill, the men of 'Tango One' watched as four bodies were carried from the island to the west bank by six captured terrorists and assisted by a couple of troopers. Two other troopers were lugging a large heavy canvas bag.

After carefully scanning the area along both banks of the river to ensure there were no other suspected insurgents, the PATU men hurriedly packed up their gear and slid down the steep side of the hill.

On their arrival at the RV, Tom and his men were met by a cheerful bunch of young army troopers, all still wet and fired up by the successful outcome of their mission. Only two of them had been hit by terrorist bullets and wounded, one in the upper arm and one in the thigh, but even they were cheerful, although in some pain. The medic was dressing their wounds. The large bag they had recovered was full of ammunition, rockets, grenades, and tins of food.

················

Creeping away quietly from their hiding place, Mamba and his men continued on the course that would take them around behind the hill as fast as they dared move. If they could reach the higher ground, they would have a better chance of avoiding capture by hiding among the large boulders.

Moments later they heard the sporadic crackle of gunfire accompanied by a lot of shouting. Mamba knew that he had lost another two units under his command. He was fuming and wanted to see for himself what was happening on the island. Within minutes they had reached a point where they could watch the drama unfold below.

Six of his men and two white soldiers were carrying four others who appeared to be dead and were being escorted by about ten soldiers, with another two carrying the bag containing their re-supply of ammunition and food. Two military trucks drove into the clearing near the river to collect the soldiers and their prisoners. To see that these young white soldiers, wearing only shirts and shorts, could so easily capture and kill most of his men, angered Mamba even more.

How had it been possible that they had been caught by surprise again and so easily? After the captured comrades and the four bodies were loaded onto the first truck, the troops stood around talking and laughing happily. They did not appear to be in any hurry to move away. Mamba was tempted to open fire on them and kill as many as he could, but quickly dismissed the idea; they were heavily outnumbered, and he felt it was not worth the risk.

Mamba was startled when, from an outcrop less than twenty paces from where they were hiding, five men appeared and scampered down the steep slope. As they slid past where he was hiding, he was close enough to see the badge they wore on the shoulders - the print of a

Leopards Paw, the insignia of PATU. He knew of these farming men and their reputation in the bush. They must have been directing operations from their lookout position and had probably been watching them on the island for days.

The last two, a tall white man and a shorter black man, looked familiar to him, and wondered where he had come across them before. Then he remembered - could they possibly be the two policemen who had given him problems during his rioting days in Salisbury all those years ago?

Mamba recalled the hill alongside the path leading to Sengwe and wondered if this same unit had been watching them there. He had lost most of his men in an ambush not long after they had passed that hill. On that occasion, he had also been lucky to escape.

Putting on his dark glasses, he watched as the soldiers climbed onto the two troop carriers and disappeared in a cloud of dust. He had to return to Mavue in time to stop the last unit going into the Sabi River area, and walking into a trap. He would have to get more men before re-organizing his plan of infiltrating that part of the country.

Once again his operations had been ruined, and he would have to abandon any idea of operating in the area for a while. The two men he had seen were obviously the cause of his failures, and his rage grew. They would have to be stopped.

....

"Well you guys did a bloody good job up there and thanks to you it looks like we have bagged the lot of them," the Lieutenant said as he greeted them.

"I hope so Lieutenant. We reckoned there must have been at least ten of them. Others could easily have moved off in the night," Tom replied.

"We will have to let Special Branch find out for us. As a precaution I have sent a group of my men to sweep the vicinity, and to check for sign of any others," the Lieutenant said.

"Good idea. Can we bum a ride back to base with you chaps?" asked Tom.

"Of course you can. You don't think we would have left you to walk back do you?"

Once the scouting party returned not having found anything, they all piled onto the back of the two troop carriers and headed back to base. As it was Saturday, a portable radio in the cab was switched on enabling all the troops to listen to messages and music being broadcast on RBC by the forces favorite Sally Donaldson. These morale-boosting messages from home meant a lot to the boys in the bush.

On their arrival back at Chiredzi base, the captured men were handed over to Special Branch for interrogation. Tom, still wondering about the familiar figure with the dark glasses he had seen the day before, studied the captured men carefully then examined the dead terrorists. None of them looked familiar. Had the man escaped? After being debriefed 'Tango One' was stood down, and they went home.

Interrogation of the captured terrorists later revealed that five men had left the island in the early hours of the morning heading in a westerly direction towards Chiredzi. Their leader was the man called Mamba. It was the third time Tom had crossed paths with this terrorist who had managed to escape on each occasion. He had to be the man who wore dark glasses, and his image was etched on Tom's brain.

****

Chapter 20

Mamba was not a happy man. By this time he should have had many successful attacks under his belt, with lots of whites killed, but it was not working out that way at all. Every time he planned and set off on a good-sized operation something went wrong; he lost soldiers and was forced to abandon the mission. The more he thought about it, the more he blamed the two policemen for his failures. He would have to hunt them down and kill them both as quickly as possible.

On his return from the abortive drive into the Eastern Lowveld, he needed to take his frustration and anger out on somebody. At Mavue, he pushed his way into the bar demanding beer. Soon he was hungry for a woman. Getting up, he staggered outside. Just his luck a good looking girl was passing by; he had seen her before. Rumour had it she came the Gona-Re-Zhou game ranger's camp in Rhodesia. She was short and well developed with a clean, round, shiny face and wearing a colorful dress and sandals. Her look of innocence inflamed his desire.

Grabbing her by the arm and ignoring her protests, he dragged her off to the nearest patch of undergrowth about 50 paces from the rear of the bar.

"I know who you are," he said as she sobbed and squirmed, trying to free her wrist from the vice of his fingers. "There are two policemen in your country who have been chasing me," he continued ignoring her pleas. "One of them is black, and the other one is a white pig. You are the one who has been informing on me," he accused her working himself up into a rage.

"No, I am not the one. I do not know these men you are talking about. I am not an informer. Please do not hurt me," she cried.

"My name is Mamba, don't forget it."

With that he raped her, and when he had finished, he took out his knife and sliced off part of her bottom lip. That would guarantee her silence. Walking back to camp he felt a lot better; he always felt better after he came and had taken his revenge out on a woman, but the anger still smoldered inside him.

Having had his operations compromised in that part of the country, he decided to move back to the southern area again, believing the security forces would have moved away because of the lack of activity since his previous attacks. When he made his report to his seniors, it was agreed that his move to the south was a good idea. Their leader, Comrade Robert Mugabe, intended making a massive push into the country from the southeast and supply lines would be needed.

....

Maria had to see Tom. She had some news he needed to hear. Once a month she attended a meeting at the hospital, to make her reports on the general health and wellbeing of the families on the sections. She also collected supplies of malaria tablets and general medication used for minor injuries and ailments on the sections.

It was at one of these meetings that they were all told of a woman who had been brought to the hospital by the Game Ranger from Gona-re-Zhou. The woman had been severely beaten, her bottom lip had been sliced off, and she had been raped.

As a rape victim herself, Maria got permission to visit the woman and to offer support. She was young; at the most, she was in her early twenties but looked frail and like a child. She lay in bed with a dressing on her lip, staring at the ceiling. After sitting with her for a while, talking gently to her, Maria managed to get her to speak.

With tears rolling down her cheeks like running water she explained that she was the daughter of a man who worked for the Game Department and lived at the main camp in the Gona-re-Zhou near the Chilujo Cliffs on the Lundi River. Her grandmother lived in Mavue in Mozambique, not far from where she lived with her parents. She had gone to visit her grandmother and to buy a few items that were not available in Rhodesia because of sanctions.

As she walked past the bar on her way to the store, a man who had had a lot to drink, came staggering out, grabbed her by the arm and ignoring her protests, dragged her into the bush where he thrust himself inside her. He accused her of being an informant, blaming her for 'selling out' to two 'Majoni's' (policemen) who were trying to capture him. One of them, he said was a white man and the other one was black. When she said that she didn't know what he was talking about, he casually took out his knife and cut a piece off her bottom lip. She ran to her grandmother who wrapped her face in a cloth and helped her home to her parents 25 miles away.

He told the girl before he raped her, that his name was Mamba. Maria went cold at the sound of this name. Perhaps it would have helped the girl to hear that the same man had raped her at school; it might have shown her that you could survive such things. But Maria could not bring herself to say it. In an instant, she was right back in that lonely spot again breathing his stench. Rushing out of the ward, she vomited in the ladies toilets.

Tom and his family had gone to South Africa for a holiday but were due back the following week. She had to meet with him as soon as he returned. He would know what to do. She contemplated going to the Police Station in Triangle to discuss what the girl had told her with Lucas, but dismissed the idea quickly. She had to wait for Tom to return.

The days dragged by but finally, the morning arrived when Tom and his family were due back. She went to his office and on the pretence of working on her medical records and registers, waited where she would be able to see Tom's car. He arrived late in the afternoon and on seeing him, her spirits lifted. She walked down to the house to greet him.

"Welcome home Sir. Did you have a good holiday?" she asked.

"Thank you, Maria. Yes, we did. But it is good to be back at home. How is everything here on the farm?" he looked so relaxed that now she wondered if she should tell him; why disrupt his peace of mind?

"We are all well. There have been no problems on the farm," she assured him.

"You look worried Maria. Are you alright?" he wanted to know.

She fell silent for a moment. "I have something that I must discuss with you as soon as you have the time," Maria told him.

"I must first unpack and have a cup of tea. I will meet you in my office in an hour."

Thanking him, she returned to the office to wait.

The clerks, who had finished work for the day, asked her to lock up when she left the office. She was pleased that she would be on her own when Tom came. Her stomach was in a knot. She was excited to be with him but worried about what he would have to say when she told him her news. He had only been away for three weeks, but to her, it felt a lot longer. She had missed him so much.

At last, Tom arrived and together they went into his office.

"Ok Maria, what is the problem? I can see that you are very upset."

"Oh Tom!" she exclaimed, and then unable to control herself any longer she rushed into his arms and cried. ,

"What is it?" he asked hugging her he gently asked

"There is some terrible news I must tell you."

She told him all she had heard and that she had known a bad man at school who had called himself 'Mamba.' She told him how this man had beaten the younger children at his school and had attacked her and beaten her badly with sticks when she went to their rescue - he had even raped her friend - a white girl. She omitted the part where she had been raped - that she would never tell anyone.

"I am so sorry the bastard hurt you like that," Tom said putting his arm around her shoulders when she finished telling him her long story.

They sat in silence for a while, and then Tom turning to her said. "It looks like we have a problem. This man you know seems to know who I am and also knows Lucas. I must have a meeting with Lucas tomorrow to discuss our plan of action. Security will have to be notified, and I will give them the man's real name."

"Please. You must not reveal where you got the information or I will be a target and will not be able to get any more information for you," she begged.

"Of course I will keep you out of it," Tom assured her, squeezing her.

Maria slept properly that night for the first time since hearing about Mamba. Tom would look after her and would not allow the monster anywhere near her. She had enjoyed being comforted and held by him as well as the intimacy of their meeting.

....

Tom was worried by the information Maria had given him, and the fact that she was so upset by it all. She lived a lonely private life. She had told him that she did not have a boyfriend yet she was a very attractive young woman with a light olive colored skin making her look almost Mediterranean. Her parents were Portuguese, and she had been born in Mozambique which explained her coloring. He did notice that she spent a lot of time at the office and seemed to enjoy her meetings with him, which she dragged on for as long as possible. Why then was she so upset?

As soon as he was able to get away from catching up on the farm activities, Tom went off to meet Lucas at the Police Station. As usual with these meetings, they sat on a bench under the Flamboyant Tree.

He told Lucas about the woman in the Hospital and what she had told Maria. Lucas assured Tom that he was aware of the woman and her assault. He had questioned her shortly after her admittance into hospital.

However, he was most interested to hear that the suspect was a terrorist going by the name of 'Mamba' whose real name was Titus Ngopi. He would investigate through the police channels and see what came to light.

They agreed that it would be a good idea to call a meeting of their PATU stick to discuss 'Mamba' and his operations. It seemed obvious that he would be targeting Tom and Lucas and had the confidence or the arrogance not to be too worried about them finding out who he was.

"Lucas. How the hell does he know that I was with you in the police?" Tom asked Lucas.

"I don't know Tom. The only thing I can think of is that he must have seen us together during the riots in Harare. Apart from PATU, it is the only time we have worked together."

. . . .

When Tom finished speaking there was a long silence around the table as all the men of 'Tango One' digested what Tom had just told them.

"Tom and I have had a long hard think together. We cannot remember anyone operating in Stodart in those times that went by the name of Mamba. I have sent the name that was given to us to the Special Branch to see what they can come up with," Lucas was the first to break the silence.

"When do you think we will get feedback?" asked John.

"I should get something back within the next few days. As soon as I hear anything I will pass it on to Tom," Lucas replied.

"It looks like we are going to have a personal manhunt if we are to get rid of this fellow," Gary said.

"Let's hope we don't get a call out before we have some feedback," Nick put in.

"Do you think this Mamba chap will still be operating in the Sabi area?" asked George.

"No I don't think so. There has been very little activity in the south lately, and we know that he has been very active in both the areas.

Perhaps he will move back to that area or perhaps even further north," Tom gave his opinion.

"Okay we'll just have to wait and see what comes back from SB then," said John.

Two days later, Lucas contacted Tom to tell him that he had received a report from Special Branch in Salisbury. Apparently 'Mamba' was, in fact, the same man Maria had suspected it to be. His name was Titus Ngopi and had been educated at Morgenster Mission, but had run away from school. He turned up again later in Harare Township and was wanted for political activity. He had escaped the net during 'Operation Cordon Sanitaire' in 1964 and was thought to have left the country to go for military training in Tanzania.

Tom got in touch with the Special Branch officer based at the JOC (Joint Operations Command) in Chiredzi and arranged a meeting with him and the members of 'Tango One.' It was getting personal now, and decisions had to be made; the man was obviously going to target them, and they had to be ready. Would he come looking for them or would he wait for them to go to him?

The meeting was held in the Police Mess the following day with all members of the stick, the Member-in-Charge of Triangle Police Station and the Special Branch detective. Inspector Lark explained that the terrorist going by the name of 'Mamba' had been responsible for a number of attacks in the country with a recorded number of kills to his name. He had been recruited by ZANU in Harare in 1963 where he had been a youth leader. This confirmed what Lucas had told Tom earlier.

Apparently, Mamba had joined ZANLA, the armed wing of ZANU and was one of the most highly trained insurgents operating in the country and known to be ruthless. He was thought to be responsible for preventing any information coming out of the areas in the South Eastern Lowveld. Having been positively identified at Mavue, they suspected that he would be starting his ruthless intimidation in the Sabi area in the near future. Inspector Lark further informed them that he had been responsible for one of the early hits on a farm in Mrewa, and had been the only terrorist to escape from what had been Tom's first follow up operation and ambush.

This all confirmed their suspicions that he had escaped from three contacts with terrorists that Tom and his stick had been involved in, and the SB man stressed the urgency of taking Mamba out of the equation as quickly as possible. He would issue instructions that all units should try to capture this wanted man and, if not possible, eliminate him. He must not be allowed to escape again.

"Make no mistake gentlemen. This man Mamba is ruthless and brutal. Do not underestimate him; he has been linked to most of the attacks in the Lowveld including the murder of the telephone technician a while ago," Lark warned.

"If he attacked that girl at Mavue not long after he got away in the Sabi operation, he must have seen and recognized you there," John whispered to Tom and Lucas.

"It sounds like he is pissed off with you guys," Nick said.

"If he knows who you are and is bent on getting his own back, you two had better be very careful. We will keep you informed of any news we hear about his movements. By the way, he always wears dark glasses. It seems to be his badge of rank."

The description of Mamba matched that of the terrorist Tom had seen leading a large group into the country near Crooks Corner. It must be the same man they had seen at the Sabi River contact who had escaped. It was all starting to fit together.

"Listen up you guys. This monster might very well decide to make a deliberate attack on my family and me. Lucas and I have already discussed the possibility. He is pretty safe in the Police Camp for the time being, but he might well get attacked when he is on one of his local patrols," Tom said, expressing the seriousness of the situation. "If any of you chaps feel that you would like to transfer to another stick, please do so. I don't want your families exposed in any way. I will understand," he finished.

"And then what? Are you two going to pull out of PATU?" John asked Tom and Lucas.

"No. Of course not," Tom responded quickly.

"Well, as far as I am concerned we are a team and will continue as we are. You can't take the bastard on by yourselves," John said forcefully. Then turning to the others, he asked: "What do you guys think?"

All agreed that there was no need to split up.

"Thanks, guys. We appreciate that. I agree we should not allow this man to get to us. I'll make sure that my family takes more care when I am away, and stay off the farm altogether," Tom said.

"I think that if he is intent on having a go at us, he will find us sooner or later," John finished.

After the fiasco in the Sabi River area, Mamba moved his depleted force back to their camp in the south opposite Crooks Corner. Again replacing the men he had lost, he proceeded to launch some attacks into the Limpopo River area. Using different entry points, he was able to wreak fear and havoc among the local inhabitants.

Through his brutal methods of persuasion, Mamba established reliable supply lines well into the lower end of the country. He attacked and killed one of the Naunetsi ranch managers at his dipping tanks. This attack he carried out in broad daylight, knowing that he would be able to escape long before Security Forces arrived on the scene.

He attacked, captured and tortured a white telephone technician who was repairing the cut telephone lines to the Nuanetsi Police Station. He had the white pig stripped of his clothes and made him march for a day before cutting off his genitals, and forcing them into his mouth. Then he left him to die in the bush.

Mamba would have preferred to take him back to his camp as a prisoner, but he would never have survived the long march. It was a pity, as it would have been a feather in his cap.

Over a period of six months, he had taken control of the lower south-east of the country, creating a safe pipeline for large numbers of comrades to infiltrate the country. His operatives now had a number of varying roles; some were even cross-dressers wearing dresses and wigs to gather vital information at beer halls. Others were made to use dagga (Marijuana) then sent to busy centers further inland as suicide bombers. He was most pleased with himself and was praised by his superiors for his success in that area.

At the end of the winter, Mamba was ordered to return to the north and, once again, base himself at Mavue where he was to carry out similar operations in that area.

Pleased to be moving back to the area where he had last seen his two tormentors, he looked forward to the opportunity of stalking them and ridding himself of them once and for all. It had become an obsession, and his hatred for the two had grown stronger by the day. He still blamed them for his earlier failures. He was more experienced now; much stronger and better prepared. It would not happen again.

****

Chapter 21

Two days after arriving back at Mavue, with a larger force than before, Mamba sent his first four units into Rhodesia. Their instructions were to secure the supply lines. He sent units he sent up the east side of the Sabi River towards the Chisumbanje and Middle Sabi, and the other two to the west to the Mkwasine and Nandi farming areas where there were some isolated Settler Farms and ranches. They would make good targets for his planned attacks.

Each group now had a political commissar with them, to subvert and re-educate the locals as they moved from village to village. Mamba took his unit on a far more dangerous mission, and without a political man; where he was going, there would be no one to re-educate.

Some time back he had received a report of a white farmer and a policeman who had rescued some of his informants from an island in the middle of the flooded Lundi River. It had been a white policeman, so he had dismissed them as they were not the men he was seeking. The two men he was looking for had to be in the Lowveld, and as there were only two police stations in the Lowveld, they had to be from either Triangle or Chiredzi.

He would start his search in Triangle and work his way back. Their route took them along the banks of the Lundi River, past Hippo Valley Sugar Estates, and on to the junction of the Mtilikwe and the Lundi rivers. Moving upstream, along the Mtilikwe River, they found a suitable campsite near the sugar cane fields and hid their weapons.

Leaving two of the men posing as fishermen, Mamba and two others continued to Triangle to gather what information they could. Knowing that the main command center for the Lowveld was in Chiredzi, he had decided to start his search in Triangle, and work his way back to Chiredzi, where the risk of being caught was greater.

None of them were wearing a uniform; this was a clandestine operation, and they posed as civilians. They walked along the main roads through the sugar farms individually and as casually as they could, so as not to attract attention to themselves. Arriving at Triangle shopping area, they wandered around without seeming to attract any attention. In the evening the three of them returned to their temporary camp to compare notes.

Late in the afternoon on the second day, Mamba was drinking a cool drink he had purchased at the Service Station when a white van pulled up to buy petrol. His anger rose like bile. Approaching the pump attendant, after the van drove away, Mamba asked, "Who was that man in the white van?"

"He is the manager on Section Sixty One," the attendant told him.

"Oh. Where is Section Sixty One?" he continued casually not wanting arouse suspicion.

"Out that way near the Mtilikwe weir," the attendant replied pointing with his arm in the general direction of their hiding place. "Why do you want to know?"

"I am new in Triangle and have just come to work in the Cotton Gin. I must still learn my way around," he told the attendant with a smile before taking his leave.

So the white policeman was now a farmer. He could hardly believe his luck. He walked back along the road past the hospital and into the bush, to where they were camped about 5 miles from the village. The other two men were already there.

He would have to find Section Sixty One and work out his plan of attack. He had noticed that all the tractors had the Section numbers painted on them so he did not think it would be too hard to find the one he was seeking. He would carry out a reconnaissance the following day.

. . . .

Tom dropped Maria off at the hospital for her meeting on his way to the Triangle Main office. He would collect her on the way back to the farm. After her meeting and with a bit of time to spare, she wandered off into the hospital garden and sat on a bench in the shade of a flamboyant tree. From there she could look out across the road to the sixties and onto the dam in the middle of the village. She would see Tom arriving from there.

She was in a cheerful mood, her life was going along nicely, and she was happy in her job. She did not mind that she could not have Tom, as long as she could be near him. And she was getting closer to him all the time.

Tractors, cane haulage trucks, vans, bicycles, and pedestrians passed along in front of her while she sat there. It was a lovely day, warm as usual, but pleasant with the odd fluffy white cloud drifting lazily across the blue sky. Maria could smell the scent from the roses in the garden.

She watched a solitary man walking along the road towards the farm; there was something familiar about him. It was not the way he kept his head down, or that he kept on looking around. There was something else. When he was almost opposite her, he glanced in her direction. He was wearing dark glasses. Her heart stopped!

Not wanting him to see her, Maria quickly lowered her head as if reading a book, but glanced at him frequently out of the corner of her eye. She watched him disappear around the bend in the road beyond the hospital. Her legs felt too weak for her to stand. Tom arrived a little while later and came to find her.

"What is it Maria?" he asked as he sat down next to her and put his arm around her.

"He is here!" she blurted out of her dry mouth and trembling lips.

"Who is here? What are you talking about?" he asked her.

"Titus Ngopi is here," Maria said.

Tom tensed. "Calm down Maria." He said pulling her to her feet; "Come, we must go to the Police Station right away."

. . . .

By eleven o'clock Mamba and one of his men had crossed over the weir on the Mtilikwe River and located the Section he was looking for. Working their way through the thorn scrub running alongside the river, they reached a position where they were able to observe the homestead from the rear.

The approach to the house from there was not good for a daylight attack. The scrub had been cut out, leaving only the larger trees and a few small Jessie bushes. The elephant grass, with no competition from the scrub, had grown tall and dense. The barbed wire fence around the house was more than ten foot high with strands running across as well as up and down to form small squares and was virtually impenetrable. They would have to attack the house with RPG rockets and wait for the occupants to emerge before killing them.

There was an orchard of fruit trees to the one side of the house with chicken runs at the rear. A large Baobab Tree stood between the house and the office on the other side. In the front of the house, there was a swimming pool and a summer house. An avenue of Flamboyant trees led from the main road up to the entrance. There were some shrubs and bushes in the garden. Sisal plants a meter tall had been planted close together, two paces from the fence around the outside, preventing access to the fence. A small gate provided access from the house to the office and a large gate for vehicles in the front.

The van Mamba had seen the white pig driving, was standing in the driveway. No other vehicles were to be seen, apart from the tractors moving in and out of the yard, to what appeared to be a workshop. While they watched, they saw 'the man' cross from the office in the yard to his house. He had an FN rifle slung over his shoulder. An hour later he emerged from the house and went back to his office where he remained.

Mamba decided to launch their attack from the rear of the house. Under cover of darkness, they would be able to crawl up to within a few paces of the high-security fence surrounding the homestead. Using the sisal to hide behind, they would be able to attack from three sides. In that way, the front escape route would also be covered.

. . . .

Lucas was in a meeting behind closed doors when Tom and Maria arrived at the station. Soon the door opened, and the petrol attendant from the garage emerged. He took their place on the bench outside while they went into the office to see Lucas. Before Tom could say a word, Lucas turned to them saying:-

"The petrol attendant outside, who is a Police Reservist, has just made a report to me of a stranger who has been asking about you. The man, who was wearing dark glasses, was at the petrol station when you filled up with fuel about an hour ago," Lucas told Tom.

"The hell he was! Well, that is just what we have come to tell you. Maria saw him not half an hour ago. He was walking along the road in the direction of the sixties sections," Tom confirmed the sighting.

"He told the attendant that he worked at the cotton gin and had just started work there recently. I have just phoned the personnel department at the Gin who told me that they have not taken on any new employees for at least three months," Lucas added.

"Maria here has positively identified the man as being Mamba."

"Yes I saw him. It was definitely Mamba I saw walking along the road," Maria said.

"Let's get moving," said Lucas jumping up from his chair and summoning a couple of constables.

They piled quickly into the Police Land Rover with two other police constables and automatic rifles and were soon heading out on the road past the Hospital. Lucas got on the radio and alerted JOC in Chiredzi. Two other vehicles were dispatched to join the search which proved fruitless. Mamba had gone to ground and disappeared once again.

Back at the Police Station, Tom contacted the members of 'Tango One.' Of one thing they were positive. Mamba was going to attack Tom's home and family within the next couple of days. They had to be ready and set an ambush!

. . . .

"Julia I want you and the boys to come into the village right now," Tom said to Julia over the radio.

"Why, what's the panic?" Julia asked. She knew by the tone of Tom's voice not to argue.

"The police have received information that there is a bunch of terrs wandering around the area. I want you out of the way while we carry out a sweep. Go to the club and stay there until I get in touch with you," Tom told her.

"The boys are already in the village, so I'll pack a few things and head in within the next fifteen minutes," Julia said.

"Try to follow as close behind one of the other vehicles on the road if you can. Better still, try following a cane haulage truck. Just in case there are any ambushes along the road."

"You are starting to frighten me, Tom. What is going on?"

"It's just a precaution. I don't want you exposed. I'll be coming home shortly but I want you in the village as soon as possible and before I get home."

"Stop worrying. I am on my way."

This was the first time Tom had sounded worried, and so Julia wasted no time in doing as he told her. The pressure of the war had been intensifying for some time, and it was difficult to sleep at night. Every time there was a strong gust of wind, small branches would be blown onto the security fence, around the house, setting off the alarm. Everyone startled out of sleep would rush to their allocated places - the boys to the shower for their safety, Julia, armed with the automatic shotgun, to a window facing the sector of the fence where the alarm had been set off, while Tom would take his FN rifle and go outside to check the fence.

Although the bright security lights on top of the house, directed outwards, made it difficult for anyone to see Tom, it always worried her that terrorists could be outside the fence waiting to kill him. Once it was all clear, they would all try and go back to sleep. Sometimes this happened a few times in a night. They all began to live on their nerves.

Tom's two boys were trained to crawl into the shower room (the only room with two walls from the outside) as soon as they were awakened by the siren screaming. There they could reload magazines if it became necessary. They had practiced for long hours and could load magazines in almost the same time as Tom could.

Now with Tom making her leave the farm and rush into the village, she was really worried and hoped that it was just a false alarm. When she was on radio duty the previous day, there had been no mention of terrorists having been sighted in the area.

It was still too early to pick the boys up from school, and so she called Jill and arranged to meet her at the club where they had lunch together. While they were eating, Julia was called to the phone.

"Julia I want you and the boys to spend the night at the club. No questions. There is a strong possibility of a terrorist attack on one of the sections out our way tonight. Our stick is going out to guard our house. Jill and the other wives of our stick members will also be staying there until this is all over. You will be safe there," Tom said.

"How serious is this?" Julia was starting to feel nervous. There had been some scares recently, but nobody took much notice and left the police and military to deal with it.

"A known terrorist was seen this morning in the village and was asking directions to the sections out our way."

"Why would he pick on our sections?" Julia asked.

"Well, I suppose it is because it will be easy for them to escape from there. There is nothing but bush between our sections and the Mozambique border," Tom surmised.

"Jill is here with me now. I will let her know what is going on."

"Okay. But keep this to yourselves. We don't want to start a panic, or for word to get out that we are on to this man. John will be in touch with Jill. You might tell her to go home and get an overnight case," Tom suggested.

"We will be fine. Make sure you find these animals Tom and don't worry about us," Julia reassured him.

"I will let you know what the outcome is, first thing tomorrow."

. . . .

Within an hour they were back at the Police Station, kitted out and ready. George, who lived further out, did not have time to go home but, like all of them, always had his FN rifle with him and only needed to borrow some kit from the police. Tom would get his kit when they got out to the house. Leaving Maria in Lucas's house for her safety, they drove out to Tom's farm.

Arriving just before sunset, Tom pulled up alongside the kitchen door, and they all slipped inside. They all agreed that the most likely direction of attack was from the rear of the house. The kitchen light was switched off allowing them to move outside, and take up positions on either side of the house, facing towards the bush at the rear. George remained inside the house to man the radio (all farmsteads were equipped with Agri-Alert radio systems linked to the police station) and to guard the front in the unlikely chance of a frontal attack. If this happened, he would switch on the security flood lights around the house, enabling them all to get back inside in the shadow behind the bright lights.

A ten-foot security fence encompassed the house and garden. Each sector of the fence had sensors linked to a control box located in the master bedroom which was also linked to high-powered security lights, strategically mounted on top of the house, pointing in all directions and a siren. When the lights were switched on, the whole area outside the fence was lit up making the house almost invisible from anyone wanting to launch an attack.

Tom activated the fence every evening as soon as it got dark, only switching it off in the morning after he had made a sweep around the perimeter. In the event of any sector being touched, the lights would come on, and the siren would start to scream. The control box in the bedroom indicated which sector of the fence had been breached enabling Tom to get outside and counter the attack.

The fence itself was made up of ten strands of barbed wire running horizontally and strands threaded vertically nine inches apart. It was designed to snag the fins of an RPG rocket slowing it down sufficiently so that it would explode before reaching the house. The rockets were capable of penetrating an eight-inch concrete wall.

The trap was set, and the PATU stick was ready for Mamba. It might be a long wait, but the men were used to laying all night in ambush. Tom locked the dogs inside the house with George. After a long uncomfortable night with no disturbance, and no sign of any attack, they were all stiff and tired.

Before dawn the next morning they left their hiding places, and one by one went into the house where they cleaned up and ate breakfast before having a sleep. In the afternoon, feeling refreshed, they sat around the dining room table to refine their trap. Now that they had more time, the ambush could be set with more care.

. . . .

"Julia we are fine. Nothing happened anywhere around here last night. We are going to lie low and see what happens tonight," Tom reported to his wife in the morning.

"How long is this going to take? We can't stay here at the club indefinitely," Julia began to think this was just another false alarm.

"We would like to catch the buggers. If they don't appear tonight, the army will search the area tomorrow, and try to flush them out."

"Make sure you feed the animals and don't mess up the house. I know what the five of you are like."

After taking all the children to school, Jill, Anne, and Judy went off to their homes for the day. Megan lived too far out for her to go home and so she and Julia spent the day together at the club. Although she knew there was nothing she could do about it, Julia hated not knowing what was going on. Eventually, she reluctantly settled down with a book from the library, but still found it difficult to concentrate. She did, however, feel there was something she was not being told. Was there going to be an attack on her home?

The other three women returned later in the afternoon, and after collecting their children from school, they all settled down to wait. They, like their husbands, were used to this sort of thing, and all being together at the club was the next best thing to being at home.

. . . .

Happy with his plan, they went back across the river to their hiding place. Mamba was excited with the prospect of finally getting rid of one of the men who had hounded him for years and had been responsible for preventing him from rising up the ranks of ZANU. (The black traitor he'd deal with later) He had intended moving at midnight, but was edgy and decided to move before dark.

Gathering up their weapons and clearing all evidence of their presence, they crossed the river once more and made their way back towards the homestead on Section Sixty One.

Two hours later, just before moving into position, Mamba changed his mind. He had a bad feeling that if they waited another day before attacking the white settler and his family, the chances of being compromised would be greater. His mind kept going back to his brief discussion with the petrol attendant. What if he decided to report the fact that he had been questioned about the manager of Section Sixty One? To wait another day might be fatal.

They would attack as soon as they were in position. He and his men were heavily armed, and amongst them, they had two RPG (Rocket Propelled Grenade) launchers with two rockets for each. They each carried an AK47 rifle with four magazines of ammunition, and each magazine taped upside down onto another. They each carried four hand grenades. Mamba would be in the center and would signal the start of the assault by firing the first rocket into the house.

At 9 o'clock they started their approach. Leopard-crawling through the elephant grass, they slowly made their way towards the sisal plants on the outside of the security fence. The lights in the house were going off one by one as the occupants retired for the night. Half an hour later they were in position.

Mamba cursed under his breath when he allowed the rocket to 'clink' on the RPG tube as he loaded it. Slowly he raised himself on one knee and prepared to fire.

....

Once again, that evening, they took up their positions after dark and were ready by 7 o'clock. This time they hid behind the sisal on the outside of the fence and had time to get comfortable. Minutes ticked by as they waited. In the house George wandered around, switching lights on and off, making it look as if everything was normal. By 9 o'clock the only light burning was in the lounge and on the veranda at the front of the house.

The cicadas suddenly stopped their screeching; it was nature's way of warning them that danger was approaching. The silence was almost deafening as they lay in wait. Tom heard a faint 'pssst' from John on the right alerting him to a possible presence of their attackers. Tom passed the 'pssst' along to Gary. The adrenalin started to pump making the hair on Tom's neck stand up like wires on a steel brush. Was that a shape he saw in the dark? As he stared at it, his eyes started to water, and he blinked to clear his vision.

The dark shape he was watching suddenly moved, and he could see that it was a man about ten paces out in front of him. Tom heard a faint metallic 'clink' that was the unmistakable sound of an RPG being loaded!

As he watched, the man slowly got up into a kneeling position, ready to fire his weapon. Without hesitation, Tom fired a burst at the figure and saw him fall over sideways firing the rocket as he fell. The rocket went high and wide exploding in the air.

As soon as Tom opened fire with his first burst, the rest of the stick opened fire with repeated 'tap-tap' 'tap-tap' of double shot fire. The cacophony of combat and the zinging of ricochets filled the air. No sooner had the rocket exploded than George, inside the house, flipped the switch, and the whole area outside the fence was flooded in light.

The terrorists were visible and didn't stand a chance. Within a minute, and with very little return of fire from the figures lying in the grass, they stopped firing. Getting up quickly, they rushed forward to check their victims and to sweep the area behind the attackers.

The terrorist, who had fired the RPG, was wounded by Tom's burst. He was lying on his side with the launcher still gripped in his right hand. His left hand was clutching a hand grenade, but he had not had time to pull the pin to release the detonator. Tom bent quickly to remove the grenade from his grip, and check the condition of his victim. He had been shot in the arm holding the grenade launcher, his left knee was in tatters, and he had a wound on his head. He was alive but unconscious.

Another of the terrorists was badly wounded, and three were found lying dead in the grass. George had alerted JOC who dispatched a helicopter from Buffalo Range to pick up the bodies, and the two wounded and captured terrorists. (All the farms had helipads marked with a large white "H" near their homes) The dogs were let out and ran around excitedly investigating and sniffing everywhere. Gunfire and the smell of gunpowder excited them. The security lights were left burning all night, to deter any possible follow up attack.

'Tango One' returned to the Police Station to make their report leaving one of the other PATU sticks to guard the house on Section Sixty One.

....

When Tom left her in the Police Camp and went off to wait for the monster, Maria was terrified. The whole of the next day and into the night she waited in the police Mess. She felt quite ill fearing that Tom would get killed and that Mamba would escape then come after her. One of the other wives in the camp brought her food and kept her company. She made small talk to try and take Maria's mind off what was happening, but to no avail.

At about 10 o'clock that night, she was disturbed by the sound of vehicles starting up, accompanied by loud voices and shouted orders and instructions. There was excitement and activity in the camp. She pulled on her coat and hurried out. Bumping into one of the constables she knew, she grabbed his arm. "What has happened? Where are you all going?"

"There has been an attack on Section Sixty One manager's house."

"I work on Section Sixty One. Is the manager alright?" Maria asked with her heart in her mouth.

"I am not sure. They're on their way here now," he replied. "Please go back to the Mess and wait there. I will bring you news as soon as I know anything."

Back in the Mess, Maria stood at the window looking out towards the entrance of the police station, hoping to catch sight of Tom. What had happened out there?

It seemed a lifetime until Lucas arrived, accompanied by Tom. They were both in high spirits, "We got the bastard, Maria. We wounded and captured Mamba. I will take you to see him in the morning," he told her. "You must spend the night here, and I will collect you first thing." Then seeing the tears running down her face he asked more gently. "What is wrong?"

"I have been so worried about you. I am just happy that you are safe," Maria replied. "Please Tom; I don't want to see that monster ever."

Relieved that Tom and his men were safe and that Mamba was locked up, Maria slept well that night. It was the first full night's sleep she had had since Mamba's reappearance in her life.

Julia and the four women were just finishing their game of cards, when the men, still kitted out in their camouflage, arrived at the club at 11 o'clock that night. They were loud and full of nonsense, demanding that the barman keep the bar open.

"Julia those bastards tried to attack our home! But we were waiting for them and culled three of them. Two others are wounded and in hospital," Tom was still on an adrenaline high.

"What happened? Are you guys all okay?" Julia said looking at each of them as they ordered their drinks.

"Yes. We are all fine. The gooks didn't even get a chance to fire a shot. Come on let's all have a drink."

Julia felt the tension drain out of her as she relaxed and joined the others at the bar. She would find out from Tom later why the terrorists had chosen to attack their home.

. . . .

After carrying out a wide sweep of the area in the morning, Tom and his men crossed the Mtilikwe River and found the spot where the terrorists had been hiding.

Special Branch confirmed that the captured terrorist Tom had shot and wounded, was Titus Ngopi alias 'Mamba.' The other captured man was unknown. No one had escaped.

After dropping the boys at school in the village, Julia returned home. Tom and Julia returned to the village in the afternoon to attend the 'post-mortem' at the Police Mess, with the other members of the stick and their wives. The boys were spending the night with friends in the village.

Knowing that the man responsible for such terror in that part of the country had finally been captured was a tremendous relief and a personal victory for Tom. He had wounded and captured the man who had been stalking him, and who had hurt Maria in ways he did not understand.

Tom had crossed paths with Mamba on five separate occasions in fourteen years. He was out of the way now and would spend a long time in jail.

. . . .

Mamba sensed that he was in strange surroundings even before he opened his eyes. What had happened? Why was there a smell of antiseptic? His head was pounding, and his body felt broken. His mind kept wandering as he struggled to concentrate.

Suddenly his eyes shot wide open when he remembered the last thing he had been doing. Looking around now, he realized that he was in a hospital bed. A black policeman was sitting on a chair in the corner near the door, reading a newspaper. On the other side of the room near the window was another bed in which Tendayi, one of his men lay.

He had a tube going into his nose and a drip in his arm, and he was handcuffed to the bed. Only then did it dawn on Mamba that he was a prisoner.

His left leg was extremely painful, and he could not move it. His right leg he could move slightly, but it too was manacled to the foot of the bed. His throbbing head was wrapped in a bandage.

What had happened to the other three men? Had they escaped? How had it gone wrong?

He spent most of the day lying there trying to put the pieces together. He or one of his men must have been spotted or followed. It must have been the petrol attendant; he was the only person Mamba had spoken with when he had asked him about the white man in the van, and where he stayed. That had to be it. He would get the traitor, later on; he thought as he drifted off to sleep.

The following morning, when he looked over towards Tendayi's bed, he saw that it was empty. The nurse later told him that he had died during the night.

Mamba knew he would be interrogated as soon as he was fit enough. He would not be giving out any information, and would escape his captors as soon as he got the chance. He would have to try to delay the interrogation and stay in the hospital as long as possible to regain his strength. He would have a better chance of escaping from there.

****

Part Two – Malawi & Swaziland
(1977-1989)

Chapter 22

In the morning on the fourth day of their two-week patrol, the radio crackled to life. "Come in Tango One." They had been on the move for about an hour, and the orange sun was climbing above the distant hills in the east. It was already warm and going to be another hot day in the Lowveld.

"This is Tango One. Go ahead," Nick said responding to the call.

"There has been an ambush on the convoy traveling to Ngundu Halt. We believe the attackers are escaping to the south in your direction. They could be heading for Boli."

"Roger that. We will move and attempt to intercept them. How many terrs are we looking for?"

"We believe there are at least four. Over."

"Are there any casualties?"

"No further information is available at this stage. We believe there are one serious injury and a few with minor injuries."

"Thank you for that. Please keep us posted. Out."

Calling a halt in a thicket of Mopani scrub, they gathered around Tom to discuss the content of the radio message. Knowing that the terrorists would be in a hurry to avoid their pursuers and to get out of the country, they studied the map to work the most likely route of escape. After some discussion, they all agreed that the terrorists would cross the Tokwe and the Lundi Rivers, keeping well away from populated areas, as they made towards Mbizi before turning southeast directly towards the Mozambique Border. It would be the quickest and most direct route for them to take in the hope of avoiding security forces.

"It is going to be like looking for a needle in a haystack. Our only hope is to try to cut across their escape route and pick up their spoor," Tom said.

"I am bloody sure it must be some of our friend Mamba's mob again. We know he had other groups working under him in this part of the country." John said.

"I agree. It looks like Mamba was the leader in the whole southeastern Lowveld. His name has been popping up all over the place," Gary stated.

"I wonder who was in the convoy. I hope none of our families were caught in that ambush," Nick said expressing all their concerns.

"We will all know the people who have been injured, unless they were visitors to the Lowveld," John observed.

"Okay, guys we have to pull our fingers out. We must be in a position to stop the bastards getting to the border and escaping," Tom said, giving the signal to move out and trying to put out of his mind the thought that Julie might have been in the ambushed convoy.

Three weeks had passed since the attack on Tom's home, and now 'Tango One' was on patrol in the Matibi Tribal Trust area. It was a good will mission to try and restore the confidence of the locals in the Government Forces.

There had been reports filtering back to the police of people being intimidated with a number of children having been abducted. The children over the age of ten were forced to march across the border to camps in Mozambique where they were indoctrinated and trained by the insurgents.

This area was not far from Chikombedzi where there had been an attack a year ago in which women and children had been slaughtered. Tom knew that Mamba was responsible for that attack and felt sure that he had been responsible for the intimidation in this area.

The previous weekend had been a training weekend with concern being expressed by all PATU members regarding the shortage of equipment and ammunition. This time the men of 'Tango One' were quite happy to have been assigned a relatively easy task for a change. Knowing that insurgents were operating in the area, they would have to be vigilant as always but had not expected to come into contact with any of them. Until now!

....

Maria arrived at her regular meeting with the Matron early and to collect her normal supply of medication for the month. She had to be back on the farm before the boys got home from school. Julia had joined the morning convoy to Fort Victoria and had asked her to look after her children until her return in the late afternoon. She glanced over to the bench where she had been sitting when she saw Titus Ngopi and shuddered.

The day she heard he had been wounded and captured while trying to kill her man was the happiest of her life. She was pleased that Tom was the one who had shot him and she felt like a huge weight had been lifted from her shoulders.

Now Tom was back in the bush, once again, leaving her to look after Julia and the two boys. After her meeting with the Matron, she enquired after the injured terrorist who was in the hospital.

"The police took him away last week. I think he is in the High-Security Prison at Buffalo Range. He had his leg amputated and is crippled for life. He is not a very nice person, and I was very happy to see him go," Matron said giving her the good news.

After a cup of tea in the Nurses Home, Maria picked up her supplies and made her way towards the Hospital entrance. Just as she reached the main gates, an ambulance with the siren screaming came flying past her and stopped outside the casualty entrance. She had plenty of time to get back to the farm and, allowing her curiosity to get the better of her; she hurried back to see who was in a bad way.

Maria was dumbstruck when she saw Julia being lifted out of the ambulance and wheeled into the operating theatre. She approached the driver and learned from him that the convoy had been ambushed. She had to do something before the boys heard the news. Rushing to the Matron's office, she explained the situation to her and then used her phone to contact Jill.

. . . .

Picking up their pace, 'Tango One' set a course to the south-east in the hopes of cutting the escaping terrorists off mid-way between the Lundi River and Boli. It was the middle of summer and hot in the Lowveld. Their sweat attracted the ever-present Mopani bees, which incessantly pestered them as they hurried along.

They were moving through an overgrazed Tribal Trust area with little grass. The almost bare ground was hot and dusty, but the going was easy, and the 'stick' was able to pass through the Mopani forests quickly, enjoying the shade offered by the butterfly leaves that rattled in the breeze.

The stick had covered 20 miles since the call came in and were entering the Gona-re-Zhou Game Conservation Area. They found a suitable ambush site and rested. Nick tried to contact HQ for an update but could not get a signal or even the sound of static; the radio was dead.

The sun was setting and the air starting to cool. Synchronizing their watches and positioning themselves two to three paces apart, they attached a string from one to the other. With one tug they could wake the next man for his watch duty or warn him of any impending danger.

Tom was wakened from his light sleep when the string attached to his finger snapped back. Raising his head slowly, he concentrated on the path and waited. A few minutes later he heard the crack of a twig. Someone was coming along the path. They were all awake now and watched the shadows. Something out there was moving very slowly and cautiously, stopping every few paces before moving on again. With racing pulses, they waited at the ready.

At last a dark shape took form. It was a Buffalo cow with her calf! She must have got a whiff of their scent and was moving along slowly, taking a few steps then stopping briefly before taking a few more. Five minutes later they had disappeared and, relieved; the men went back to sleep. In the area where they normally operated, it was not unusual to come across herds of buffalo, elephant, zebra, kudu, and impala, and they were always wary of the presence of lion and leopard.

At first light, after a hasty breakfast, the 'stick' was on the way again, this time following the path. An hour later, John, who was out in front, stopped suddenly and, signaling to Tom, crouched down to examine the ground in front of him. Fresh tracks crossed the path, going towards the east.

Checking the spoor card, Tom identified the tracks as belonging to four or five insurgents. No effort had been made to cover their tracks. They must have crossed 'Tango One's' tracks during the night. The 'stick' would have to move fast if they wanted to catch them by nightfall and prevent them from escaping into Mozambique.

Coming across the tracks was a stroke of luck. They were in a vast area of game conservation land, and although they had put themselves directly in the path of the fleeing terrorists, they had not dared to hope that they would find any trace of them. Now the tables had turned, and they knew that the men they were hunting were ahead of them. They would have to track them down, taking extra care not to walk into an ambush.

Before moving on again, Nick tried to call JOC to request that a stop group be put in place before the afternoon. The radio was still dead, and this was cause for concern – not to have communication when going into a possible contact situation made them all very nervous.

By mid-morning, with the sun high in the clear deep blue sky, they crossed the road from Chilojo Cliffs to Boli. They were following a well-worn game trail leading straight toward the border, now only 10 miles away. The trail led along a small gully and around a large anthill. Thinking it would be a good place to check what lay ahead; Tom called a stop and climbed to the top of the anthill.

He slowly stood up, then using his binoculars; studied the vista ahead for any signs of movement. About 200 paces ahead and right in their pathway he could see the backs of a large herd of elephant feeding on the leaves of the Mopani scrub. He could hear them ripping off the branches of the trees.

If the fleeing terrorists had passed in that direction, the elephants would have been disturbed and moved off. They had to have gone around downwind behind them. A busy hoopoe was tap-tapping on a dead tree trunk, trying to entice insects to come out of hiding and, high overhead, the shrill cry of a circling Bateleur Eagle attracted his attention briefly.

As Tom started to climb down from his view site, he heard 'frritt, frritt, frritt' in the scrub Mopani leaves around him that sounded similar to the sound of a Fiscal Shrike (bird) but when the sound was followed by a faint crackle, Tom realized that he was being fired at, and quickly jumped to the ground.

It was uncharacteristic for trained terrorists to take pot shots and give their position away, so Tom suspected that by presenting such an easy target, they had opted to fire at him to slow them down.

With their prey so close, and now aware of their presence, it was possible that the hunted had now become the hunters. The terrorists had the advantage of knowing where the PATU stick was. Tom was very lucky not to have been hit by one of the bullets, but then again, most terrorists were poor shots. To follow up in the direction from which the shots had come would be suicide.

The border was so close that 'Tango One' would have to move fast if they were to stop their target escaping. If they were too cautious, they would allow the terrorists to get away, but if they did not take care, they might walk into an ambush. Quickly changing their direction, they took a course well in front of the herd of elephants. Then, making directly for the border at a fast pace, they hoped to get ahead of the terrorists who would also be moving fast.

Throwing caution to the wind, the stick moved as fast as they could, Reaching the border fence at about 2 in the afternoon but with no further sign of their quarry. They swung around to the south-west and followed the fence in a last-ditch attempt to cut the insurgents off.

The rumble of an engine warned them that a large military troop carrier was approaching. It appeared over the rise on the road inside Mozambique, grinding its way northwards. The road was only about 20 paces from the fence.

"Quick. Take cover before the bastards see us," Tom urged his men. There was no time for caution.

Scrambling for cover, in the sparse Acacia thorn scrub, they watched as the vehicle drove slowly past them. The troop carrier was full of Frelimo soldiers, all looking hard into the bush on the Rhodesian side of the fence. Lying only partly hidden below the high sides of the vehicle, Tom could almost feel hot lead pumping into his back. If the soldiers had just looked down, they would have been seen.

No sooner had they moved back from the fence, into better cover after the Troop carrier disappeared than they heard it coming back again. It re-appeared in a cloud of dust moving quickly to the south and stopped 200 paces further down the road. Four figures from the Rhodesian side dashed across the open fence line and were hurriedly helped up onto the back of the truck. The terrorists must have had a radio.

Once again, the vehicle turned around coming back on its original route to the north. The soldiers all moved to the left side of the truck and started firing short bursts, with their automatic rifles, into the bush on the Rhodesian side of the fence. The escaping terrorists must have told them that security forces were pursuing them.

Tom and his men were so intent on trying to stop them that they had neglected to move into a position where they could have retaliated effectively. They were still far too exposed and were slow in moving into thicker bush. Nick, struggling to heft the radio he had dropped when he removed it from his back, lagged behind the rest.

He was spotted and attracted a hail of bullets as he ran for cover. Gary and Lucas doubled back quickly to help him, while Tom and John returned the fire, covering the retreat of the other three. Moving away quickly, the troop-carrier soon disappeared in a cloud of dust. Luckily most of the shots fired at the 'stick' had been well off the target having been fired from a bouncing platform.

Nick had been wounded twice; in the left shoulder and leg. Gary patched him up as best he could and gave him a morphine shot to ease the pain. They constructed a makeshift stretcher using two Mopani poles and their ponchos. Tom tried the radio which finally came to life.

"One of my men has been injured. We need a 'casevac' (casualty evacuation) ASAP," he told the controller.

"Roger that. What is the situation regarding the insurgents? Over."

"They have escaped through the border fence and have been picked up by a Fred RL (Frelimo Troop carrier). Over," Tom reported.

"Roger. Remain in your present location and stay on radio watch. Over."

"Roger. Wilco. Out."

Five minutes later they received a call.

"Is there a suitable LZ (Landing Zone) near your location?" The controller asked.

"Affirmative. There is one on the other side of the border about 200 paces from our present location. Over."

"What activity is there on the other side?"

"Nothing at this time. We expect the troop carrier will be coming back sometime later today."

"Roger that. We have a fire-force unit on its way to you. They will give you cover while you cross the border to board the chopper."

"What is the ETA of the chopper?" Tom asked.

"Forty-five minutes. Over."

"Roger. Copied that and thank you. We are standing by. Out."

Making Nick as comfortable as possible and leaving Gary and Lucas with him, Tom and John walked down the fence looking for a good site to cross. Nick was then moved 200 paces south, to where the insurgents had escaped through the fence.

On schedule, the chopper arrived with the familiar clatter of its rotor blades and landed on the other side of the border. A unit of RLI soldiers leaped out to cover while Tom and his men scrambled through the fence and loaded Nick into the chopper before climbing aboard themselves. An hour later they had landed in Chiredzi. The soldiers remained behind to carry out a 'hot pursuit' operation into Mozambique.

Nick was rushed off to the hospital, where Anne, his wife was waiting. The rest of them went for debriefing. On his way to the debriefing room, Tom was summoned to the Member-in Charge's office. He hoped this meeting would not take too long as he was tired and wanted to get home to Julia and the boys.

John's wife, Jill and Gary's wife Judy were in the office with Roger Tomkins, the Member-in-Charge. Tom got a bad feeling as soon as he saw them but still managed a cautious smile.

"Tom I am very sorry, I have some really bad news for you. I want to tell you kindly, but there is no way. Julie was in that convoy that was ambushed; she was injured and rushed to Triangle hospital, but the doctor was unable to save her. She passed away noon yesterday," Roger said.

Tom felt all the blood drain from his face. He could not believe what he was hearing. He felt like the heavens had fallen in; all the breath was sucked from his body, his head started to spin, and he slumped down onto a chair. It had to be a nightmare.

"Why the hell wasn't I told when we were first informed of the ambush?" he asked Roger as soon as he was able to get the words out.

"At that time, we didn't know who had been wounded," Roger explained. Jill, she put her arm around him trying to comfort him.

"As soon as we knew Julia had been wounded we did try to contact you. But we were unable to raise you on the radio. We put a chopper on standby to pick you up as soon as we heard from you. We had estimated when you would get to the fence and where you would be." Roger told him "I am so very sorry. We all loved Julia."

"Oh my God, what am I going to do? She was my life," Tom sobbed.

His beloved wife and partner had died alone, and he had allowed her murderers to escape. What was he going to do without her? How was he going to cope? What were the boys going to do without their mother? They had such plans for the future. He felt raw inside.

He had to pull himself together and go to the boys. They did not know that they would never see their mother again. Tom went with John and Jill back to their home. Jill had fetched the two boys from school the previous day as soon as she had heard from Maria that Julia was in hospital.

Breaking the news to the boys was the hardest thing Tom had done in his life. They cried their hearts out as the three of them clung to each other. They had been born and brought up in a country at war and were used to hearing of people being killed by terrorists, but to be told that their mother was a victim of one of these cowardly attacks on people, was horrific. They were good boys who had loved their mother, why had it happened to them?

With him being away from home such a lot, he had been forced to leave most of the parenting to Julia. He had not had the time to do 'boy' things with his sons. What was their life going to be like without their mother? How was Tom going to raise the boys by himself with this godforsaken war? What was the point of it all?

....

Julia's funeral service was held at the Chapel on the Hill with Julia's parents and most of the people in the Lowveld attending to pay their last respects. It was a beautiful spot overlooking the whole of the Triangle area where Julia had been so happy and enjoyed her life to the full. Tom was proud of Stuart and Kyle who handled themselves with dignity as they silently shed their tears. The wake held at the Country Club was a somber affair, with the realization that everyone was vulnerable. Julia was the first woman non-combatant to have been killed in the Lowveld by terrorists.

"Listen here, you guys. I really think we must go away to the coast for a short break. Your Mum would not want us to stay here and be sad," Tom said to the boys as the three of them lay in bed together that night.

"Dad, is Mum up in Heaven now?" Stuart asked.

"Yes, my boy. She will be up there watching over us."

"Why did she have to go and leave us behind?" Kyle asked.

"Well I think that God wanted her to go and help him up there."

"But what about us Dad?" Kyle asked again, struggling to understand.

"She will just want us to be brave and to get on with our lives. You must talk to her in your prayers. Although you will not hear her, she will hear you."

"Well then I think it would be good for us to go to the beach. Will we stay with Aunt June and Uncle Pete?" Stuart asked.

"Yes. We will go on Friday."

It would give them all a break away from the emptiness of their home without Julia. They were used to her bustling around organizing everyone, taking care of their every whim and fancy and just being there to keep them all in line.

The healing power of the sea and a three-week break from the war zone worked wonders. It was good to see the boys sleep peacefully right through the night. At home they were used to leaping out of bed in the night and dashing into the bathroom ready to reload FN magazines for Tom every time the alarm was triggered, usually by the wind or a falling branch.

With the country completely isolated, and with no help from the Western Nations, it was becoming apparent to Tom that this war was being lost. Two political leaders, Joshua Nkomo, and Ndabaninge Sithole had recently been released from restriction and were now busy running across the country, and traveling overseas to drum up support for their cause.

To endorse his fears, the 'Hunyani,' one of Air Rhodesia's fleet of Viscount Aircraft, was shot down by ZIPRA insurgents using an SA-7 Grail surface-to-air missile, shortly after taking off from Kariba. All 59 passengers and crew were killed - those who survived the crash were lined up and slaughtered by the terrorists.

He had lost his beloved Julia to this senseless war. The boys had lost their mother, and he was not prepared for them to lose him or for them to be exposed to any sort of terrorist activity that would endanger their lives. He was going to have to change his long-term plans. He made his decision; he was going to take his family out of the country as soon as possible.

On his return from South Africa, Tom made contact with a friend in Malawi who worked on a Sugar Estate there. After explaining his situation, Tom was invited to fly in for an interview, and he liked what he saw. He was offered an excellent contract, which he accepted before returning to the Lowveld to make their preparations. A fresh start – that's what they needed. Not only would a move get them away from the place in which they had lived happily, but it would give them time to build up finances, most of all, they would be away from this damned war.

Despite the strong motives to leave, however, Tom found it surprisingly difficult to leave the Lowveld and country he had put his life on the line for. Logic prevailed. He knew that the war was all but lost so what sort of life would they have if they stayed? The time had come to move on, he told himself. He wanted to leave all the pain behind.

****

Chapter 23

Tom was sitting in his office staring out of the window when Maria knocked on the open door. She sat down in the chair alongside his desk. He had been crying and quickly wiped the tears off his face before turning his attention to her and her health log book.

"I am sorry Maria, but I am just not in the mood to examine your records today. Can we leave it till tomorrow?" he asked her.

"Of course we can." She replied. "Do you want me to go now?"

"No. Please don't leave now. I need to talk to you."

"Let me fetch you a cup of tea. I'll be back in a minute," and getting up she went to the kitchen giving him time to regain his composure.

After Julia's funeral, Tom had taken his two boys and gone off to South Africa for a break. They all needed to get away, be together and learn how to deal with their loss. Maria's heart felt like breaking when she saw the suffering in Tom's face. If only she were able to go with them to help. She missed his laughter. It would take a long time, but she was going to be there to help him get through this.

They had been back on the farm for two months now, and he seemed to be picking up the pieces of his shattered life, or so she thought, until today. Maria returned to Tom's office and they sat in silence. Tom seemed to be gathering his thoughts.

"What have we done to make the world hate us so much? Too many people have been killed in this senseless war. Why Julia?" Turning again to look at Maria he asked: "What am I going to do?"

"You must not go into the bush again. You must look after your boys. They have already lost their mother, and they don't need to lose you as well," she told him sternly, trying to focus him and ground him again.

"Yes. I realize that, but all I want to do is to go and find the bastards responsible," Tom replied angrily.

"Where are the boys? I have not seen them this afternoon," Maria said changing the subject and giving him time to calm down.

"They are staying with their friends tonight. Will you come to the house this evening to keep me company? I don't want to be alone."

"Of course I will. What time shall I come around?"

"Come at six. You can eat with me."

"Thank you, Tom. I look forward to that."

With that Maria went hurrying off to shower and change. Although she felt desperately sad for Tom, she could not suppress her joy and excitement at the prospect of spending the evening with him. She was going to do her best to cheer him up. She wanted him to lean on her and not to go looking for another woman to console him. She had all the love in the world to give.

Tom led her into the lounge then sitting her down on the couch, handed her a fruit juice. He sat down on his chair and took a swig of beer

"I am glad you came. I promise not to be miserable; I just need the company. Would you like something to eat?"

"I am happy to be here with you Tom." Maria almost whispered, but he did not seem to notice the intensity of emotion behind her words. "I don't want to eat anything just yet," she tried to regain her composure. "We can just sit and talk for a bit."

"That would be nice," Tom said. "Tell me a bit about your life before you came here."

Maria looked down and seemed to tense.

"I am sorry. Have I said something to offend you?" Tom asked.

"No. It's alright. I want to tell you about myself," Maria said.

Knowing now was the time to let it all out, she told Tom about her history with Mamba and how the memory of what had happened that day in the field never left her. It was a part of her now, always with her like a shadow no matter how hard she tried to push it to the back of her mind. She hated him for what he had done to her.

"Why didn't you tell me this long ago?" Tom demanded.

"I didn't know how to. You are the first person I have ever told this to."

Tom softened. "Good God! You poor girl. You must have been going through bloody hell all these years. I am so glad I was the one who shot that bastard. It's a pity I didn't kill him. No wonder you refused to go and see him in the hospital. Everything makes sense now."

"I am sorry I'm crying. I am supposed to be comforting you," Maria tried to smile as she dug in her handbag for a tissue.

Tom moved to the sofa and placed a comforting arm on her shoulder. "You do know that he is now locked in the High-Security Prison. He refuses to speak to anyone," he said.

"He must rot there for all the bad things he has done. They must never let him out." This was the first time Tom had seen venom from Maria, she was a gentle soul.

For a long time, the two of them just sat there talking quietly, enjoying the comfort of each other's company. She wanted to go to lean into him and kiss him, but did not want to push too hard or to be rejected by him. It was still much too soon.

"Maria I have decided to leave the country," Tom said suddenly. Standing up he started pacing about the room. After a long silence, he stopped and turning to Maria, said: "I have landed a contract to work in Malawi, and will be going at the end of next month."

"What about your two boys? Will they be going to school in Malawi?" Maria asked, feeling like she had been punched in the stomach.

"No, they will be going to school in Marandellas. I have already booked them in. I'm getting a house in Salisbury to use as a base and will have to have someone to manage things from there while I am away."

"Who?"

"I am going to take Samuel, the gardener, and I was hoping that you might like to be my manager. You could look after the boys for me as well as keep the house running smoothly."

"Tom, I would love to do that for you," Maria said, so grateful that she was a part of his future. "Do the boys know your plans?"

"Yes, they do. I had to make sure that they would be happy to have you acting as 'mother' before I approached you. Are you sure you will be happy doing this for me?"

"Of course," she almost jumped up and shouted. "I will hand in my resignation tomorrow."

"I am so relieved you will be coming with us. There is one thing we must do as soon as possible, and that is to get you a driving license. You will need it. I will come down to Salisbury from Malawi for a couple of days every six weeks to catch up with things."

Maria was on top of the world. The man who had almost destroyed her was in jail, and she was going away with the man she loved. She had waited a long time, but it had been well worth it. She was excited about the future and what it might bring. She was only sorry that her happiness had come at the cost of Julia's life. They had been good friends.

....

Tom's farewell party was a drunken affair held at the Country Club. He was accused, in a good-humored way, of 'Taking the Chicken Run' and leaving the country. His accusers did, however, admit that if they were offered the same opportunity, they wouldn't hesitate to do the same.

Tom had handed the leadership of the PATU stick over to John, who had been voted in by the other members, at a rather emotional get together at the Police Mess. They had spent the better part of six years working in the bush together as a tight-knit fighting unit, and they trusted each other with their lives. In all their operations, only Nick had ever been wounded, and fortunately had fully recovered.

....

Lucas understood Tom's reason for leaving the Lowveld, and the country, after the loss of wife. He had been a good leader for the PATU stick, and he had enjoyed working with him. On and off the two of them had a history going back many years, and it was hard to see him go. John was a good replacement for Tom, and he was happy to go to war with him.

The vehicle transporting them to their place of deployment, on the first patrol 'Tango One' went on after Tom left, hit a land mine. It was a boosted mine, and it destroyed the front end of the troop carrier. They had all been thrown off the vehicle by the explosion, but none of them were injured. The stories Lucas had heard that you only know you have hit a landmine when you found yourself lying on the ground were not true - he heard himself screaming, as he flew through the air, before landing on the ground in a heap. The screaming must be the body's way of protecting the eardrums.

He lay on the ground for a short time, sucking air back into his lungs, waiting for his ears to stop ringing. After pulling the pieces of two by four rifle cleaning cloth from his ears (they all put pieces of cleaning cloth in their ears as a precaution when there was a possibility of hitting a landmine), he regrouped with the others. The driver and his assistant were not injured and had to wait, with another unit, for help to arrive.

They must have hit the mine within minutes of it having been buried in the road. In next to no time, they found the perpetrators tracks and were quickly on their trail. Two hours later, they caught up with the terrorists, who were hiding in a village, and quickly killed all four of them in the ensuing fire-fight. A helicopter arrived to collect the bodies, and they continued their patrol of the area.

By their obvious nervousness, and reluctance to talk every time he questioned one of them, Lucas knew that the inhabitants of the reserve were assisting the insurgents. Towards the end of the patrol, they found the proof of their presence - a woman, whose lower lip had recently been sliced off by a terrorist because her son worked on a sugar estate, and she was accused of being a 'sell-out' and an informant.

There had been numerous reports of this type of atrocity being committed around the country, resulting in information about insurgent's movements almost drying up completely.

· · · · · · · · · · · · · · ·

Tom found a nice four bedroom house in Umwinsidale, a suburb of Salisbury, and the boys were going to boarding school near Marandellas. They would be safe there. Maria who had also given her notice helped with the packing and the move to Salisbury. The boys happily accepted her and were now looking forward to being boarders at their new school.

Maria stopped at Chibi on her way to Salisbury, to visit her mother. When she walked into the shop to greet her, her mother burst out laughing.

"Why are you laughing Mother?"

"It's because I am happy. I see you drive up to my shop in a car by yourself. And I can see that you are smiling for the first time since you were at school. What has happened to make you smile again my child?" her mother asked her.

"It is because I am in love," Maria beamed.

"Go and make us some tea, then you can tell me all about it."

Maria told her mother all about her life and about Tom. She also decided that the time had finally come to tell her mother about Titus Ngopi.

"Oh Maria, why didn't you tell me this dreadful thing had happened to you?" her mother cried. "I could have shared your misery with you and helped you."

"I was so ashamed, and I didn't want anyone to know," Maria confessed to her mother.

"I am so glad that you have found happiness now with this man who has also suffered great pain. I would like to meet him soon."

Promising to bring Tom for a visit, Maria said goodbye and drove on to Salisbury, her new home.

The house in Umwinsidale was small but cozy. It was sad unpacking things that had been collected by Tom and Julia during their 13 years together, but in her heart, she knew that she would be happy for them. She had got on very well with Julia during the years she had known her. Tom helped with arranging the furniture and hanging the curtains and pictures. Some of the more personal pictures and photographs he packed away for the boys to have when they grew up.

Samuel the gardener, who had moved from the Lowveld with them, got stuck into the garden while Maria busied herself in the house, arranging things as she and Tom wanted them. It was soon time for the boys to depart. With their trunks packed and dressed in their new uniforms -Stuart helped Kyle with his tie- they all piled into the car, and Tom drove them to school. On arrival, the boys and Maria were introduced to the staff, and the two settled into their dormitories. Both put on brave faces when they said goodbye and hurried off to meet the other boys.

After dropping the boys off at school, they sat together on a bench on the veranda having a drink and watching the sunset.

"Maria, I'm going to miss you while I am away in Malawi."

"I am going to miss you a lot too Tom. Are you sure you will be coming home every six weeks?" Maria asked taking the initiative and cuddling up closer to Tom. She put her head on his shoulder.

"Of course I am sure. I will even try to come back more often when I get the chance." Tom put his arm around her.

At last Tom lifted her head with his other hand and gently kissed her on the mouth. She willingly and eagerly opened her mouth to respond to his kiss putting her arms around his neck as she did so. Tears of joy filled her eyes. Silently they got up and Tom led her inside the house. She was very nervous, but he was gentle, and their lovemaking was wonderful.

Lying in his arms, Maria quietly said to Tom. "I have loved you for a long time."

"I know you have. I have seen it in your eyes. I have also fallen in love with you. Why do you think I asked you to move here with me?"

"I did suspect that you might have ulterior motives," Maria teased him happily.

After a little while, they rolled together again; this time their love-making was long and slow, with them both relishing every moment.

Two days later Tom caught the flight to Malawi.

****

Chapter 24

Apart from the quick trip to attend the interview, Tom had never been to Malawi before. The feeling of being released from military duties and not having to spend so much time in the bush was amazing, but he felt naked without his trusty FN rifle.

His only worry was the ongoing security of his two sons and Maria; he had left them on their own to fend for themselves in a country still at war. Tom had left his two vehicles with Maria in Salisbury. He would need one whenever he was at home and she would need the smaller car to run around doing her chores and to ferry the boys to and from school for holidays, long week-ends and days off.

The sugar estate was situated in a vast floodplain 80 miles south-west of Blantyre, in the Lower Shire Valley and at the end of the Great Rift Valley. The altitude was less than 700 feet above sea level and like the Lowveld in Rhodesia; it was very hot and humid.

Tom's contract was to bush clear and develop 1500 hectares of sugar cane fields from virgin bush. This involved the use of two large bulldozers linked together with a large chain with a two-ton steel ball in the middle of the chain. Moving 30 paces apart the bulldozers pulled the chain through the bush after knocking the larger trees down with their blades. The flattened scrub, brush, and trees were all pushed into huge piles and burnt.

These big bonfires attracted a variety of insect-eating birds that swooped in and out of the smoke catching the insects carried up in the thermals. There were Swallows, Starlings, Drongoes, Kingfishers and Lilac Breasted Rollers in numbers. The cleared area was then leveled, ripped, plowed, harrowed, and then was the sugar cane planted. The disturbance of virgin lands brought all sorts of worms and bugs to the surface and attracted other species like Glossy Starlings, Doves, Herons, and Grey Storks.

The hard work kept Tom's mind from dwelling on the loss of Julia. Although there was now a new love in his life, all his plans for the future had been made with Julia, and he still missed her terribly. He had known for a long time that Maria had strong feelings for him and he too had been attracted to her, but he had loved his wife and the thought of having an affair with Maria had never been an option. Over the Mamba business however, his feelings for her had grown stronger, and when Julia died, it had been Maria who brought him to his senses and was there for him when he was at his lowest point.

When they went to bed together, Tom felt no guilt nor did he feel that he was betraying the memory of Julia. It seemed the natural thing to do. He had fallen in love with Maria, and they would move forward together, once they had both dealt with the traumas they had been though. Given time, he was sure that his two sons would not have a problem in accepting her.

Tom spent most evenings socializing in the Sunset Country Club because he hated being on his own at home. After a while, he became restless but could not put his finger on what was bothering him. Eventually, he realized that he missed the camaraderie of his old PATU stick. He had become so accustomed to the regular two-week trips into the bush every four to six weeks and of being on constant stand-by, that he actually missed the feeling of being 'on the edge' all the time. The fear and adrenalin rush must have been addictive. It was going to take a while to get used to the luxury of not having to live on his nerves.

He was allocated a house in the village that was built in the colonial style, framed by a wide gauze enclosed veranda. It had been standing empty for a while, and the swallows had built their nest under the eaves. In the evening after rain, they darted across the sky catching flying ants. The mosquitoes in the flood plains were a problem, and malaria was rife in that part of the world. Because of the massive marsh adjacent to the estate, there were even more 'mozzies' (mosquitoes) than there were in the Lowveld.

The house was comfortable and it had been renovated with all the fittings and cupboards upgraded or replaced. It was fully furnished and air-conditioned. Tom employed a gardener, Mapepa, and a cook cum houseboy called James. Malawi was renowned for having excellent well-trained cooks. Basic commodities and perishables, milk, bread, etc. were available in the shop on the estate, but it was necessary to make a trip to Blantyre every couple of months to stock up on other items.

Holiday time came for the boys and Tom had them flown into Chileka Airport, outside Blantyre where he picked them up. His sons were growing up fast - Stuart was now 12 and Kyle 10 years old. When he met them at the airport, he was pleased to see that they were happy, excited and full of fun and laughter. They seemed to be dealing well with the death of their mother and were enjoying being at boarding school. Maria was looking after them well.

After a tour of Blantyre, they drove down into the valley. Arriving at their second new home, Tom introduced the boys to James, who greeted them happily with a generous white-toothed smile. Then taking their luggage, he led them off to their room. He had taken a great deal of trouble to make it as welcoming as possible.

The boys were eager to explore their new surroundings, and so Tom took them through the village and down to the river. It was late in the afternoon, and with the sun setting, the birds were coming in to roost on the mangrove and fever trees lining the banks. The pink eyes, ears, and nostrils of a pod of hippo were sticking up out of the water as they wallowed in the murky water, grunting and snorting. The odd crocodile could also be seen gliding through the water in search of prey.

By the time they got back to the house, James had a feast prepared for them. After showering and changing, they sat down to a lovely rich stew with veg. The boys wolfed it down hungrily, making James' ever-present grin even wider than usual. After supper, they sat outside on the veranda. The boys told their father all their news; about new friends they had made, their teachers, sports they played, and what they had been up to on their long weekend in Salisbury with Maria. Promising to take them fishing the next day, Tom and his boys happily retired for the night.

It was a long holiday weekend in the country, and added to the couple of days Tom had taken off to spend with the boys, they had a week to explore the area together. But first, they wanted to go fishing in the Shire River. Dropping the boys off at one of the fishing jetties in the morning with Mapepa, their fishing tackle, a cool box filled with drinks and sandwiches, he warned them to watch out for crocodiles.

Both boys were fluent in Shona and although Mapepa spoke Chi Nyanja, his time as a contract worker in Rhodesia for some years enabled them to chat away happily. Tom rushed off to play a round of golf at the club. It was a knockout competition played over a couple of months, and his match had to be played that day.

Much later when Tom picked the fishermen up at the river, he was pleasantly surprised to see that they had a keep net full of fish. The sun was low over the distant hills making the surface of the river shimmer with dancing golden lights. A Fish Eagle sat in a branch of a dead tree and two Giant Kingfisher birds on another. A hippo surfaced close by and snorted loudly disturbing a flock of ibis that took to the air with loud squawks.

"Dad, what are we going to do tomorrow?" Stuart wanted to know, after their supper of fresh fish and chips.

"Well Stu, I haven't made any plans. What do you guys want to do?" Tom responded. "There are a lot of interesting places; I haven't explored, not far from here. Would you like to go up into the mountains?"

"Let's go fishing again," Kyle piped up.

"No Kyle. We went fishing today. Let's go to the mountains tomorrow. We can go fishing again the next day," Stuart said overruling his younger brother.

"Oh, all right. As long as you promise we can go fishing the day after tomorrow," Kyle conceded.

"Okay, we'll go to Mulanje. I will get James to make us a picnic basket of grub. We'll go after an early breakfast," Tom agreed.

With the boys tucked up in bed, Tom made a few inquiries to a friend who suggested they have lunch at Lujeri Tea Estate and Lodge, set at the base of Mount Mulanje.

Not forgetting to take their costumes, towels and lunch pack, they were on the road by seven the following morning. It was a two and a half hour drive with the route taking them via Blantyre and Thyolo to Mulanje. The massif of Mount Mulanje could be seen from a considerable distance away as it jutted out of a sea of green tea plantations and rose to dominate the skyline. As the three of them got closer to the mountain, deep gorges could be seen with the white lace of waterfalls plummeting down from the summit. Tall Cedar trees grew on the lower slopes.

"Shucks Dad. The mountain looks just like a gigantic rock that had been dropped from heaven. It is humongous," Stuart exclaimed as they got closer.

"Yes, it looks as if a giant has put it there. How high is it Dad?" Kyle asked.

"I believe it is the third highest mountain in Africa, but I am not sure exactly how high it is. We'll have to ask them at the office when we get there," Tom said.

Parking at the Lujeri Tea Estate they set off along one of the many trails around the foothills. As they walked along, they spotted a black eagle circling lazily in the air, looking for tiny antelope or other small mammals to swoop down on and capture for a hearty meal. The trail led them through a cedar forest to a deep crystal clear pool at the base of a waterfall. It was a hot, still, day and the pool beckoned to them.

"The last one in is a rotten egg," said Stuart as he threw off his clothes and, not bothering with a costume, leaped into the water.

"Dad is a ninny. Look he is putting on a costume," said Kyle as he too leaped naked into the water.

Tom threw his trunks aside and also dived in making the boys laugh. He splashed water in their faces, which made them laugh even more. After playing in the water for a while and feeling refreshed, they sat down on a rock at the side of the pool to eat their sandwiches, washing them down with cool drinks that James had packed for them. Satisfied, they continued along the trail back to the Tea Estate, passing some white-necked ravens that 'craw-crawed' at them as they went by.

Back on the Estate, they were taken on a tour of the tea factory. They watched as huge baskets full of green tea leaves were emptied onto drying racks. The dried leaves were then shredded in a machine and spread out on cooling trays to ferment. When it was golden brown, the tea was dried in hot air chambers until dark brown. It was ready to be bagged and packed into chests, ready for delivery to the tea merchants. Tom and his young boys were fascinated and found the whole process most informative.

The strong aroma of tea inside the factory made them thirst for a cup of the brew that was served in the reception area with fresh cream and jam scones. After tea, they piled into the car and set off home.

"Where will we go to next holidays Dad?" Kyle asked, already thinking ahead.

"I am not sure my boy. We'll have to just wait and see when the time comes,"

"I think we must go to the lake," Stuart decided.

"If we do go to the lake, we'll go for a couple of days. It is too far for a day trip," Tom said. Both the boys agreed this was a good idea.

All too soon the holiday was over, and Stuart and Kyle were flying back to Salisbury. Tom missed seeing them every day. The remaining four days had been spent fishing, and they had even played a little golf. Stuart was starting to get a reasonable swing, but Kyle was struggling and tended to get irritated and impatient.

Maria phoned to report that she had collected the boys at the airport and that they had given her a full account of their holiday in Malawi. After putting the phone down, Tom realized how much he was missing Maria. He had invited her to come up to Malawi with the boys, but she decided that he should have the time alone with them. Besides, it was still too soon after Julia's death to break the news of their relationship. She would only come once they had accepted the situation. In the meantime he would have to be satisfied with seeing her every few months when he went to Salisbury to see them all, and to watch the boys play their sport.

****

Chapter 25

Every morning, when she woke up, Maria felt as if she was living a dream. Was this real? She often asked herself as she settled into the life of an urban wife, and spent her time fixing up the house or helping Samuel in the garden. She went shopping and applied for a number of jobs around the area. Every Sunday she went out to visit the boys at school. Sometimes she also went on Saturdays, to watch them play their sport. Tom phoned her every Sunday evening, to catch up on her news, and to tell her what he had been doing that week.

Holiday time came for the boys, and they were going to spend a week in Malawi with their father. Maria helped them pack, and put them on a plane. When Tom had asked her to accompany them, so that they could all be together, she had turned down his invitation. She did not want to get between him and his sons. It would be better for them to be together, without her getting in the way. Their time would come.

Aside from being separated from Tom most of the time, Maria was happy with life. Knowing that Samuel was close at hand, if she needed help, was comforting. His cottage at the bottom of the garden was only a shout away.

The only thing that made her unhappy was that she would never be able to have children of her own. When she was working in the hospital in Bulawayo, the gynecologist had examined her, and given her the bad news. It had something to do with having been raped. It had never really worried her before she met Tom.

When she collected Stuart and Kyle from the airport ten days later, they rushed to greet her. She had not realized how much she missed them and was pleased to have them back under her wing. On the way to the house, the two boys were in such a hurry to share their experiences with her, that they kept interrupting each other. They had brought small gifts and mementos, made out of dark teak wood and colorful beads, especially for her. She was touched.

Things were difficult to find, with no imported goods coming into the country and Maria often wondered if it would ever be as good as it had been before the war. She enjoyed running around in her little car but had to preserve fuel for her visits out to the school. Everyone in the country was on fuel rationing, and her allocation of coupons did not give her much to spare, considering she also helped at the local clinic.

The boys never went short of anything, when they came home for weekends, and they never asked for much. They too understood the situation and knew that they would have to wait, until they holidayed in South Africa, for the special things.

The news in the country was not good; it all seemed to be swinging politically in favor of the insurgent forces. When was the war going to end so that they could relax and get on with their lives?

．．．．．．．．．．．．．

The house was quiet and seemed lifeless after Stuart and Kyle had returned to Rhodesia. Tom had gotten used to having them around. Even James was at a loss and did not know what to do.

"When will Stuart and Kyle come back to stay with us again Bwana?" asked James.

"In about two months, when they have another holiday from school," Tom said.

"That is good Bwana. Your children must be with you all the time when they are not at school," James offered up his advice.

"Thank you, James. I will try to have them here whenever I can."

Tom was on a three-year contract and had decided that he was going to make the most of it. With plenty of free time in the evenings and on weekends, he began to investigate possible farming ventures for the future. If nothing turned up by the time his contract expired, Tom decided they would move to South Africa and find something to do there. With this in mind, he booked his sons into his old school in Natal. (A Province of South Africa)

With the deteriorating situation in the country, Rhodesia looked set to become yet another African state, where democracy meant 'One man, one vote, one time.' Greedy leaders are inevitably led to corruption, with all opposition being suppressed, and the collapse of law and order.

Mozambique was a shambles, as were Zambia, Uganda, Kenya and Tanzania and the Nationalist Government in South Africa remained unchanged and still out of favor. The only countries that looked stable were Swaziland, Lesotho, and Botswana. Having come from Swaziland, Tom knew there were limitations in the small country too.

He would plan a trip there at some stage, to see for himself how it had changed since being granted independence. In the meanwhile, he would sit tight; make as much money as he could while the 'winds of change' blew around him. It would all settle down in the end.

....

Julia's parents, the Preston's, were up from South Africa and had invited the boys to spend part of their holiday with them in Inyanga. They would collect them from Umwinsidale, and return them two weeks later. It was two years since Julia's funeral, and Tom agreed it would be good for them to spend the time with their grandparents. The boys had not seen them since their mother died. The last part of their holiday they would spend with Tom in Malawi.

Maria and the Preston's got on well, and she communicated regularly over the phone with Mrs. Preston; they were very pleased Maria was there to look after their grandsons. As they all disappeared in the car, Maria stood in the drive wondering what she was going to do with herself, while the boys were away. There was no fuel to go and visit her mother.

Just then the phone rang. Rushing to answer Maria heard Tom's voice on the other end of the line.

"Have the boys left yet?" he asked.

"They have just driven out of the yard. Is there a problem?" she asked, concerned that he had phoned at this time of the day. He usually only phoned in the evening.

"Yes, there is a problem my girl. You have two hours to get to the airport. You are booked on the next flight to Blantyre. Chop-chop now, you'd better get moving. I'll be there to pick you up."

She was so excited she could hardly think. Tom had been in Malawi for over a year, and although he had been back and forth several times, this was the first time she was going to stay with him. Organizing the Security Guards to give extra cover while she was away, she gave Samuel money for dog food and notified the neighbors that she would be away. She packed a bag and took a taxi to the airport.

Maria had never flown before, and it was only after she passed through the immigration and customs checks, that she suddenly became very nervous. Were it not for the fact that she was going to see her lover; she might well have turned back. She was beside herself.

Strapped into her seat, she gripped the armrests tightly as the engines started. She closed her eyes when felt it shaking as it picked up speed. Then the shaking stopped as it left the ground and started to climb into the sky. Maria soon relaxed and enjoyed watching the scenery slowly gliding past way below, and the Zambezi River was visible as they flew over it.

Two hours later they descended to land in Malawi, where Tom was waiting. She rushed to meet him, and they were soon on the road. Tom laughed at her happy chatter about her flight. Then after giving him a summary of events in Salisbury, she settled back to admire the scenery, as they dropped down towards the Shire River. The anticipation of getting to the house created an electric atmosphere that grew more intense as they drove along.

Tom had given James the evening off, telling him that they would eat at the club that night. Arriving at the house, Tom threw Maria's bag down in the bedroom and turned to embrace and kiss her passionately. Breaking apart breathlessly, they quickly undressed each other and fell into bed. Much later they reluctantly showered, changed and went to the club for a meal. Two hours later they hurried back to the house and leaped naked into bed; they couldn't wait to be intimate again.

Lying in the dark, with Maria snuggled in his arms; Tom decided that the time had come.

"Maria I love you so much. You have become a big part of our lives. Will you marry me?"

"Oh, Tom you know I will. I have waited a long time for this moment. I love you more than you can imagine," she said hugging him tightly.

"Thank heavens for that. I was afraid you might say no," he teased her. With that, she playfully punched him in the ribs before leaping on top of him.

"You have unfinished business to attend to," she said dreamily, as she leaned down and kissed him.

In the morning James brought them breakfast in bed. Setting the tray down, he greeted Maria.

"Good Morning Madam. I am James, the cook," he said proudly introducing himself.

"Good morning James. It is nice to meet you," she said, responding to his greeting.

"What must I make for dinner tonight, Madam?" immediately accepting her as the lady of the house. "I have good beef topside. Can I make a roast for dinner?"

"Thank you, James. I am only on holiday here. You are in charge of the house. We will eat whatever you prepare for us," Maria told him.

"Thank you, Madam," he said. "Will you be here for lunch today?"

"Yes James, we are not going anywhere today," Maria quickly replied, before Tom could say anything. Her plans did not involve leaving the bedroom, let alone the house. They had a lot of catching up to do!

The next ten days passed all too quickly. It had rained and was too wet for Tom to do any work and so he took a few days off. Deciding that they just wanted to spend time together, Tom took Maria to stay at Nyala Lodge in the Lower Shire Valley. It is a lovely thatched lodge right at the bottom end of Malawi on the banks of the river near Port Herald - probably the lowest part of the country and extremely hot.

They spent three wonderful days there, wandering along the river, swimming in the pool at the lodge and watching the birds flitting in amongst the trees in the grounds. They visited the Murchison Cataracts; a spectacular series of waterfalls and rapids where the river dropped down into the Mpatamanga Gorge to the Kapichira Falls on its way to join the mighty Zambezi River.

Back at Tom's home, they went fishing, went to the club for lunch and toured the area where Tom was preparing and planting sugar cane. All too soon it was time for Maria to return to Salisbury. They decided not to set their wedding date until Tom had spoken to the boys. Stuart and Kyle would be spending the next holiday with him, and he would speak with them then.

****

Chapter 26

From a distance, Tom followed developments in Rhodesia and the state of the war. He phoned John on a regular basis, for updates and to hear his thoughts. Normally always the optimist, he too was beginning to sound negative and a little depressed.

"Tom, everyone is sick and tired of this bloody war. We are not going to win because the whole world is against us. The only trouble is that this country will not be worth living in if it is handed over to the gooks," John said.

"Well I am sorry to say it, but that is the way it is starting to look from the outside," Tom replied.

"I think most of the whites, who were able to leave the country, have done so now. The rest of us, who were born here, will just have to stick it out and see what happens. Unless of course, we are chased out," John said.

"I don't think you have any option, John. You should try to get an offer of employment in another country; then you will be able to get out."

"This is the country of my birth Tom. We are not giving up just yet."

....

With more and more white Rhodesians leaving the country, there was added pressure on those remaining, both black and white, in the fight against insurgent forces. The situation was not good. South Africa was no longer helping with supplies and equipment, and so, to Lucas, it seemed as if the war would soon be over.

He had never been concerned before, always confident that the insurgent forces would be defeated, and normality restored. Now as it looked as if it was going the other way, he worried about his future. He had never considered or even imagined that one day the enemy might take control of the country.

What would it be like working as a policeman under a black government, run by the very people he had been fighting against all these years?

Needing advice, he contacted Tom in Malawi. "You see the situation from outside the country now. What do you think I should do Tom?"

"Lucas, as you know I have always worried about what might happen to you, as a black policeman, if the insurgents won the war. But if there is to be law and order in the country, they will still need trained policemen."

"Yes, I know. But I don't think it will be too long before they start looking for those of us who actively fought against them, and killed some of their numbers," Lucas said expressing his fears.

"It looks like a peace agreement is just around the corner. I think you must just hang on and let's see what happens. In the meantime, we must keep our ears open for other opportunities for you."

"I suppose you are right. But you must keep in touch with me. Don't just throw me away and forget about me," said Lucas.

"Of course I won't throw you away!"

Lucas agreed with what Tom had said; there was nothing much he could do at this stage. He certainly could not leave the country; no other country would accept him as he was a Shona, born and raised in Rhodesia. He was pleased that he did not have a wife and children to worry about if the terrorist forces won the war. He had been involved with some women but was not ready to take a wife. He was too committed to the war and his career as a policeman— only the security of his parents that was a worry for him.

The war dragged on for another year, with life getting progressively harder; call out's and patrols were more and more frequent; with military commitments draining their numbers, the police station was always short staffed.

Now with the senior political prisoners being released, from restriction camps, as a condition stipulated for the progress of peace talks, the future looked bleak. Lucas had never imagined that one day the enemy might take control of the country.

Eventually, due to the lack of equipment and other supplies needed to fight a war, the government was forced to sit around the conference table and work out a peace agreement beginning again. Ian Smith wanted a responsible interim shared government, leading eventually to majority rule. An internal agreement was agreed, an election was held, which the UANC party won, and on the 1st June 1979, its leader Bishop Abel Muzorewa became the new prime minister. The country's name was changed to Zimbabwe-Rhodesia, and a new government was formed.

America and Britain refused to recognize Muzorewa's Government and the 'Bush War' continued unabated. A second Viscount aircraft, the 'Umniati' was destroyed in 1979 with 50 civilians being killed. After further talks lasting three months in London, UDI ended with Rhodesia reverting to the status of a British Colony

The war was over. It had lasted for fifteen years and resulted in the loss of thousands of men on both sides. During the war the terrorists committed huge numbers of atrocities, sometimes killing whole villages if the people resisted them. There were also reports of atrocities being committed by the security forces. The Rhodesian forces had won the battles but lost the war. Sanctions and international pressure eventually worked, forcing Ian Smith's Government to capitulate.

An internationally supervised election was held in 1980. Maoist Robert Mugabe, the leader of ZANU, used his terror and intimidation tactics, even threatening to continue the war if the people did not vote for him. The nation, tired of the long war, just wanted peace and so Mugabe won the election. He was sworn in as the Prime Minister in 1980, and the country was renamed Zimbabwe.

Not wanting a mass exodus of whites from Zimbabwe, as had happened in Mozambique, causing utter chaos in that country, Mugabe reassured Ian Smith that the whites could and should stay, promising to abide strictly to the terms of the Lancaster House Agreement. Any changes in Zimbabwe would be gradual and by the proper legal process – he said. He needed the white commercial farmers to help maintain the economy.

On the downside, and a major blow for Tom's long-term plan was the cancellation of the Lowveld Settler Farm Scheme. In spite of what was happening in the country, he still had hopes that once the dust settled, he might get his farm in the Lowveld.

On reflection, it was probably appropriate, that the venture he had planned with Julia was not to be. He would once again have to change his direction but remained determined that he would still have his farm.

One of the first things Robert Mugabe did, after his inauguration, was to release all political prisoners. This meant that Mamba if he had survived prison, was a free man.

What had it all been for in the end, Tom wondered?

****

Chapter 27

It was only a short holiday for Stuart and Kyle. They arrived in Malawi, dumped their suitcases, changed into shorts and t-shirts, grabbed something to eat and drink, picked up their fishing tackle and headed for the river. By the time Tom found them, they had already caught a couple of bream.

He had been unable to pick them up at the airport due to the pressure of work. One of the company drivers had been there to collect visitors to the estate and had brought the boys with them. So intense was the competition between the two of them that they barely had time to break off and greet their father. Naturally, they ate fresh fish for supper that night.

Tom's contract work was progressing on schedule and in spite of the early teething problems he had encountered in the beginning; he had developed and planted 1000 hectares. The boys were doing well at school, and he was about to get married to the woman he loved. He was enjoying his work as a contract land developer and was making good money. But it would not last forever; he would be completed in less than a year, and he still did not know what he was going to do when he completed the work. He still had plenty of time though, and so would worry about it after he and Maria were married.

"I have something I need to discuss with you chaps," Tom said to his sons at dinner that night. The boys turned to look at their father expectantly.

"Your mother has been gone for two years now. We will never be able to replace her, and we will always love the memory of her," Tom continued starting to get tongue tied and with a lump in his throat.

"Yes, Dad. We know that, and we will always miss Mum. But what do you want to discuss?" asked Stuart, coming to his rescue.

"Well, I want to get married again. I need to know how you feel about it."

"I hope you want to marry Maria," Kyle piped up, with a naughty grin on his face.

"Why would you think that?" Tom asked his younger son.

"Because we have seen the way you look at each other when you think we are not watching," Kyle revealed, with Stuart smiling and nodding his head in agreement.

"Would you be happy for me to marry Maria?"

"Sure Dad. She is already like a mother to us, and she looks after us while you are here," Stuart gave his approval. Then turning to Kyle, he asked him "You like her don't you Kyle?"

"Of course I like her. She always comes to see us at school and watches us play sport," Kyle responded to his brothers' question.

"So you boys will be okay for me and Maria to get married in the Christmas Holidays?"

"Yes. That will be great. We thought you might want to marry some other old bag we didn't like," said Stuart

"That is great Dad. Maria has been like our mum ever since we moved to Salisbury. Will we all live together like a proper family?" Kyle said.

"Yes we will, but you guys will still have to go to boarding school."

"That's okay Dad. We like it at boarding school anyway," Stuart said with Kyle now nodding in agreement.

"Well, that's settled then. Thank you both, I will let Maria know the good news. Would you chaps like to go flying tomorrow?"

"You bet. That will be brilliant," Stuart said.

"In a small plane or do you mean in that stupid big one we fly here in?" Kyle asked.

"No Kyle. In a small one and I will fly it."

"Yeah Dad that will be so great," Kyle responded eagerly.

As soon as dinner was over, Tom got on the phone, to tell Maria the good news. They were both overjoyed by the happy response from the boys, and with their immediate agreement. They could now make their wedding plans.

The company kept a light aircraft, on the airstrip on the estate, which Tom was able to hire; if it was not being utilized by them. He had made a few flights over the area he was developing, for aerial inspections of his work. These flips proved invaluable from a work point of view, and he also caught up with his flying hours.

The boys had never flown with him before. At first, they circled the estate so the boys could get their bearings, and see their house from the air, before heading south-east to the Elephant Marshes. The marshes had been named by David Livingstone when he saw a single herd of

800 elephants in the marsh. It is the floodplain of the Shire River and is about 900 square miles in extent.

Flying in a wide circle around the central area of the marsh, they could see, below them, a network of channels crisscrossing through the thick mat of vegetation floating on the water.

"Dad, look at all those Jumbo down there!" exclaimed Kyle excitedly, as they flew low over a large herd of Elephant in the northern section of the marsh.

"Yes, I see them, my boy. There used to be thousands in this area," Tom informed the boys.

"Where have they all gone?" Stuart wanted to know.

"A lot were hunted in the old days, and a lot have been killed by poachers who want their tusks for the ivory," Tom replied.

They passed over a few more small herds of elephant, before turning to fly over the wetter part of the marsh. Here they saw large pods of hippos, their bodies quite clearly visible in the water as they wallowed. Some large crocodiles were on the banks of the river, sunning in the morning sun, their mouths open absorbing vitamin D.

The occasional heron and stork could also be seen gliding just above the water, looking for a place to fish. On the eastern perimeter of the marsh, they spotted a solitary fisherman poling along one of the channels in his dugout canoe, on the way to check his fish nets.

Tom promised the boys he would take them flying again the next time they came to Malawi on holiday. Over the next week, they settled into some sort of routine. The mornings were spent with Tom, in the fields, while he supervised and managed his operations.

In the afternoons, they either went to the river to fish, or they went to the club to play tennis with other children who were home on holiday. At the end of the week, Stuart and Kyle flew back to Salisbury. Each time they left Tom was a little lonelier than he had been before.

••••••••••••••

The wedding was not going to be a big fancy affair. Maria and Tom wanted a small intimate wedding with close family and their friends. She would take a trip to tell her mother and would speak to her father on the phone. Tom contacted John in the Lowveld to give him the news.

"Are you telling me that you are marrying Maria? Isn't she the girl who worked for you in the Lowveld and who now runs your home in Salisbury?" John asked.

"Yeah you got it," confirmed Tom. "You jealous or what?" he teased.

"Well she is a beautiful woman, and she has certainly been bloody good to you guys," John stated emphatically. "Are the boys happy about it?" he wanted to know.

"Yes. They have given us their blessing."

"Well good luck to you all. I will pass on the news. Where are you getting married?"

"Here in Malawi in December. I want you to be my Best Man and Maria would like Jill to be her Maid of Honour. Can you make it?"

"We would be honored. We wouldn't miss it for the world. You can count us in."

Invitations were sent to the other members of Tom's old PATU stick, Gary and Judy, Nick and Anne, George and Megan and Lucas and all their children. They all gladly accepted the invitations. There were no longer military commitments to worry about; that was now a thing of the past.

....

A lot had happened, since her first visit to see Tom in Malawi. Maria cried with joy when Tom told her that the boys were happy for them to get married. Fuel was no longer in short supply, and so Maria was able to drive to Chibi to visit her mother and explain to her what was happening.

Maria's mother came out onto the veranda to greet her as she approached the store. They had not seen each other for more than a year, and it was a relief for Maria to see her still looking so fit and well.

"To what do I owe the pleasure of this unexpected visit?" the elderly woman greeted her daughter.

"I have some exciting news to tell you," Maria beamed.

"Well, we had better have some tea. Put your case in the bedroom, while I put the kettle on."

Feeling like a young girl obeying her mother's instructions, Maria went off to her bedroom to unpack and freshen up after her long trip from Harare.

"Well then, let me hear your news," she said to Maria as soon as they had their mugs of tea.

"Mother, Tom and I are getting married, and we want your blessing," she blurted out.

"Maria that is wonderful. I am so happy for you," her mother exclaimed clapping her hands to her cheeks. "Tom is a good man, and I have hoped you two would marry. You both deserve happiness. Of course, you have my blessing," she finished hugging Maria tightly.

"Will you come to our wedding? We are getting married in Malawi."

"I would love to come to your wedding my child, but I cannot leave my shop alone," she took her daughter's hand. "These days there are a lot of thieves wandering around the countryside, who think they can just help themselves to whatever they want," she said by way of an explanation.

"Mum you never go anywhere. You have been stuck in this shop of yours, all these years, without a break. It'll do you good to get away. Is there nobody you can ask to look after things?" Maria pleaded, but her mother was adamant that she could not leave. Disappointed, Maria returned to Harare the following day.

. . . .

Things were moving quickly at home. Stuart and Kyle had finished school for the year and left Springfield for good. The boys were moving to a new school in South Africa. Jill came up to Salisbury from the Lowveld, with John and their children, to help Maria choose her wedding dress, and to lend a hand with the planning. There would be no time once she got to Malawi.

"John is coming to Malawi, with Stuart and Kyle tomorrow, as you suggested Tom. I will be coming up with Jill next week. It will give you guys some time to do whatever you have to do, and to be with the boys."

"You're starting to sound like a wife already," Tom teased her, and then more solemnly asked. "Are you organized at your end?"

"Yes darling, everything is under control," Maria beamed. "Jill has taken over, and I am just following her around. I'll see you in Zomba," she said hanging up the phone.

A rowdy bull's party, held for Tom at the Country Club, was an all-night affair, ending with a large breakfast. The participants all retired to bed for the rest of the day. Early the following morning, Tom, accompanied by his sons and John, drove up the mountain to the Zomba Plateau. Taking the scenic drive around the plateau, they crossed some small streams leading to tumbling waterfalls and still lakes way below.

The views were stunning. They could see Mount Mulanje to the South East, and far in the distance, the Shire Valley disappeared into the haze. They spent the night in a lodge set amongst the Cedar, Pine and Cyprus trees. After the extreme heat of the Shire Valley, it was lovely and cool at an altitude of 6000 feet.

Outside the Zomba Magistrate's office, Tom and his escort awaited Maria's arrival. The bridal party had spent the night at another lodge on the plateau. Tom felt like a love-sick schoolboy as he waited in anticipation of the arrival of his bride. The car drew up, and he rushed to open the door and hand Maria out.

"Maria you are so beautiful," Tom said admiring his bride.

"You don't look so bad yourself you great oaf," Maria responded. "I think this is the best I have seen you look," she added smiling radiantly, then turning to John said. "Thank you for looking after my men so well - they all look very smart."

The Court orderly ushered them into the Magistrate's rooms where a brief ceremony was conducted, and the register signed. Tom hugged and kissed his new wife, and the boys joined in as did Jill and John. After a few photos were taken and a bottle of Champaign cracked on the veranda of the courthouse, they drove the 140 miles to Lake Malawi.

Tom had booked rooms for everyone at the Nkopola Lodge, on the southern shores of the lake near Monkey Bay. The lodge, which was made up of a series of thatched buildings and bungalows, was to play host to a wedding lunch in the garden and as they sat down, Lucas arrived with a very special gift.

"Oh my God! It's my mother," Maria said knocking her chair over in her haste to get up. "I thought you said you would not be able to come."

"Well my darling, you have a very persuasive husband and some good friends," the old woman replied.

"This has made it the happiest day in my life," Maria said shedding tears of joy.

It was the best wedding gift she could have received. Unbeknown to Maria, Tom had made a special trip to Chibi to persuade the old woman to attend the wedding. Maria did not mind sharing their time with their friends and her mother; they would have the rest of their lives together. Her day was complete.

Then the four-day party began. The Lodge was only thirty paces from the water's edge giving easy access to scuba diving, snorkeling, water skiing, and sailing. Warm days, white sandy beaches and crystal clear freshwater - life could not get any better than this.

****

Chapter 28

Mamba had been in prison for over two years. His leg had been amputated just above the knee, as a result of the injuries he had sustained when he had tried to attack his old enemy's house. He hadn't been given an artificial leg so used crutches to get around in prison, and was kept in isolation most of the time. He was an angry man, who allowed his hatred, for white people, to grow like cancer inside him. He did not know what was happening outside the prison walls or how the war was progressing.

During one of his few exercise breaks in the yard, he heard from one of the other prisoners that the war was over and that the whites had surrendered. If what he had heard was true, he knew it would not be long before he would be released. Once free, he would get his revenge on those responsible for the loss of his leg and his capture.

He had envisaged marching into Salisbury (now Harare) as one of the heroic leaders of the victorious ZIPRA forces but, having missed the last two years of the Chimurenga; Mamba had been robbed of this recognition and this added fuel to his hatred.

Two months later, Comrade Titus Ngopi, alias Mamba, was released from prison. Hastening to Harare, he reported to the leaders of ZIPRA and was just in time to attend the victory celebrations following the election of his leader, Robert Mugabe, as the Prime Minister of Zimbabwe. The Chimurenga (the war) was won.

At last the white settlers had been defeated. Now they had to be driven out of the country for good. What was Comrade Mugabe talking of reconciliation for? Surely he was not expected to mix with his former enemies.

Once he had taken care of his future and secured a position within the structure of this new Zimbabwe, he would turn his attention to dealing with those who had humiliated and injured him so badly.

As an ex-leader of a combat group, he was appointed a sector head of the War Veterans Association, with a branch of the Youth Brigade falling under his command. He was also paid a salary, and a disability allowance. He was pleased with the recognition he received, but the hatred of the men who had destroyed his chances of really rising to the higher levels within the new government burned inside him. He would get his revenge one day; if they were still alive. He had waited this long and so did not mind waiting a little longer.

The time had come for him to return to the area where he had grown up. He wanted to strut around and show everyone there that he was a hero who had killed white farmers, and of course, he would exaggerate the numbers, to make it more impressive. He wanted them to cower in front of him. He had been fitted with an artificial leg and walked with a limp, but as it was a war wound, he was proud to show it off.

Meeting up with other war-vets in Fort Victoria, the four of them toured the province, and over the following few weeks, assessed the damage they had caused to white farmers. Visiting Triangle in the Lowveld, he made inquiries about the manager of Section Sixty One. He heard that the man had left the country, not long after Mamba himself, had been wounded and sent to prison. His wife had been killed in an ambush on the Ngundu road.

He also heard that a woman who had been working for him by the name of Maria da Silva had left at the same time. Could this be the same woman he had raped at school all those years ago? It almost seemed impossible but all the pieces fitted.

What sweet irony and showed it was meant to be. Things like this were not a coincidence, and it was almost poetic how it had all come together. They were intertwined now like twisted lovers. He was more convinced than ever that he would have his retribution.

Mamba did not bother to pay a visit to his parents – they had been supporters of the Smith Regime, and should be punished.

The region to the east of Fort Victoria, where he had dispatched groups of freedom fighters during the war, seemed untouched. All the farmers were still operating, and none of them had been attacked during the Chimurenga. The white farmers had not left their farms as planned. They still had a lesson to learn.

When would those who fought for freedom finally be given this productive land? When would they be the ones making money? What had happened to the great liberation?

Comrades from all over the country were making their way to see a witch near the Zimbabwe Ruins, Sophia 'Mbuya Nehanda', who claimed that she could expel evil spirits and offer forgiveness for misdeeds, they had committed during the Chimurenga.

She advocated the killing of all white farmers if the land was to be liberated. She believed that there would never be peace in the country, as long as the forefathers of the Shona Nation remained angry with the white man, for stealing stone birds from the Zimbabwe Ruins. According to her, the Chimurenga was only the beginning; there would be four more wars before peace could be restored; a war of fire; a war of rain; a war of bees and a war of locusts.

With her help and some of those who came to see her, he organized and planned attacks on three of the farms in the proximity of Kyle dam. As a result, four white farmers were killed in their homes at night, by the men he recruited for the work. By the time these killings were reported to the police, Mamba had left the area and moved on to the Gweru district with his two henchmen, a driver, and a bodyguard.

From Gweru, he moved on to Bulawayo where he helped to organize the supporters of ZANU. He had not been in Matabeleland for very long when he was forced to return to Harare. He was a Shona in Ndebele country and had become a target. There was a great rivalry between the ZANU supporters and ZAPU, the party of Joshua Nkomo and most of the Ndebele people. Guerrilla activity and armed resistance to the government by the Ndebele pushed him back to the Shona dominated part of the country.

The uprising was quickly crushed by the elite, communist Korean trained Gukurahundi or 5th Brigade. They killed thousands of civilians in the rural areas, disposing of their bodies down old mine shafts and mass graves. Nkomo and his ZAPU party were forced to join up with ZANU. The new party was called ZANU-PF.

Mamba could not understand why the killing had stopped. There had only been 20000 civilians killed; surely it would have been better to kill them all off. After all, the Ndebele tribe had stolen the land from the Shona people and chased them away to the north.

He learned later that all those men who had been involved in the killings near Lake Kyle had been arrested by the police, including the witch Nehanda. All were sentenced to death, but somehow Mamba's involvement was never discovered. The fools should never have been caught.

****

Chapter 29

Back on Shire Valley Estates, after the wedding festivities were over, Tom took the family flying. Going up in a light aircraft for the first time, Maria was a little nervous, to begin with, but the boys, as excited as ever, soon made her relax.

"Look at Mount Mulanje in front of us. Isn't it massive?" Tom said

"It's like an enormous rock. I don't see any other mountains around, is it part of a range?" Maria asked.

"No. It's an old volcano and stands on its own. You will be able to see the crater when we fly over those high cliffs. The peak, Sipitwa, is over 7000 feet high," Tom said, glancing at the altimeter on the dashboard, as he took the plane higher.

"Is this the same mountain we walked around when we came to the tea estate Dad?" Stuart asked.

"Yes, it's the same one. We were down there at the base of the mountain," Tom pointed out.

"It looks different from up here in the sky. It sure is big," said Stuart.

"Wow! Look at those cliffs. They go all the way from the top to the bottom of the mountain. I reckon they must be a couple of thousand feet high," Kyle said.

"Look at all those waterfalls cascading down the rock faces and the cliffs," Maria said, appreciating the beauty. "What a magnificent spectacle!"

Flying over the crater above the cliffs, they looked down into a deep gorge dividing the main massif in the center, with two outer circular protrusions standing almost separated from the main. Dense forests surrounded the mountain on all the lower slopes and extended into the gulleys. Tea plantations extended from the edge of the forests, away from the base of the mountain.

In the south, Mulanje village looked small and insignificant at the foot of this magnificent mountain. Air turbulence, caused by the mountain, made the plane bump around from time to time, which worried Maria a little. After circling the massif, Tom turned the plane and headed for home. Still flushed with excitement from their flight, the family went to the club for supper.

They spent Christmas at the club, joining in with the other families who had not gone away on holiday. The mill had shut down for the year, and only a few people were left on the estate. After New Year, again enjoyed at the club, they flew to Harare.

Both boys were booked into Tom's old school, in Natal, so early in January, they drove to South Africa, to put them into their new school. The school had changed somewhat since Tom had been there 25 years before. In his time, it had been a junior school only. Now it had expanded and was both a junior and a senior school, with three times as many pupils. However, Tom was pleased to see that the sporting facilities were still as good as ever.

Once Stuart and Kyle were settled, they traveled to Swaziland. Tom was keen to show Maria where he had grown up, and to explore any opportunities there might be in that country. He had heard a whisper that there might be a new sugar project being developed in the Bushveld. This gave him a good excuse to visit his old employers on the ranch.

The ranch was in the middle of nowhere and was a hot, dry, dusty place. Tom had told Maria that Mike and Bunty were a little 'bushed,' but she found them to be good friendly people whose company she thoroughly enjoyed.

"Good Lord lad, it's grand to see you after all these years. You might have missed us if you had come any later. We are about to retire," Mike said, greeting them on the veranda outside the store.

"It is bloody good to be back with you guys again. I thought you would be here forever; where are you retiring to?" Tom asked, after introducing him to Maria.

"We have bought a little place in the Drakensberg, in Natal. Take Maria up to the house. Bunty is there now. Then come back to the store, and talk to me while I lock up."

Sitting on the veranda, having sundowners in the evening, Maria had to endure tales from Tom's past, while he had been working on the ranch, and in Swaziland.

"Mike, have you told Tom what is happening to the ranch?" Bunty asked.

"Not yet. Well, Tom, the ranch has been sold to the Swazi Nation. They are going to plant cane on most of the place. The rest of it will be incorporated into Hlane Game Reserve; hence the reason for our imminent departure, and retirement."

"When is this all happening?" Tom was not surprised by the news. "I believe it will be kicking off within the next couple of months. I hear there will be bush clearing contracts coming up for tender soon, so perhaps you should look into it."

"Well, I certainly am very interested. Do you know who I should see?"

The following morning, Tom was met at the back door by Themba, his boyhood friend who had grown up with him and was now Mike's assistant. They had a lot to catch up to do.

"Where is Danger? Does he still work here or has he been in more trouble?" Tom enquired after the big Shangaan ranch mechanic.

"Yes Nkosaan, he still works here, but he is up at Blue Jay Ranch doing maintenance."

"Okay, Themba. Tell him I will see him next time. I must go now. Perhaps I will be back soon."

It was just what Tom was looking for, and so armed with contact details in Mbabane, Tom and Maria said farewell to their friends and rushed off to submit a tender for the bush clearing. Maria loved Swaziland and found it a beautiful country with friendly people.

The hills and valleys around Mbabane were a mass of wattle trees in blossom, and the air was filled with the fragrance from the bright yellow flowers. Maria was fascinated by the names of towns and places; Hlatikulu and Mankayane, two towns in the mountains on the west of the country; Ezulweni, Sipofaneni, Balegane, and Manzini in the central area with Bulembu, Tshaneni, and Vuvulane on the east.

That night Tom worked on the tender documents, and after submitting them in the morning, they motored back to Zimbabwe. The decision would be made before the end of March.

Leaving Maria to tidy up their affairs in Harare, and to prepare for their move to South Africa, Tom returned to Malawi. With his contract rapidly coming to an end, and with no sign of any other work, he was becoming anxious. Time was running out.

"Tom I have just heard on the radio that all political prisoners have been released. Does this mean that Mamba will be out of prison?" Maria said when she spoke to him a week after he had returned to Malawi.

"I am afraid so. He will probably be one of the liberation heroes now, and could very well be looking for revenge, seeing as I shot his leg off."

"What are we going to do Tom?" Maria sounded worried.

"He doesn't know we are connected. He'll find out that I have left the country and that will be the end of it. Don't worry, if this Swaziland contract comes off, we'll be moving there shortly. If we don't get it, we'll move to South Africa and try to get something organized there," Tom reassured her.

With groups of 'ex-guerrillas' wandering around, taunting the whites whenever they had the opportunity, Tom was concerned for Maria's safety in Salisbury and urged her to avoid the city center, and not take unnecessary risks when traveling in the country. When he had moved to Malawi, his intention was to one day return to his beloved Rhodesia to farm. Now things had changed, and once again he was forced to change his direction. With the likes of Mamba on the loose, he had no intention of settling there.

After completing the last of the cane planting, Tom made a hurried trip to Swaziland. Flying directly from Malawi to Matsapa, he was met by a representative of Swazi Trust, who drove him to their headquarters in Mbabane. His tender was discussed at length, with Tom agreeing to a few minor alterations

In the morning, Tom was told that the committee had decided that as Tom was originally a Swazi National, and he could speak SiSwati, (the language of Swaziland) he was being awarded the contract. He would have to be on site in the Bushveld and ready to start by the end of April. He only had a month to get organized.

Catching the two o'clock flight from Matsapa, Tom arrived in Harare three hours later where Maria was waiting to meet him. On the way back to the house, she did her best to pry news from him.

"How did the meeting go Tom? Do you think we might get the contract?"

"The meeting was okay. I had to make a few small changes, but nothing too drastic. Now we have to wait and see what happens," Tom replied, stringing her along.

"But what do you think? What was the mood like at the meeting?" Maria asked, not letting go, as they drove through the gates into the yard.

"Well. I think we are still in with a chance," said Tom, dragging it out as long as he could.

"When will they let you know? We have arrangements to make," she said, as she parked the car and they got out.

"Okay, you win. We got the contract!" Tom said, grinning and unable to keep the good news from her any longer.

Leaping on him in a flash, she punched him playfully in the ribs, before kissing and congratulating him.

"Isn't that wonderful," she exclaimed delightedly. "When do we go?"

"I still have to finish off in Malawi. But I do have to start work in Swaziland in May. So there isn't much time."

****

Chapter 30

After the failure of the Muzorewa government, and the election of Mugabe as the new Prime Minister, the Bush War ended. The name of the country was changed to Zimbabwe, and all political prisoners and captured guerrillas were released.

Under the new government, life for the white members of the police force became almost impossible. They were transferred from one end of the country to the other, every few months. No sooner had they settled in one area, than they had to move their children to another school. In this way, the government managed to force the majority to resign, soon after independence.

The police were losing senior members and officers, with a wealth of experience, and were being replaced by untrained political appointees. Lucas began to look in earnest for a new career. He was not happy with the way the police force was being run and wanted no part in it.

Lucas heard that the Mozambique government had started to clear land-mines, and were looking for experts to locate and remove them. It was just the thing he had been looking for and seeing as relations had been re-established between the two countries at the end of the war, it would not be a problem going there on a contract basis.

Contacting the office of the Governor of Manica Province in Chimoio, Lucas arranged an interview and went to Mozambique. There were signs everywhere of their recent civil war, and of the even more recent invasions by Rhodesian Troops on hot pursuit operations. The town itself was in a state of disrepair; the roads had potholes everywhere, the streets were lined with litter, and most of the buildings were badly in need of maintenance. Mozambique had reached the bottom and was struggling to recover by encouraging foreign investment.

At the Governor's Office, Lucas met a large white Rhodesian from Matabeleland, by the name of Jan Van Rensburg. He had been in the Special Air Services during the war, and he too was there to discuss landmine removal. After waiting in the small, hot reception room for two hours, the secretary explained that the governor had been delayed and would only be in the office the following morning.

Van Rensburg was staying at Chicamba Dam, not far from Chimoio, which he said was very pleasant and quite comfortable. Lucas followed his new friend, booked in and then joined Jan in the restaurant. Swapping tales over a few drinks, they discovered that their backgrounds were very similar. Jan had opted to leave the SAS at the end of hostilities; he was not prepared to work alongside former enemies.

Getting on well, they agreed it would be beneficial for them both if they presented themselves to the Governor as a team. If awarded a contract, they would draw up the necessary partnership agreement.

They were awarded a contract starting three months later. The money, for the removal of land-mines in Mozambique, was coming from foreign donations. That night, after discussing how to set up their operation, they made plans to meet in Harare.

Excited with the prospect of working for himself, Lucas phoned Tom and told him about Jan, and their success in winning the contract.

"Congratulations Lucas. That is bloody good news. Just make sure that you have a water-tight agreement with Van Rensburg," Tom advised.

"He is coming to Harare to meet with me next month. We will be signing an agreement then."

"You are going to need some capital, to get the equipment you need and to pay your workers."

"We have already discussed that Tom. As soon as we know what equipment we need, we will raise the money to get going. I have a little saved up, and so does Jan."

"It sounds good to me. Keep me posted. I will help if I can."

Lucas felt no regrets, resigning from the Police Force. In the past year, it had changed dramatically for the worse, and so he was better off out of it altogether. He had accumulated six weeks leave which he had to take before leaving the force. He used the time to visit his family in Mvurwi (used to be Umvukwes), before concentrating on setting up their operation.

First of all they had to work out an efficient method of locating and diffusing the mines, without blowing themselves up in the process; then they had to work out what capital they required; they had to obtain the necessary 'Diri' or work permit to work in Mozambique; accommodation had to be found; staff and workers had to be employed and trained. There was a lot more to be done than Lucas had even thought of in setting up a business.

Lucas went to Malawi, to attend Tom and Maria's wedding, and to spend four days with his old friends. He was very happy for them. Spending time in the company of his friends with their families, Lucas began to think that it might be time to look for a wife and start a family of his own. But now that would have to wait; his work in Mozambique was going to be dangerous.

The slow pace of bureaucracy in Mozambique had been frustrating, requiring several trips, before everything was in place. Three months later, Lucas and Jan moved to Mozambique. They found suitable accommodation on a farm near Chimoio. They both changed their cars for bakkies (pick-up trucks), then purchased the metal detectors, explosives and other equipment they were going to need.

Just before Lucas and Jan moved to Mozambique, he heard that Tom and Maria were moving to Swaziland. He wondered if he would ever see his friends again.

....

At the end of February, Tom closed his operation in Malawi and moved to Harare (the name had now been changed from Salisbury) to help Maria with the moving arrangements. A week later, they departed for Swaziland. Samuel, who was going to work for John, was dropped off in the Lowveld en route.

Stopping to say goodbye to Maria's mother on their way to the south, they were shocked to hear that Mamba had survived prison, and was operating in the area around the Zimbabwe Ruins. It was rumored, that he was responsible for the murder of four white farmers, in the Kyle Dam area, since independence. That these people could be allowed to continue with their atrocities a year after the country had been granted independence was shocking news.

Maria was glad that they were leaving the country. It was the start of a new chapter of their lives. By the end of the contract in Swaziland, Tom was hoping to have sufficient funds to buy his farm.

****

Chapter 31

Tom had always loved Swaziland. The country was handed over to King Sobhuza Dlamini in 1964 when Britain so hastily pulled out of Africa. He had grown up in the misty mountainous area around Mbabane, the capital, where there were huge forests - Piggs Peak and Usutu Forests (Mhlambanyati). With its good rivers supplying an abundance of water, the country is very fertile, with a variety of crops grown in the different climatic zones.

At the foothills of the mountains surrounding Mbabane, the fertile Ezulweni valley produces pineapples, granadillas, and avocado pears. In the valley, there is a hot sulfur spring or 'Cuddle Puddle,' where Tom and his friends had great fun when they were growing up.

Further east beyond Manzini is the hot low lying bushveld suitable for cattle ranching and growing cotton, sugar cane, and citrus. There is a lot of game in this part of the country, and Tom and his father enjoyed many hunting trips here before Tom went to work on Mlaula ranch, and before joining the Rhodesian police.

Tom found it strange being back on the ranch, where he had worked as a young man, after having been away for 18 years. It had changed and was no longer a hive of activity. His old friend and ex-employer had retired and moved to Natal. The move from Harare to the Bushveld, in Swaziland, had gone smoothly enough. They arrived well ahead of time, a week before the end of March, and were soon settled into the old ranch house, recently vacated by Mike and Bunty.

With Maria busy setting up the home, employing a gardener and house servant, Tom set about getting his operation organized. He had the equipment to hire, operators and laborers to employ and train, and housing for his staff to arrange.

After being awarded the contract, Tom had contacted Mike who had arranged for Danger, the ranch mechanic who had worked for him on Mlaula Ranch, to wait there for him. So Tom knew he had a good mechanic. He would have liked to employ his boyhood friend, Themba, but he was now a Section Manager for a large ranch in the South of the country.

He used the old ranch store as an office and workshop, had overhead fuel tanks erected, and fenced the whole yard off. It was a little further from the work front than Tom would have liked, but with a mobile service truck and fuel tanker, it would be fine. The contract, much the same as in Malawi, involved bush clearing, deep ripping, plowing, and digging of drains and trenches for underground irrigation pipes. The planting was to be done by the estate once he finished harrowing and the lands levelled, and then handed over. The heavy machinery arrived on site two weeks later, and he was ready to make a start.

The estate lay at the foothills of the Lebombo Mountains with the Mbuluzi River, which was to supply the water for irrigation, running along the northern boundary and with the Hlane Game Reserve on the other three sides. The gravel roads, leading to and from the estate, were in poor condition because of the heavy traffic bringing equipment and supplies for the construction of the sugar mill and were not easy to travel.

A club, with tennis and squash courts and a cricket field, as well as a golf club and a large dam in the vicinity provided recreation for the people in the area.

"When we came on that flying visit to see Mike and Bunty, I didn't realize that so much sugar-cane was being grown in this little country," Maria said when Tom was showing her around.

"Yes, there's a big area under cane. There are two other sugar estates nearby, and to the south, there is Big Bend. Now, with the 9000 hectares that are being developed at Mlaula, Swaziland will have about 50000 hectares under cane and will be producing a hell of a lot of sugar for export."

It was a lovely, warm, clear autumn day with only a few wispy clouds high in the sky. From the small town of Siteki, on top of the Lebombo Mountain Range, they were able to look down the other side of the mountains eastward into Mozambique and towards Maputo (used to be Lourenco Marques).

Because it was that time of year, the countryside was brown and grey, except for the emerald green of the cane fields on the sugar estates, which were visible in the distance. Looking south-west, they could see the Bushveld stretching for miles and in the distance, a low line of blue hills, marking the start of the climb out of the low-lying areas up into the middle of the country and then into the high hills of Mbabane, 130 miles away.

There were thousands of cabbage trees dotted about along the mountain slopes, with protruding prongs like giraffe horns, sticking out all over them, and there were Corkwoods, Silver Cluster trees, and mountain aloes among the acacias. It was autumn, and all the acacia trees and scrub had already lost their leaves.

Siteki itself was no longer the bustling colonial town Tom had known; it was now an untidy mess, with weeds and scrub growing everywhere. He remembered the good times he had had there and was disappointed to see the poor state of the town. When Tom was a young man, the farmers and ranchers from the Bushveld lived in Stegi because of its cooler temperature and healthier climate it also had fewer mosquitoes. Now all the grand homes were unoccupied and falling apart - some had even been burnt down.

"It is so much cooler, up here on the mountain, than it is down where we live. Is that why so many people used to live up here?" Maria asked.

"Yes, Stegi was a very pleasant place to live, with a close-knit community. There was a country club with all the sports facilities, and golf course, as well as two hotels and all the usual shops. A lot of traffic passed through here on the way to Lourenco Marques from Johannesburg, and some people stopped overnight. Quite a few of the residents had planes and would fly back and forth to their ranches in the bushveld. It was very colonial," Tom explained.

"Then what happened? It all seems pretty run down now," Maria observed.

"When the road, past Mlaula to the border post at Nomaacha, was built and the Goba border near here was closed."

"What a pity. Do you think there are many white people living here now?"

"Only one or two I should think. There is nothing for them to do now, and a lot of them left the country soon after Independence in 1964."

Stuart and Kyle had both settled into their senior school and made some friends, who also lived in Swaziland. Every holiday, when all the youngsters came home, activities were organized for them; tennis tournaments, golf competitions, water-skiing, sailing and fishing on the dam with trips to the Kruger National Park and other places on interest in the Eastern Transvaal.

Maria, who enjoyed being part of the community, was fully involved with the organizing of these events. She was popular and made a lot of friends. The country club was the hub of all activities for both children and adults. It was a wonderful life, and there was never time to be bored or have nothing to do.

During the summer months the work was hard for Tom under the punishing sun, but in the winter months, it was pleasant. As in Malawi, bush clearing and the turning of virgin soil attracted multitudes of birds that came in large flocks to feed on worms and grubs, exposed by the work. Others came to catch flying insects swept up in the thermals when they burnt the piles of brush. Lilac-breasted rollers, blue-jays, and European bee-eaters joined the other species in the insect feast. Large Maribu storks, looking like mourners at a funeral with their black feathers and white breasts, strolled around the refuse dump site, searching for tasty morsels.

Whenever they felt they needed a break from the hectic life of a developing sugar estate, Tom and Maria would take a trip to the Kruger National Park, where they spent a couple of days game viewing and relaxing in the quiet atmosphere of the camps.

Driving around slowly through the woodland areas, they were treated with numerous sightings of elephant, rhino, cheetah, giraffe as well as kudu, nyala and impala antelope. If they were lucky, they would have sightings of lion and even leopard. On the banks of the Crocodile River, when they stopped to watch a large herd of Buffalo slaking their thirst, two large baboons males jumped onto the car and peered through the windows at them, hoping for titbits of food.

At a nearby waterhole, a family of Warthog was rolling in the mud, happily cooling off, and covering themselves with mud as protection against the sun. Once their toiletries were done, the mother turned and trotted off with her piglets following behind, all with their tails sticking straight up in the air like aerials with tufts on the ends. One late afternoon, just before getting back to camp, they stopped along the Sabi River, to watch the animals come down to drink. A huge herd of Wildebeest, accompanied by a herd of Zebra, were lined up along the water's edge.

"Maria, look over there," Tom said excitedly, pointing to the other side of the river.

"Do you see those two lionesses stalking those wildebeest?"

"Oh yes, I see them. It looks like they are going for one of the calves," Maria said.

They watched as the lionesses closed in on their prey. Sensing their presence, the Wildebeest spooked, turned away from the water, and galloping off to safety. The lionesses singled out a young beast, and despite the attention of the mother, trying to protect her offspring, quickly caught up to it. One of them leaped onto its back, bringing it down, and the other two were quick to join the kill. Realizing that her calf was doomed, the mother galloped off to join the rest of the herd leaving the lions to devour their kill. The whole herd stopped and turned to watch the lions, as though in total disgust.

Maria closed her eyes. "How horrible!" she whispered. "Nature can be very cruel at times."

Tom bought a ski-boat, which they used for water skiing on the dam, and to go deep-sea fishing. It only took three hours to get to Sodwana, on the coast of Zululand, where they went for four days every second month. They took two other couples with them on these fishing trips and were usually accompanied by one or two other teams, with their ski boats and crews.

Usually arriving at the camping ground in the late afternoon, they would set about pitching tents under a large tarpaulin. Shade cloth was pinned to the ground, and the tents pitched around the edge, and a special kitchen tent, with a camp stove and fridges where food was kept and prepared. Tables and chairs were placed in the center. One of the boat boys had to be left in camp when they were out fishing, to make sure it wasn't raided by vervet monkeys and mongooses. Stuart and Kyle went with them whenever they could.

Early every morning, just as the sun was peeping up over the horizon, they would launch their boats from the beach. The sea was usually calm at that time of day before the wind got up. Launching off the beach took a certain amount of skill, which came from experience. The skipper had to pick the right gap, throttle the motors to take the break and shoot over the incoming waves, at just the right speed to avoid being flipped over backward as the boat leaped into the air.

Five or six hours later, depending on the catch and the wind, they would return to the beach. Tom never tired of the thrill of hearing the reel scream when he hooked a 'big one' and the fight to land the fish. They caught Barracuda, Bonita, Kingfish, Yellow-fin tunny, Dorado and if they were very lucky, even Sailfish and Marlin. The smaller fish were cooked and eaten for supper, and the larger ones were frozen and taken home. Far too much alcohol was consumed during these breaks, but it seemed to come with the territory!

In February 1984, the country was hit by Cyclone Demoina, which came in from the Mozambique Channel and passed over Swaziland and the Eastern and Northern Transvaal. It left a path of destruction in its wake. Accompanied by torrential rains (600mm falling in 24 hours) that brought all the rivers down in flood with bridges and roads being swept away.

In Swaziland, massive high-level bridges, over the Mbuluzi and Usutu rivers, with sections weighing hundreds of tonnes were carried some distance downstream by the raging waters. On the estate, the main river pump station was destroyed; the canals were damaged, and huge areas of the fields washed away. Mlaula was completely cut off.

Tom was contracted to repair some of the damaged fields which kept him busy for some time, and his other work had to be put on hold. As the estate grew, he was given more and more work.

Time passed quickly, and the two boys turned into fine young men. They both completed their schooling and went on to college. Stuart graduated with a degree in civil engineering and went to work on the Katse Dam project in Lesotho. While studying, he met Felicity, a delightful young Durban girl who was taking a degree in Graphic Design. After bringing her to Swaziland to meet Tom and Maria, who took to her straight away, they had got engaged.

Kyle, following in his father's footsteps, decided on a career in agriculture, and after attending the South African Sugar Association Training course, earned a diploma in Sugar Cane Management. He found a job on a cane farm in Zululand.

The future of South Africa still appeared to be uncertain, but at last, the English speaking South Africans were being assisted by the land bank. The political unrest was ongoing, with the blacks wanting complete control of the country. As Tom was now only a temporary resident of Swaziland, he was unable to purchase land there, and so was undecided as to where to look for a farm. The sugar estate was fully developed, and there was no other work available in Swaziland. Once again it was time to move on.

****

Chapter 32

Lucas and Jan did well with their landmine removal contract. Starting in areas around Chimoio and Catandica, in central Mozambique, where terrorist camps had been during the Bush War, they cleared large areas.

In the beginning, they only used metal detectors and probes. Then they discovered that they could use large rats to sniff out mines. They strung long wires across minefields, then the rats, wearing collars attached to the wires, were released to work their way from one end to the other. Because meal porridge was used to tamp the fuses down when the mines had been laid, the rats were able to sniff out the location of mines, which were then marked and removed or blown up.

From the Chimoio district, they were sent to clear mines in the Gorongoza Game Reserve. A new road was being made from Dondo on the Zimbabwe to Beira road, through the game reserve to Caia, on the Zambezi River where a new bridge was being built. Two other mine removal teams were also working on the road line, so they leap-frogged each other, from one cleared area to the next un-cleared area further up the line.

As it was too far from their base in Chimoio to commute daily, they camped with the road crews. The road construction contractors set up campsites with all the basic amenities; store, bar, canteen, ablutions and so on. This was more convenient and sociable

The work was stressful and dangerous; the hours were long, and it was hellishly hot. Lucas and Jan both had malaria several times. After working for two weeks, they would take a three-day break back at their base, visiting Lake Chicamba, Beira or going to Zimbabwe to see friends and family.

In their third year, and on one of his visits home to his parents in Mvurwi (was Umvukwes), Lucas was disturbed to see that his father did not look well. He asked Lucas to return home, and help him with his duties on the farm he managed.

Concerned about his fathers deteriorating health, Lucas discussed his predicament with Jan on his return to Mozambique.

"What do you want to do?" Jan asked him.

"Will you be prepared to buy my share of the business?"

"No problem. We'll work out a price that we're both happy with when we finish clearing the section we are busy on now. Is that Okay?"

"That sounds fair to me."

A month later, Lucas sold his share of the business to Jan's new partner. Lucas had been in Mozambique for three years and had built up a substantial nest egg. He was pleased to be going home where he hoped to settle down. Although the mine clearing work had been very lucrative, he was tired of camping and needed a break from the nervous tension that came with the job. He looked forward to his new life.

Having worked on the farm before joining the Police Force, Lucas soon settled back into the work and found that he enjoyed the life. It was 22 years since he had left the farm, and operations had become far more sophisticated.

Instead of having to stoke the barn fires manually they now had automatic stokers, controlled by thermostats. These timers also operated the vents, controlling the humidity and temperatures in the barns. Other than that, the operations had not changed much. His father explained the position to his employer, who was more than happy for Lucas to gradually take over from him.

Lucas was 40 years old and still a bachelor. His mother decided that it was high time he found a suitable woman and settled down. She had traditional values, which Lucas agreed with in all but one; he would choose his own wife.

Lucas joined the Mvurwi Country Club and played tennis most weekends.

"Hell it was hot out on the tennis court this afternoon," Lucas said to Tandi, his attractive doubles partner, after a game of mixed doubles one Saturday afternoon.

"Yes, almost too hot for tennis. I don't think I am going to play another game today," Tandi said.

"Okay. I have a better idea. Will you join me in the bar for a couple of drinks? At least it is air-conditioned in there."

"What a good idea. I'll meet you in a few minutes after I have had a shower and changed."

They had met before at the club but never spoken much. This afternoon they had been drawn to play together and got on well. Now they were enjoying each other's company in the cool, relaxed atmosphere of the bar.

"Why don't we stay and have some supper?" Tandi suggested.

"That's a brilliant idea. I'll book a table," Lucas was quick to agree.

Tandi was medium in height with an athletic build. She had a light brown complexion and a wide, generous smile that showed off her beautiful white teeth. She was easy to talk to and had a wonderful sense of humor. She worked as a receptionist at the Mvurwi retirement village. Her parents lived in Centenary.

Lucas, for the first time in his life, was bowled over by her and fell in love. Their romance developed from there, and after courting for a while, he took her home to meet his parents. Then he went to meet her parents, to ask for permission to get married. The Lobola or bride price was agreed and paid.

They were married two months later. Lucas would have liked all the members of the old PATU unit to come to the wedding, but he was unable to contact any of them. Tom and Maria were somewhere in Swaziland or South Africa. John and Jill, who were the only people who knew how to contact Tom, were away on holiday. The rest of the old team were scattered far and wide, and he didn't know how to contact any of them.

Lucas lost touch with Tom when they moved to Swaziland, and at about the same time as he went to Mozambique. Communication from Mozambique had been almost impossible.

A year after returning to the farm, Lucas's father retired. Although his health had improved, he was not up to the hard work on the farm. Lucas was promoted to Farm Manager and took over all his fathers' old duties. His parents returned to their home in the Chiweshi Tribal Trust, and Lucas and Tandi moved into the manager's house.

At that time there were problems in the south and western parts of the country. Nkomo, the leader of ZAPU in Matabeleland, had been ousted from the cabinet when his party he was accused of planning a coup, and of being "the Cobra in the house."

This prompted Nkomo supporters to rebel, resorting to acts of terrorism. Thousands of troops, including the Korean trained Fifth Brigade, were moved to Matabeleland to quell the uprising. They did it by committing full-scale acts of genocide, killing over 20000 men, women, and children. It was almost double the number of casualties incurred during the Bush War.

The military also stopped food supplies from reaching many areas in Matabeleland, resulting in many more people dying of starvation.

In Mashonaland and Manicaland where the population was mostly Shona, there was little or no trouble. (Mvurwi was in Mashonaland). They lived in relative peace, with little interference from the government - apart from occasional threats of land confiscation for re-distribution to the ex-guerrillas. This didn't cause them too much alarm though as the vast areas of commercial farming land that had been taken over by the government, shortly after independence, still had not been re-distributed.

****

Chapter 33

John, Tom's old friend, still a professional hunter in the Lowveld, told him of a farming project that was about to be started in central Mozambique. As Tom had always been interested in that part of the world, and with the Mozambican government encouraging farmers to reinvest in the country, he was keen to find out more. They decided to join an organized party that was to be shown around by the developers. Tom drove to Zimbabwe, spent the night in the Lowveld with John, and then the two of them drove on to Lake Chicamba near Chimoio, in Mozambique, where they spent three days investigating the proposed development.

"Wasn't Lucas operating somewhere in this area, with his Landmine removal business?" Tom asked John, as they traveled around with 30 other interested farmers.

"Yes, he was. But he packed it in five or six years ago. He called me on the phone when he returned to Zimbabwe," John told him.

"I wonder what he is doing now."

"He said something about going to work on a farm in Mvurwi with his father," John recalled.

"It might be a good idea to try to get hold of him. He would know where the mines have been removed, and more important, where they have not," Tom said.

John agreed to try to locate Lucas.

The areas they were shown around, and the proposals for the development project, were of great interest to them both, and Tom committed himself to it, on the assurance that the start date was imminent. Being one of the first to pay the deposit, Tom would be in the initial group to get started. He also had the advantage of having a wife who was fluent in Portuguese.

Back in Swaziland they packed up, put their furniture into storage and took their animals to Kyle in Zululand to look after. They sold the boat and bought a caravan, had a farewell party at the club and were on their way. They would be based in Harare until they were given the go-ahead to move to Mozambique.

Once again they were heading off into the unknown. Maria and Tom had enjoyed ten wonderful years in Swaziland where they led a very hectic social life; playing golf, tennis, squash and being involved in everything that was happening in the sporting and social scene. They toured the whole of the Eastern Transvaal and the Kruger National Park, and they went deep sea fishing at the coast every second month.

Maria was nervous for two reasons; she was going back to the country where she feared her enemy was, and she did not know what was in store for them in Mozambique, or how long she would be living in a caravan. On the positive side, she knew that they would only be in Harare for a short while, before moving to Mozambique. Both she and Tom were sad to leave Swaziland and their friends – Swaziland had given them many happy memories.

Late in the afternoon, they struggled up the steep incline and over the top of the high red tinted sandstone mountains, of the Soutpansberg range, before reaching the Zimbabwean border on the Limpopo River.

Maria's mother was in her seventies and still looking strong and fit when they pulled up to the front of her store the next day. The store tailor was sitting at the far end of the veranda, with his treadle sewing machine going flat out. Maria was always amazed at how good these store tailors were. A couple of children were playing in the dust outside the store, and two elderly men were also sitting on the veranda, in earnest conversation.

Under a large mango tree, two donkeys stood, harnessed to a cart loaded with bags of meal, which had been milled from the maize they had carted earlier. They were waiting patiently for their owner to finish drinking beer before heading home.

Having left South Africa early in the morning, and then spending two hours clearing customs and immigration at the border, it was a welcome stop to have lunch with her mother. Besides, Maria had not seen her for some time.

"Mother, you hear everything that is going on around here from people coming to your shop. Have you heard any news about that awful man Mamba? Has he been back to the Kyle area again in the last few years?" Maria asked.

"No Maria, there hasn't been any trouble down here."

Pushing on after a short stay, they arrived in Harare late in the afternoon and set up camp.

....

The consultant company, responsible for organizing the farming venture in Mozambique, had its headquarters in one of Harare's suburbs. Tom went to see them, and he was told that he was in the first group and would move to Mozambique within two weeks. While he was there, he met a few of the other farmers who were also in his group. He and Maria spent the next two weeks making final preparations for their new venture.

It was ten years since Zimbabwe had gained independence, and apart from appearing untidy and in need of maintenance, seemed to have settled down with no apparent problems. Tom, who had put his project proposals together before leaving Swaziland, was armed with all the required documentation to apply for their temporary residence permits, or 'Diri,' to live in Mozambique.

Three weeks after they had expected to move to Mozambique, their permits were eventually approved. They moved to Chicamba Dam where they set up their temporary camp, and to wait for the allocation of farms. Two months later they were still waiting. They had been allocated an area where, during the Bush War, there had been a huge base camp for terrorists operating into Rhodesia. Although the camp and its 5000 terrorists, had been wiped out by Rhodesian troops, there was still the likelihood of land-mines buried in the vicinity. It seemed as if they were going to be used to clear the land mines left behind!

John and Jill came from the Lowveld to spend two weeks camping with them. While they were there, the four of them explored and put their markers on suitable farmland. John had not been able to locate Lucas to find out where there might be mines. Eventually, they decided to split from the main group, opting to find their own farms. It seemed a far better option and gave them a much better choice. The area that interested them was between Mercado and Sussendenga, about 60 miles to the south of Chimoio. The soils were good, and there was an abundance of good water in the rivers and streams.

During their explorations, they came across a farm being worked. Curious to find out more about the area and conditions, they drove into the farm and were met by a young Afrikaner with his wife and their two young daughters.

"Good morning. My name is John, and this is Tom," John said as they got out of their van.

"Good morning Meneer (mister). How can I help you?" the young man replied, in a broad Afrikaans accent. "My name is Piet, and this is my wife, Sannie."

"We want to come and farm here and are looking for vacant farms in this area. Have you been here long?" Tom asked.

"*Ja Oom* (yes, uncle). There are plenty of empty farms here. We have been here for a year now."

"Did you come here on your own from South Africa, or did you come in a group?"

"*Nee Oom*. (No Uncle) We came with the Viljoen Group five years ago. We all went to the far northern part of Mozambique. It was a mess. A lot of the people died of malaria, and some of them were murdered. All the others have gone back to South Africa," he said sadly.

"But you stayed and moved here?"

"Ja. My wife said that we must not *sommer* (just) give up and go home with our tails between our legs. We must stay and make our life here," he said proudly.

"What crops are you growing?" John asked.

"I have been trying burley tobacco and sunflowers," Piet told them.

"Have you had any problems since you moved onto this farm?" Tom asked.

"It was hard to get all the papers authorized; it takes a long time."

"We have to go to Mutare to buy our groceries. There is very little in Chimoio except for beer," Sannie said, smiling at her husband.

"What about schooling for your daughters, Mevrou (madam)?" asked John.

"I am teaching them myself. I get the books from South Africa. My mother sends them to me," Sannie replied.

"Perhaps we will be neighbors," smiled Tom. "Goodbye and thanks."

"Ja. That will be good. *Totsiens* (goodbye)," Piet and Sannie waved them off.

Tom had great admiration for these young people who had such courage and determination. Turning to John, he said; "Hell, that is a strong young family. She must be one tough bird. Those are true pioneers."

"You can say that again. They have had a bloody hard time. It looks like he is making some progress. I wish them all the luck in the world," John summed it up.

Maria and Jill agreed that they would never have stayed by themselves like the young couple had chosen to do.

Driving on, they noticed that all the farms in that area had remains of what must have been good homes once. The houses, sheds, and outbuildings appeared to have been built to the same design; they all had avenues of old gum trees leading from the main road to the homesteads and were all close together. Tom decided to find out who had been there before.

Paying a visit to the local chief, they learned that before the Second World War a group of 200 German families had settled there. They had stayed for about ten years, and their farms were productive, until one night, seven of them returning from a meeting in Vila Peri (now Chimoio), had been ambushed and killed. Within two weeks, the remainder had hurriedly packed up and returned to Germany. The reason for the ambush was not known.

Wherever they went in the Manica Province there were signs of the civil war, and damage caused by the Rhodesian Troops on hot pursuit operations in that country. There were blown-up bridges and roads, buildings that had been demolished by rocket fire and bombs, and most disturbing; some people without limbs – lost mostly from exploding anti-personnel mines, set during the civil war. Many of the legless people had tri-cycles with pedals where handlebars would normally be; an ingenious solution that enabled them to get around.

The airport outside Chimoio surprised them. When they went to investigate, they found that it was a fully equipped but unmanned, International Airport, complete with a full-length tarred runway, a Control Tower with an up-to-date terminal building, fire tenders and other emergency equipment. It would be ideal for any export produce they might grow; such as fruit, vegetables, and flowers.

Time went by slowly as they waited for the start of the project. The organizers went back and forth, meetings were held with the Governor of the province, with the local Chiefs in the proposed areas, and with the banks and overseas investors. Eventually, after waiting for three months, the potential investors got cold feet and decided not to finance the scheme.

Tom and Maria, after having put all their efforts, and a fair amount of time and money into the project were bitterly disappointed. It looked as if the project would never get off the ground, and that the organizers had misled them.

They packed up their caravan and returned to Harare. They were not prepared to wait any longer in Mozambique for other financiers to be found. How wrong Maria had been to expect she'd be out of the caravan within a matter of weeks, and into a home of her own.

****

Part Three - Zimbabwe
(1989-2004)

Chapter 34

Tracking down his old friend Lucas was not as difficult as expected. Knowing that he hailed from the Mvurwi farming area, Tom made inquiries at the local co-operative, and soon had directions to the farm where Lucas could be found.

It was a typical summer's morning in the Highveld, with blue skies and early signs of an afternoon shower building up on the horizon. Parking his van under a flamboyant tree, Tom walked over to the farm office. A motorcycle was parked outside, and the Alsatian dog lying outside the door got up and wagged its tail as Tom mounted the office steps. Knocking on the open door, Tom walked in.

"Good morning Lucas," he greeted his old friend, who was head-down busy with bookwork.

"Maiwe! Is that really you Tom? What a wonderful surprise," exclaimed Lucas, leaping out of his chair. "What the hell are you doing here in Zimbabwe?"

"I finished my contract in Swaziland, and we moved to Mozambique to start a farming venture there," Tom explained.

"Yes, I have heard of some farmers interested in farms there. I understand there are problems with the organizers. There are still a lot of uncleared landmines in that area. You'll have to be very careful," Lucas warned.

"You are quite right. There are problems, and right now it doesn't look too good," Tom replied.

"Come on. Let's go over to the house for tea. Tandi would love to meet you," Lucas said, leading the way.

"And who is Tandi, my friend? Is there something you have not told me?" Tom asked as they made their way over to the house.

"She's my wife. We've been married for five years."

"Congratulations. Why didn't I know about this long overdue marriage?"

"I did try to contact you in Swaziland, but somehow we had lost touch, and I didn't know where you were, or how to get hold of you."

Two small children, playing in the garden, came to meet them as they walked through the gates, and a good-looking black woman stood watching from the veranda.

"You have done alright for yourself. That is a fine looking woman you have there," Tom said admiring Lucas' wife. "Are these your two youngsters?"

"Yes, they are. The boy is Tomas and the girl we named Sarah." Lucas said proudly.

"I am so pleased to meet you at last. Lucas has told me all about your adventures together," Tandi said, after being introduced to Tom.

"If I had known Lucas was now a married man, I would have brought Maria out with me. She is sitting in the caravan park outside Harare and not very happy. I see you are looking after my old friend. Lucas is looking very well. You must be very good for him."

"Why don't you bring your caravan out here and camp on the farm? You will be much happier," Lucas suggested after bringing each other up to date with all their news.

"That sounds like a bloody good idea. I am sure Maria will be more than happy to get away from the city."

"Do you know whatever happened to our friend Mamba?" Tom enquired when Tandi had gone inside and was out of ear-shot.

"No, I haven't heard a word. If he is alive, I'm sure he'll be up to no good somewhere in the country. He's probably in Masvingo; he comes from that part of the country. With the War Veterans getting massive compensation and back-pay, I am sure he has made himself very comfortable somewhere."

Driving back to Harare, Tom had a lot to think about. Lucas had said that the farm he was managing was up for sale; the owner wanted to retire and leave the country. When Tom had asked about the security situation and Mugabe's land reform, Lucas explained that providing the government did not want the farm; it could be purchased. It was ten years since independence, and it seemed that the farming community in Mashonaland was under no threat of having their land confiscated.

From what Tom had seen driving to and from Mozambique, and now his trip out to Mvurwi; the commercial farmers were expanding, and producing huge crops of maize, wheat, cotton, tobacco, citrus, roses, and vegetables. As they were producing the majority of the country's exports, and feeding the nation, it seemed highly unlikely that this flourishing industry would come under threat.

Before being granted independence from Britain, the Lancaster House Agreement had been signed in London by all the participating parties. The agreement stipulated that at the time of land re-distribution, land transfers would take place in an orderly manner, with adequate compensation paid to the farmers. Although by 1990 the agreement had expired, Mugabe was still encouraging white farmers to stay and had restored their confidence.

It was still possible for white people to purchase land, providing a certificate of 'Non-Interest' was obtained from the government. This meant that if the farm Lucas managed was not earmarked for Land Re-Distribution, it could safely be purchased.

Two days later, Tom and Maria were happily settled under the shade of a huge Wild Fig tree, on the bank of a small stream running through Bushlands farm. Lucas made sure they had everything they needed for their comfort.

News travels fast around farming communities, and within days they had visits from some of Tom's old friends, from his days as a policeman and a tobacco farmer. They were still on their farms and had all expanded and modernized; using the latest technology. Tom had the highest respect for the Rhodesian farmers. With their innovative ideas and methods, they had always been far more efficient and productive than their South African counterparts.

The friendly welcoming nature of the people in the district made them feel as if they were back at home. Before long, Tom and Maria were inundated with invitations to attend braai's (barbeques) and to play tennis or golf. They watched polo, went game viewing in a nearby game park and toured the Great Dyke and other nearby places of interest. The lifestyle was as good as it had been before the start of the Bush War.

A visit to the Mazarabani Wilderness Area near Centenary, with Ted and his wife Elsie, their friends from Msoneddi, was well worth it. Rhino, giraffe, kudu, waterbuck, impala, and warthog were seen in their numbers. After driving around the park, they went to where various captured animals were caged, pending their export to other countries. Most of these animals had been caught in snares set by poachers and rescued by farmers.

A couple of cheetahs, a few species of antelope and a very disturbed leopard were in the cages. Getting up close to the fence to peep at the leopard, Tom had his face against the netting trying to take a photo, when, with a sudden blur of movement, he found himself looking into its yellow eyes. He could smell its breath as it bared its teeth and snarled at him. The leopard hung on the diamond mesh fence for a couple of seconds before dropping back to the ground and retreating into the shadows.

Tom had never seen an animal move so fast and was lucky to have been wearing a cap with the peak up against the fence. Had it not been for that, he would certainly have lost his eyes and nose. This, of course, caused a great deal of mirth amongst the others.

"Tom I think you might need a change of underwear. You should have seen your face," Ted laughed at him.

On another outing - again with Ted and Elsie - they drove over the Great Dyke to see where Ted had worked in his mining days. Winding their way over the 5-mile wide range of hills Tom asked his friend. "Ted you're the mining fundi, how long is the Dyke?"

"If I'm not mistaken, it's 530 miles long. It stretches from Gwanda in the south-west to Mazarabani in the north-east of the country."

"There's very little vegetation growing on these hills. It looks almost like a moonscape. Is it like this for the whole length?" Tom was fascinated. The only vegetation, apart from grass, was an abundance of aloes and a few stunted bushes scattered around between the rocks and boulders on the hill slopes.

"The soils are very toxic because of the minerals. The Dyke is one of the most remarkable and richest rock formations in the world. It has deposits of high-grade platinum, chromium, nickel, copper, cobalt, gold and asbestos," Ted explained.

They stopped near an abandoned mine shaft on the top of the hills, for a picnic, where they had a good view of the area. Along the slopes, there were numerous narrow roads and paths leading to gaping black holes where miners had burrowed deep into the hills following seams of gold, chrome and other sought-after minerals. Cableways and coco-pan rails crisscrossed the hills like giant spider's webs.

"You know how the old mine shafts were used to hide the bodies of all those killed during the Matabele rebellion a few years ago. The old shafts along this part of the Dyke would make ideal places to hide bodies," Ted observed, as they peered into the dark depths of the old mine shaft.

"It sure would. I wonder if the ruling party has used any of them to bury so-called dissidents in this part of the country?" said Tom.

"I haven't heard of any people being 'got rid of' around here, but it wouldn't surprise me."

Moving on after their picnic, they dropped down to the foothills to explore the small mining town of Mtorashanga, where there had been a lot of mining from the early 1900s. Now it was practically a 'ghost town,' with only a few houses occupied and one or two shops still open.

"The whole area was abandoned, when major mining activities were suspended, just after the end of the Bush War. The price of gold had dropped to a level where it was no longer viable to mine, and with the American Space program slowing down, the chrome was no longer in such high demand," Ted explained.

The Rhodesian high-grade chrome and platinum, along with tobacco and maize, had been the main external sources of revenue for the country during the Bush War years. Because of international sanctions at that time, America could not buy the chrome directly from Rhodesia and was forced to buy it via Russia. Sanctions came at a price!

Near the village, there was a huge, deep hole in the granite, created by mining activities, which was now full of crystal-clear water. Divers were using the pool to train for deep-diving.

It was a fascinating area and in its heyday must have been a very 'busy' place.

When Tom and Maria were with their friends, the discussion inevitably turned to the subject of land ownership and land reforms. The consensus was that it would be a good idea if they bought a farm in the district, and put the Mozambique Project on the back burner.

At the time of independence, there had been 6700 white farmers in the country. By 1990, with funds from the West, 500000 hectares had been purchased by the government for resettlement. Seventy percent of the remaining 4000 farmers were under the age of 35 and had legally purchased their farms since independence; with the consent of the government. It seemed most unlikely that more farms would be needed, seeing as the farms already acquired, were still to be distributed to black farmers.

"Well, my darling, what do you think we should do?" Tom asked Maria, after an enjoyable Sunday braai with friends. "Are we going to take a chance, and settle back here in Zimbabwe? It looks pretty stable to me, and we seem to be running out of time and options."

"I don't know. We have been living in the caravan for four months, and I'm getting a little tired of it. We know it's going to be quite a while before we can get going in Mozambique - if ever. Those idiots who are trying to organize the project are completely useless, and have led us up the garden path with their promises. The other thing, of course, is that if we do buy a farm here, we would not have to start up from scratch, and I would have a ready built house to live in," Maria said. The idea appealed to her.

They agreed that Tom should approach the government, and find out exactly what the situation was. It would make a lot more sense buying an established farm. With the help of the Land Bank, they could be productive in next to no time.

After a long, frustrating day at the government offices, Tom and Maria were finally given the forms they needed to apply for authority to purchase a farm. They were told, quite emphatically, that as they were both citizens of the country, they could purchase a farm providing it had not been earmarked for resettlement. They were to find the farm they wanted, and then apply for a 'Certificate of Non-Interest'.

. . . .

Two months later, they moved onto their farm. Purely by coincidence, an old friend of Tom's, who owned land near Mvurwi wanted to sell. He had suffered several heart attacks and was moving to South Africa. It all happened very quickly; Bill was in a hurry to sell, and get started in Natal, and Tom wanted to start farming before the season began. Papers were drawn up and signed, the 'Certificate of Non-Interest' was granted, and the sale went through.

All the farm equipment and stock were included in the deal. Tom's funds were in Natal, which was where Bill wanted the money. They made a flying visit to Durban to arrange the transfer and for the removal of their furniture to Zimbabwe. It all worked out perfectly.

The farm, Outlook, was in the Msoneddi district and was 3500 hectares in extent with forty percent of it arable. The remainder was mainly open grassland with Msasa and Acacia flat-top trees. This area was used for grazing cattle and sheep. The farm was undulating with a few rocky koppies.

A small river ran along the northern boundary, and there was a good sized dam in the center of the farm, below the homestead. The office, workshop sheds, and barns were behind a rocky outcrop to the rear of the house. The main tarred road from Mvurwi to Chiweshi ran through the middle of the farm.

Tom grew 20 hectares of citrus, 100 hectares of tobacco, 200 hectares of maize and 300 hectares of wheat. He had a flock of 200 sheep and a herd of 150 head of cattle. All the lands could be irrigated with water pumped from the river or the dam if there was insufficient seasonal rainfall.

Views from the house were breathtaking. The Matepatepa Mountains, to the east, were jagged and broken, with the distant ranges a light greyish color and those closer, a dark grayish-blue and sometimes purple. Looking to the south-east, across the light green farmlands and cultivated areas, crisscrossed with streams and bush lines were the dark blue Mazoe Hills; strips of which turned a cream color where the sun shone on bare granite rock faces.

Before leaving the farm, Bill had completed the plowing and prepared the seed-beds for the tobacco crop. He had also sown the seed and covered the beds with mulch. It was a well-run farm, and ready to start the season.

Tom attended a five-day refresher course at the Tobacco Training College, to bring himself up to date with the latest methods and technology. Maria, with the help of her two gardeners, busied herself cleaning, pruning and re-organizing her enormous garden. In the house, she had two maids and a cook assisting her with all the domestic chores.

Buying the farm was a risk they had to take. Tom was not prepared to delay turning his dream into reality any longer. The only cloud on the horizon was the threat of land distribution.

Because of the changing face of Africa and the Rhodesian Bush War, it had taken Tom 28 years to realize his dream.

****

Chapter 35

Bushlands, the farm Lucas was managing, was up for sale and had been on the market for some time. Concerned about his position if the farm was to be sold, Lucas approached Jeremy, his employer, to discuss the situation. Assuring Lucas that there was no need for concern, Jeremy told him that he was working on a plan, and would meet with Lucas the following week.

True to his word, a week later, Lucas was summoned to Jeremy's house. He was very nervous when he met his employer.

"Sit down Lucas. Would you like a cup of tea?" Jeremy asked as he greeted him.

"Thanks, Boss. That would be nice," Lucas said, accepting the offer with a dry mouth.

"Don't look so worried. I have a proposal that I think might interest you. I have been to see my lawyer, my accountant and my bankers who have all agreed with my proposal. It now depends on what you have to say. As you know, I have had very little to do with the running of the farm for the past few years. You have been in complete control, and have done a sterling job. I am too old and too tired now. I have some property in the South of France, where I am going to retire as soon as I can finalize things here," Jeremy explained.

"Have you got a buyer for the farm sir?" Lucas asked.

"In a way, yes I think I have. I am prepared to hand over the entire running of the farm to you for the next year. You will still be using my farm account at the bank, and I will leave signed cheques with the accountant, for you to use as and when you need the money. You will still draw a salary. If at the end of the year, the bank manager is happy with the way you have performed, and you have made a fair profit, he will be prepared to finance your purchase of the farm, with my guarantee."

"That is an incredible offer sir," Lucas stammered, taken totally by surprise.

"Well, what do you think? I will ask Jack Steele, next door, to keep an eye on you, and to help you if you ask."

Lucas stood up to shake his boss by the hand. "Thank you, sir. I will not disappoint you," he said.

Jeremy clasped his hand in response. "You and your father have worked for me for a long time, and have never let me down. It is the least I can do for you. From next week, we will be partners. In this way at least I will still have an interest in the farm. Now go and tell Tandi the good news," he said.

Outside the house, Lucas had to sit down on a bench under the tree to stop his knees shaking, while he got his emotions under control. He had never even considered, or dared to dream, of one day owning a commercial farm – it was way beyond his financial means. Although he did still have his nest egg from his Mozambique venture, it was nowhere near the price of a farm. What an opportunity this was.

After a few minutes, he got up to head home, walking faster and faster as he went; he could not wait to tell Tandi the wonderful news.

"What are you looking so pleased about? Have you been given a bonus?" Tandi greeted him with interest.

"You might say that. But much better than a bonus."

"Well, what is it then?" Tandi demanded.

Without missing out a single word of the earlier conversation, Lucas told her of Jeremy's proposal. Tears of joy rolled down her cheeks as she listened quietly to him. When he finished, she hugged him tightly.

"Whoever said all white people were no good. Come on, let's go and celebrate our good fortune with Tom and Maria."

Filling a cold box with drinks, they drove to Outlook to share their news. Tom and Maria were delighted. Lucas mused that their arrival seemed to have brought him luck; first Tom had bought a farm in the district, and now he too was going to have his farm. Who would have thought all those years ago in the police together, that the outcome would be this! Their lives seemed inexplicably intertwined.

Lucas was quite confident he could live up to the challenge; after all, he had Jack and Tom to help him. He decided too that he would get his parents to come back and live on the farm as soon as Jeremy left. After so many years of service, it was his home as much as theirs, and having his family close again would be wonderful.

****

Chapter 36

At last everything started to turn in their favor and finally, they owned their farm, and   how wonderful Maria felt. It was a large, rambling, ranch-style house, with a wide covered front veranda. There were five acres of garden, with a guest cottage, a swimming pool, and a tennis court.

A giant pepper tree stood in the middle of the lawn in the front garden. Beyond the tennis court, the manager's house stood amongst a clump of Msasa trees. The entire garden was watered by a computer controlled pop up sprinkler system. The large rose garden, with its masses of highly perfumed blooms of every color and variety, kept the house filled with magnificent arrangements.

The small orchard had plums, peaches, avocados, and pear trees. The vegetable garden produced prolifically, and after the farm staff had received their weekly rations, Maria took the surplus to a retirement village in Mvurwi. As a result of her frequent donation of vegetables, Maria was invited to join the committee responsible for running the village. The senior gardener, Samuel, had come back to work for them when John and Jill moved to Zambia.

Tom was happy, and the two boys who both came from South Africa to help them settle in, were suitably impressed. Stuart was engaged to a lovely girl, Felicity, who came with them and was a great help to Maria. Kyle was a typical young farm manager, who was enjoying his carefree lifestyle. He had grown into a big strong man with a happy teasing nature. Stuart, on the other hand, was more serious, but also enjoyed a bit of fun. The two of them together were a bad influence on their father!

Tom and Maria spent most weekends entertaining, visiting, playing tennis or golf, fishing, game viewing or sightseeing. Weekly tennis afternoons for the ladies and golf day on Thursdays, as well as the normal Saturday golf at the Country Club, kept Maria fit. One of the farmer's wives had a pottery studio, and Maria, who had taken up pottery while they were in Swaziland, went to a weekly class with Tandi.

It was good to see Tom getting back to the work he so enjoyed. Before long the farm was buzzing with activity. Once a fortnight, during the tobacco sales season, she and Tom went to Harare to attend the tobacco auctions. Maria loved going and was fascinated by the sing-song of the auctioneers. She was happy with the way things were going for them. There were rumblings about the land re-distribution, but it did not worry her – they had bought the farm with all the necessary permission from the government – they would not be affected.

Tom built a runway and a hangar on the farm, for the four-seater aircraft he had bought. They used it for the occasional trip to South Africa and Mozambique for holidays, as well as touring the country and for aerial inspections of his farm. Their maiden flight had been to Durban to attend Stuart and Felicity's wedding; a year after they moved onto Outlook.

Lucas was doing well on his farm, and his wife, Tandi, had become a good friend. Lucas and Tandi's children were growing up fast. Twice a year, Maria went to visit her mother who still refused to leave her store, and come to stay with them. The two boys came from South Africa with their families, to spend Christmas every year. They all loved coming to the farm.

Every year after Christmas, the whole family went to spend five days on a houseboat on Lake Kariba. It was the middle of summer and scorching hot by the time they reached Makuti. The road from there followed the elephant trail down the escarpment and was punctuated by great mounds of steaming green elephant dung. Herds of elephant, making their way along the trail, took no notice of the vehicles on the road. Descending towards the lake, it got even hotter, and by the time they reached their destination at midday, the temperature was well into the forties.

The houseboat was middle of the range in size, but comfortable and well appointed. It came with the captain-cum-cook and the boatman. There were three decks; the upper deck was open and covered with a canopy; on the main deck, there was the wheelhouse, the kitchen as well as the cabins and bathroom. The lower deck was crew accommodation and engine room. It was 65 foot long with twin engines, and a tender-boat that was towed along for fishing jaunts and shore trips.

Lake Kariba is such a massive stretch of water, 270 miles long and 30 miles wide, that when the wind blows the water gets extremely rough and choppy. For this reason, no boats are permitted in the middle of the lake at night, and so all the houseboats find shelter in bays around the shore-line. The boat crew did all the cooking and serving of refreshments.

Every morning, the three men went fishing for Tiger and bream, returning at midday with their catch. Kariba bream is excellent eating. Tigerfish, on the other hand, is one of the best fighting fish, but does not make good eating – there are far too many bones. The girls usually stayed on board the houseboat, game viewing and sunbathing. When they were out in deep water, well away from the edge of the lake, they swam. Crocodiles were a danger along the shores. Sunsets on Kariba were always magnificent.

At night the moored kapenta rigs looked like floating cranes, bobbing around in the swell on their steel pontoons, creating a galaxy of twinkling lights in fish-rich parts of the lake. A bright light was suspended on a winch over the water, attracting the small sardine-like fish. As soon as there are multitudes of the small fish gathered under the light feeding on the insects, the light is turned off, and the frightened fish dive straight down into the nets below. The nets are then hauled up, and the fish spread out to dry, before being bagged and sent to market. Kapenta fish is one of the most popular and cheapest sources of protein in the country.

. . . .

Tom and Maria had been on the farm for five years, and just as it was beginning to show a profit, things began to change. The legislation was passed which effectively removed the 'Willing Buyer, Willing Seller' clause put in place at the time of independence. In the next five years, a lot of white-owned farms were confiscated, with only 'reasonable' compensation paid to the owners.

As before, very few of these farms were used for the resettlement programme; most ended up in the hands of senior politicians and wealthy black businessmen, and now stood empty and unproductive.

The war-vets, who had already been paid exorbitant veterans pensions, seemed to think they could forcibly take over a fully operational commercial farm, and continue to produce crops as it had under white ownership. This was impossible as the majority of them were far too idle and did not have the necessary skills or training; they simply did not want white farmers on the land. Only those who had held senior positions, and with years of experience on farms stood a chance – but they were not included in the land reform exercise.

The majority of this 'new generation' of war-vets were merely paid thugs and had not even been born before the end of hostilities. Many of the real war-vets had become terrorists because they had been unemployed, and too lazy to work.

Never-the-less, the War Veterans Association began to put pressure on Mugabe, because the land already acquired still had not been given to them. This resulted in a further 1000 farms being listed for resettlement.

A year later the second phase Land Reform & Re-Settlement Programme was announced. This time there would be no compensation as there was no money left in the coffers – it had all been used to pay pensions and back-pay to war veterans, plus Mugabe believed the British government was responsible for paying compensation to the farmers.

Tom sensed it was going to be a struggle between the farmers refusing to give up their farms, and the Mugabe backed war-vets. Wanting to hedge his bets, Tom entered into a partnership with Ted, and they set about expanding the business.

Within a few months they owned three service stations, a workshop and farmers supply business. They employed scouts to scour the country for tractor parts and equipment that, due to the lack of foreign exchange, were unavailable in the country. They even had a runner traveling to South Africa to get parts. Sourcing diesel and petrol in bulk was a challenge; the fuel had to be paid for in advance, and to some pretty shady characters; usually connected to senior government officials.

****

Chapter 37

On his way back from the Lowveld, after a meeting with 'war-vets' in Chiredzi, Mamba and his companions stopped off at Chibi for refreshments. As he swaggered into the store, he saw an elderly Portuguese woman sitting on a chair behind the counter, knitting and watching people come in and out. He suddenly remembered the girl he had raped at school. She had come from Chibi and was Portuguese.

"Is your name da Silva?" he asked the woman gruffly.

"Yes, I am Mrs. Da Silva. What can I do for you?"

"Was your daughter at the Mission School?"

"Yes, she was. Why do you want to know about her?"

"I attended that school, and I knew her very well. We were in the same class." Turning to his men he said. "Help yourselves to whatever you want from this store. The old woman will not mind."

"You are the man who hurt her at school," the old woman's voice dropped an octave; her eyes burning into him.

"She got what she deserved," he smirked, turning away from her.

"Get out of my shop. You monster," she screamed at him.

Leaping out of her chair with amazing speed and agility, she dropped her knitting, picked up a broom and rushed at Mamba, trying to hit him with it. Mamba ducked easily, drew the pistol from his belt, and shot her twice in the chest. As she dropped to the floor, her assistant fled from the shop and disappeared.

As she lay dying slowly in a pool of blood, Mamba and his men filled some boxes with goods. Loading the boxes into their vehicle, they drove to the nearest bar for a drink, and then on to Harare.

Mamba was not concerned about the killing; the police would never come after him.

. . . .

Maria received the call from her father, who was in Chibi, around midnight. She was awake, trying not to disturb Tom who slept soundly beside her; it was almost as if she knew. Her mother was dead; she had been murdered. Why hadn't she listened and come to live with them when Maria had first suggested it? She should have been more forceful.

Although Maria did not spend much time with her mother, she adored her and was close to her. She had always kept in regular touch with her by phone. Since their arrival in Chibi after being forced to flee Mozambique during the civil war, Maria had lived with her mother until she left school. When Maria moved away from home, she had been on her own, and for the past twenty years had lived a lonely, solitary life. Maria was devastated.

Tom, who had grown very fond of the elderly Portuguese woman over the years, cursed himself for not arranging a buyer for her shop before this had happened to her. She had been getting on, and vulnerable to the young thugs.

Maria and Tom immediately rushed down to her mother's home. A group of men had robbed the shop, and when her mother had tried to chase them out, she was shot by the ringleader. Phineas, the shop assistant, who had witnessed the shooting, phoned her father and the police.

He arrived in Chibi three hours later and before the police attended the scene. He had driven 250 miles, and the police station was only a mile away!

According to Phineas, the man who shot Maria's mother wore dark glasses and walked with a limp. Once again, Mamba had come into their lives and caused heartache and misery. Was there no stopping him?

. . . .

Mamba was moved up the chain of command and transferred from the Masvingo Province to Mashonaland Central. This was the prestigious part of the country and the homeland of President Mugabe. It was a big area, but he had Sector Commanders in each district. He was given a Toyota Land Cruiser and a driver; both paid for by the government.

As a Regional Commander of the War Veterans Association or 'Brown Shirts,' he felt very important being driven around the country. He always wore his dark glasses and had taken to wearing a slouch hat with the side turned up.

His duty was to monitor all the outlying rural areas and make sure that the poorer people knew where their loyalties lay. Where he thought it necessary, they were harshly re-educated and made to understand that there was only one party that counted in the country. When they were called to vote, he was to ensure they voted for President Comrade Mugabe and his party.

Mamba's role also included the recruitment, training and political indoctrination of young boys and girls in the farming and Tribal Trust areas. For this purpose he established training camps on some farms that had been taken over by the government in the early part of the land seizures; in Concession, Centenary and Chiweshi Tribal Trust. At these camps the children were taught how to march, using sticks as guns; they had to learn how to sing political songs and songs of the Chimurenga and made to dance and chant party slogans.

"Pamberi ne Chimurenga" (forward the war), *"Pamberi Zanu PF"* (forward Zanu PF), and *"Pasi ne MDC"* (down with the MDC) they were taught to chant while they danced the *'toyi-toyi'* - an intimidating high stepping dance. The Movement for Democratic Change (MDC) was the opposition party and was getting more and more support. This had to be stopped.

In the townships, Mamba organized gangs of youths who, after their training in the camps, were sent to intimidate workers and small businesses suspected of supporting opposition to the President. These gangs paid particular attention to white-owned businesses, as Mamba's main objective was to drive all the whites out of the country. They were known to be assisting the MDC financially and were not needed.

Both these roles suited him down to the ground. He could bully as many people as he wanted; teaching them to fear and respect him, and he could have his way with as many young girls as he wanted, with no danger of being arrested by the police.

Mamba reported directly to Comrade Chenjerai 'Hitler' Hunzvi, the new leader of the 'Brown Shirts.' Hunzvi was a doctor, who had learned communism in Poland, where he had married a white woman. It was rumored that he liked to beat, bully and abuse her. Although he had not fought during the Chimurenga, as a doctor, Hunzvi could assist all veterans to get disability allowances and was close to the President.

Mamba himself received a sizeable award, with back pay for the time he had been in prison, and a good disability allowance. Through Hunzvi, Mamba and other sector leaders were able to put pressure on Mugabe to get the land away from the whites. It had already taken far too long.

As time went by, Mamba became more and more frustrated that there were still so many white farmers on the land. 'Why was it taking such a long time to chase them away? They were continually being harassed, yet they still would not move'. He could not understand what the problem was. The war-vets had been promised the land, and that they would be wealthy.

His hatred for the whites was so intense it burned inside him, making his eyes bloodshot and looked as if they were smoldering. The only time this burning hatred eased was after raping women. He still remembered quite vividly, the hatred in the eyes of the girl, whose mother he had recently killed, when he had raped her at school. Just thinking about it still gave him pleasure. There would soon be other opportunities to pleasure himself, and have his way with other white women.

At the end of February 2000, the president lost the vote for the passing of changes to the constitution, which would have given him the power to confiscate land without compensation. Mamba failed to understand why he had had to ask the voters for permission to make these changes. Why not take whatever was needed, and put all the war-vets on the land?

Infuriated by the lost vote, Mugabe ordered Hunzvi to mobilize the War Veterans for a mass invasion of white-owned farms. At last, it looked as if there was going to be some action, and Mamba prepared for the invasions. Visiting his training camps and other centers where he had placed his observers, he organized his teams of militia-youth and war-vets.

A week later, he was given the go-ahead and using trucks liberated from previously-acquired farms; the teams were dispatched. Their instructions were to move onto farms, set up base camps on each farm, near the main activity and where possible, within sight of the farmer's homes and offices. Then they were to peg out plots for the war-vets.

Mamba's teams were under orders not to attack the farmers; this would cause problems for the President. They were to try and provoke incidents by antagonizing the farmers in any way possible. If a farmer reacted violently, they could retaliate with violence.

****

Chapter 38

Within days of Mugabe declaring white farmers to be enemies of the state, a truckload of brain-washed thugs arrived on Outlook. Tom was extremely annoyed when a group of eight or nine of these scruffy, dirty, aggressive individuals pitched up at his office to confront him. An 'official,' armed with a clipboard, seemed to be in charge.

"I am Gurupira. I am the leader of the war veterans in this area," the man with the clipboard, and the oldest of the group announced.

"Yes. What do you want on my farm?" Tom asked.

"I am authorized to tell you to stop farming immediately. We are taking this farm," he said belligerently, with the rest of his cronies nodding in agreement.

"This farm has not been listed for resettlement. You must leave now. You are trespassing on my property," Tom responded, struggling to keep calm and not lose his temper.

"We are not going to leave. This is our farm now. I am going to peg it for the war veterans," the man informed Tom, and then turning away he went back, with his support team, to where the rest of the mob waited expectantly.

The Farmers Organisation had warned them this might happen and had advised them not to react, but to stay calm. Negotiations were taking place, and the invasions would soon be stopped. This was easier said than done; it was not easy for Tom to stay calm, and to keep from losing his temper, with this blatant invasion of his property.

"My farm had just been invaded. They have started pegging plots for themselves," Tom told the controller, over the Agri-Alert farm radio.

"There have been some reports of farm invasions this morning. Just sit tight. The Farmers Organisation is speaking to government authorities, to get this problem resolved as quickly as possible," he was told by the farmer on radio duty.

"These sods have told me that I must stop farming."

"I wouldn't take any notice of that. Just let them get on with their pegging, and don't interfere with them. I will keep you posted."

Feeling angry and sick in his stomach, Tom watched while the group marched down the farm road. The leader strutted out in front, with his clipboard, looking very important. He paced out fifty paces and tied a knot in the grass on the edge of the road (where there was no grass, he pushed a stick into the ground) then pointed to one of the followers to indicate that that was their piece of ground. Then he paced another fifty paces and repeated the performance.

When they had all been allocated a piece of ground, they gathered back under a Marula tree near the entrance to the farm, where they proceeded to set up camp. Fires were lit and the women set about cooking food. Later, as the sun set, they started singing war songs as loudly as they could, while they danced around the fire. It carried on for three or four hours.

That night, the farm radio buzzed with reports from all the farms that had been invaded in the district. It was all very worrying. What was going to happen next? Where was law and order?

The following morning, Tom was discussing the day's work with his manager, when the 'war-vet' leader swaggered into the office, uninvited, to tell him that the farm had been pegged. He said they were going away to get 'our stuff' but would be back within a couple of days. Two hours later they had all disappeared leaving a hand-painted sign hanging over Tom's signpost; "Gurupira's Farm."

With a sigh of relief, Tom and Maria hoped that it had all been a bluff and an attempt to intimidate them, as well as a demonstration of their disregard for the law.

As a precaution, Tom decided to move his aircraft to Mount Hampden airport, outside Harare. It could easily be destroyed by the farm invaders, and he was not going to take that risk. The plane might be their lifesaver sometime in the future,

Over the next couple of days, they heard numerous reports of farmers being beaten, some executed, and of women being raped. A Rusape farmer and his manager were abducted and killed; a farmer in Matabeleland was killed in a full-scale attack on his farm, while the police raided farms in the area confiscating firearms.

"Do not retaliate. Keep calm. But do not give in to their demands," was the daily message coming from the Commercial Farmers Union, who were desperately trying to enlist help from the courts to force the government to stop the madness. But Court orders to disband were ignored.

The madness did not stop. A week after pegging Tom's farm and disappearing, some of them were back. This time they came with sheets of corrugated iron, poles, bundles of thatch grass, chickens, dogs, old wheelbarrows and old-fashioned farm implements. Chopping down trees at random, they proceeded to build huts for themselves; on the plots, they had been allocated.

One morning Maria noticed that the gardeners were exhausted, and so she asked them why they were so tired.

"Madam, at ten o'clock at night the war-vets take us from our houses. They force us to run to Chiweshi, where we are made to dance and sing songs of the Chimurenga. Then we are forced to run back to the farm. It is three o'clock in the morning when we get back to our homes."

It was a twenty-mile round trip they were made to run.

"Keep calm. Do nothing!"

****

Chapter 39

Bushlands had belonged to Lucas for six years, and he was doing well. When he bought the farm from his previous employer, a few of the workers had been '*majeras*?' (jealous) of him being the owner and their employer. It had been acceptable for him to be the manager, but as the owner of the farm, and the person responsible for paying them, it was a different matter. He was black, and so they felt they were entitled to a bigger wage and a share of the profit. He quickly got rid of them before they stirred up trouble.

Lucas' children were at boarding school in Harare, and he and Tandi were very happy with their life. That was before the troubles started. Now they were extremely worried by what was going on.

Mugabe accused the whites of being "Enemies of the country - who must give up their farms and go back to where they have come from." Lucas could not understand his thinking; was it not the commercial farmers who were the backbone of the country; was Zimbabwe not the 'Bread Basket' of Africa? Did Mugabe really think that by putting the 'war-vets' on the land, they would be capable of producing sufficient food to feed the nation and to export the surplus? It made no sense at all.

Jeremy had sent Lucas to Tobacco Training College to learn how to become an efficient farm manager, and it had taken him a long time to know how to run a commercial farm properly. He still needed the help of his friends from time to time, when he had problems. How could these people, with little or no education, or any formal training, become productive farmers? And where would they get the money to keep a farm going? The government did not have the funds left in its coffers; it had all gone due to the massive payments being made to war veterans.

When farm invasions began, Bushlands was not among those invaded. Tom's farm was occupied along with about 50 other farms nearby. Lucas presumed it was because he was a black man. Both he and Tom had purchased their farms with the authority of the government, and farms that had been purchased, since independence, with official permission, should be left alone.

When they heard that squatters had moved onto Outlook farm, Lucas and Tandi went over to visit Tom and Maria, knowing their friends would need support. It was disturbing to see that the farm signpost had been turned around and two new hand-painted signs were hanging over it; *"Gurupira's Farm,"* and below the other one read *"No go Area. War Veterans Ahead"*. Under the big Marula tree, near the entrance to the farm, was a makeshift tent where a few scruffy individuals sat on logs around a fire.

"You have always told me that Tom doesn't lose his temper easily. But I'm sure this will make him very angry," Tandi said.

"Well, I hope we don't have the same problem. I am sure it will all fizzle out soon. When they don't get a reaction, they will get bored and move away."

"I don't know about that. They look as if they have settled in for good."

"I am sure the government will soon realize they are destroying the economy of the country and have these people removed," Lucas said.

How wrong he was, that had been nearly three years ago. The year after Outlook was invaded, Bushlands was targeted, and squatters moved onto the farm. Lucas was accused of being "A puppet of the whites." He was permitted to continue farming a small portion of the farm but was expected to prepare and plant other areas for the squatters. He refused to do this.

As he could not risk having his elderly parents molested, Lucas rented a house in the village and moved them there. The two children were at boarding school in Harare and only came home on the weekends.

. . . .

Ecstatic with the early stages of the farm invasions, Mamba received reports from his commanders that they had pegged some farms. The majority of farm owners, when confronted by the war-vets, backed off and left them to carry on pegging.

It gave him a good feeling of power knowing that he was in command of a huge area of the country, and the white farmers could not stop him from doing exactly what he wanted to do on their farms.

He eagerly awaited reports of farmers becoming angry and resorting to violence. That was when he would get involved.

He didn't have long to wait. A farmer in Rusape was creating problems with the invaders, and so Mamba went to see what could be done. He issued instructions that the farmer and his black manager should be taken to another area for 'education.' They were caught in the farm office, tied up with wire and taken to another district. During their 'education,' they were both killed. Their death should have served as a lesson to other farmers, who did not like having their farms invaded.

Mamba was called to a small farm on the outskirts of Harare where the owner had sworn at his gardener. War-vet youths who received the report surrounded the house and waited for him to arrive. He was excited about this problem, as it was believed that there was a young white man, and two white women in the house.

On his arrival, Mamba banged on the door, and when it was opened by the white man, he stormed into the house, accompanied by four or five others. Two young white women cowered in the sitting room, whimpering in fear, as they watched the man being tied up, and cried out aloud when he was beaten with sticks.

Walking over to one of the women, Mamba grabbed a handful of her yellow hair, and dragged her screaming, to the bedroom. He ordered the other woman to be tied up, and the man brought to the bedroom. Flinging the woman onto the bed, and with two youths holding her down, he raped her while her gagged husband kicked and struggled desperately.

When Mamba had finished with her, the rest of the youths raped her and the other woman. Leaving them to get on with it, Mamba went back to Concession. He had a lot of work to do and had had his fun for the day.

This little incident gave Mamba a great deal of pleasure. After leaving the scene, he regretted not having had the time to have his way with the second woman. It was too late to go back, besides there would be other opportunities.

Back at his base, he checked on the progress of farm invasions in the northern area. One of the Army Brigadiers wanted to take over a farm there, and Mamba was to oversee the invasion by the war-vets before the army got there.

When he arrived on the farm, he found that there had already been a full-scale attack by the army with the farm owner, his wife, their two children, and three dogs all hacked to death. The Brigadier was strutting around the garden, inspecting his new property, while the bodies of the dead were dragged to the garage, and thrown in a pile. This was how the army worked.

****

Chapter 40

Harassment by the squatters continued month after month, with no sign of them being ordered to leave by the government. Some of them built their pole and dagga huts in the middle of lands, where crops of maize were growing. The crop was theirs now, or so they told Tom. Like most farmers in the district, Tom decided to stop farming until the nightmare was over.

All the farm workers were kept on, but paid a reduced wage and still had housing, food, medical care and education for their families on the farm. This was a huge drain on Tom's capital, but he felt it was necessary. He would need them when he was able to start farming again. They were loyal to him, and although not happy about it, they understood the situation perfectly.

All the farmer's meetings were held at the Country Club. This was also where they came to boost morale, get feedback from the CFU, and to discuss tactics and plans to try and resolve the land issues. It was a safe-haven where families could play sport, and enjoy socializing. But this changed one night when the local war vet leader accused the farmers of using it as a venue to hatch plots against them and moved a group in to occupy the club.

With an abundance of food and drink on the premises, it was an ideal place to occupy and to demonstrate their authority. The police were advised of the situation, but once again chose to ignore calls for the removal of the thugs. After a couple of days, having consumed all the liquor and food, and with no reaction from the community, they got bored and moved off. It was another attempt to intimidate and prevent farmers and their families from having any enjoyment.

A distress call on the radio from Mandini farm, adjacent to Bushlands, told them that a large group of drunk and aggressive war-vets was demanding food and drink from the farmer's elderly mother. The war-vets were having a '*Jongwe*' (gathering with intent to intimidate) and had made fires on the lawn in front of the house. They helped themselves to one of the owner's sheep and were defiantly cooking the meat on the fires. Peter, the farm owner, was not there at the time and his mother, who was on her own, had locked herself inside the house. It was a thatch-roofed house, and there was a danger that the house would be set alight.

Tom together with Ted, Jack, Lucas, and six other farmers, all bundled into their vans and drove over to show support, and if necessary, try to rescue the elderly woman. On their arrival, and stopping well short of the homestead, they were confronted by a police inspector, who angrily confiscated a pair of binoculars from one of their group.

"You are not allowed to use binoculars and cameras. You can collect the item from the police station in two weeks." the inspector shouted, obviously not wanting them to see what was happening.

"We want to know what is happening on this farm. There is an old woman alone in the house, and we want to make sure that she is safe," Steve, the group leader, said.

"I am handling the situation. It is under control," the police inspector retorted.

"It does not look like you have anything under control. We are going to wait here to make sure that nothing happens to her," Steve said.

"If you stay here, you will annoy the war-vets, and there will be trouble. You must leave now," the inspector ordered.

"Okay. We will back off a little, but we are not leaving until we are satisfied there is no life-threatening danger to the old lady," Steve told him.

The 'war-vets,' on seeing them parked on the side of the road, quickly grouped, and came running towards them, chanting and waving their sticks, knobkerries, and pangas (machetes) threateningly. The police inspector stood aside and watched.

The rescue group leader gave the farmers the order to back off. They were not armed, and to resist would have created an incident, which would give the invaders an excuse to go on the rampage. This undoubtedly would result in injuries, destruction of property, and even death.

Tom found this extremely frustrating; there was an elderly woman in a dangerous situation, and they had to back off. It was not the way he had been trained - to back off is to show weakness. After a couple of hours, the situation was diffused, and when the mob had calmed down, they dispersed. Once Peter arrived, and was escorted into his home safely, the backup group - satisfied that there was no longer any danger - returned to their farms. It had taken amazing restraint to back off and give in to these illegal invaders, but a good thing they did – the situation could very easily have turned nasty.

This had been the first militant confrontation in the district, and they all found it very disturbing to witness the police openly supporting these criminals and invaders. Tom and Lucas were ashamed to see what had become of the once world-renowned police force.

International outrage at Mugabe's involvement with the Congo's 'Blood Diamond' scandal resulted in the withdrawal of most foreign aid, leaving the government short of funds to pay for fuel. Diesel and petrol were in short supply, and people had to wait in long queues to fill their tanks. In Harare, some drivers left their cars parked for more than 24 hours before being able to get a few liters.

Most people soon became accustomed to queuing for fuel and would take deck chairs, tables, umbrellas, cards, and books; some even took picnic lunches with them as they had done during the war. With preference being given to the cities, it became more and more difficult for Tom to get supplies of fuel for their service stations. The fuel that did arrive in the tanks was second grade and full of impurities.

The shortage of foreign currency made it difficult for merchants to import food and clothing, and so the shelves in supermarkets became depleted.

Gadaffi, the Libyan leader, on a state visit after an OAU (Organization of African Unity) meeting in Lusaka, toured the Mvurwi district with his massive cavalcade. He viewed some of the properties (citrus estates, hotels, hunting concessions, and farms) he had been offered in repayment for fuel, and stopped on one of the farms to address the resident war-vets.

After praising them for their efforts, he advised them to do as he had done in Libya; chase all the white people out of the country. The 'war-vets,' taking him at his word, stepped up the tempo of farm invasions, and the intimidation of the white farmers and their families.

From then on, Tom was confronted at the gates almost every day by scruffy 'war-vets' with threats and demands.

"Your house is too big for you. There are only two of you living in the house. You must share the house with us," one of them shouted at him.

One Sunday when friends came for a braai, they allowed their children to swim in the reservoir. The war-vets were outraged. "Why are you spoiling the water? It is our water now, and you must not wash in it," they ranted.

It was getting harder and harder to ignore the jibes and turn away. Reports were surfacing from all corners of the country of farmers losing their tempers and retaliating. Inevitably they were attacked and their dogs beaten or killed. Some farmers were killed or very badly beaten and their wives raped.

....

In the spring, Tom and Maria went to Zululand to attend Kyle's wedding in Eshowe. His bride, Rosa, was the daughter of a sugar-cane farmer and so he and Tom had a lot in common and got on well. The reception was held at the country club up in the hills. Spending time with the boys was good. Felicity and Rosa were good friends, and by all accounts, the four of them spent a lot of time together. The boys had both married well.

On their return trip, Tom and Maria met up with some friends in the east of Zimbabwe, to spend a few days in the mountains. Winding their way up into the Eastern Highlands, they were fascinated by the vast amount of terracing on the sides of some of the steep slopes.

It was obvious that these terraces had been constructed a long time ago. Resembling the hillside rice paddies in the Far East, they most certainly were not made by the local inhabitants and must have been constructed under the supervision of Arab slave traders. The Chimanimani mountain range lay halfway between the Zimbabwe Ruins and the ancient port of Sofala on the Mozambique coast.

Staying in the lovely thatched Kiledo Lodge, high in the mountains, they spent their days exploring the Chipinge area. In the early morning, as the mist lifted, they were treated to a spectacle of unparalleled beauty. The high peaks which surrounded them, looked as if they had been carved from blocks of quartzite. Patches of white sparkled like sugar candy on the slopes. Numerous crystal-clear streams flowed through the valleys, bordered by ferns and wild orchids, with bushes of wild sweet peas and masses of purple heather. The whole area had a magical, fairytale quality.

While sitting on the balcony of their lodge, enjoying lunch-time drinks, they were entertained by a family of vervet monkeys showing off in the trees, while a variety of birds called to each other.

With very little war-vet activity in the area, they were able to visit tea and coffee estates and a large natural forest. The forest was an unspoiled area, full of immense Mahogany, Teak, and other indigenous trees. A long walk through the forest took them to the 'Big Tree.' This giant Red Mahogany with a height of well over 250 feet and a diameter of 15 feet, had been one of the tallest in Africa before part of the top was broken off during a recent cyclone. The hushed quietness at the base of this magnificent 1000-year-old giant, with the sunlight and shadows chasing each other around, seemed to make time stand still.

The wonderful peaceful break made going home that much harder. Getting back to the farm was no longer a pleasant experience. As they drove through the farm gates, they were confronted by yet another new hut.

....

Any distraction from the stress and strain of the constant harassment was welcome. On the 21st June 2001, there was a total eclipse of the sun. Tom and Maria joined friends in the hills on the edge of the escarpment, beyond Centenary, where the road dropped down into the Zambezi valley. It was the most northern part of the country, and where they would get the best view of the eclipse. Hundreds of people gathered there, mostly from Harare. Beer and food were available from the vendor's tents that had been set up.

At midday, as the moon moved in front of the sun, it gradually grew darker, until day turned to night and it was pitch black. The birds stopped singing, and nothing stirred. The silence and stillness, in the middle of that hot day, was eerie. Then as quickly as it had vanished the sun reappeared from behind the moon and seemed to breathe life back into everything; the people, the birds, the animals, and even the vegetation and countryside. It was a phenomenon not many had witnessed before.

....

Early in 2002, the drums started beating again, summoning everyone to a Star Rally (ZANU PF) or 'Pungwe' in Mvurwi. The farmers were ordered to provide transport for their workers to attend. Most of them refused to do so, but for some refusal was not an option, and they had to oblige.

The Agricultural Supply office was situated at the intersection of the roads from Chiweshi Tribal, Harare and Centenary. A large number of the supporters passed the office, en route to the meeting, including truckloads of paid ZANU PF youths, wearing yellow party t-shirts. These supporters were brought in from other areas to intimidate the locals. As they passed the office where Tom, Ted, Maria, and Elsie were watching, they chanted loudly and shook their clenched fists, iron bars, and machetes. It was very frightening for Maria and Elsie, who had never before been exposed to such threatening behavior.

Most businesses closed their doors for the day, and the farmers kept well away from Mvurwi. The sight of a white person was likely to spark a violent reaction from the crowds. A few hours after the crowds had passed Tom's office, he decided that he should go into the village to make sure everything was in order and that none of his staff were being subjected to violence.

Arriving in Mvurwi, he was surprised to find it almost deserted. The big rally had fizzled out when the so-called supporters had not been given the t-shirts or the beer and refreshments they were promised.

Two weeks later, an announcement was made over the national radio ordering all farmers to leave within 24 hours or face prosecution and imprisonment. Again, the order was ignored resulting in 19 farmers in the Chonhoyi area being arrested. Their heads were shaved, and they were released 17 days later, on the eve of the 11th March elections.

Most of the men in the district also shaved their heads, so that those who had been imprisoned could not be singled out. This incident was more than a little unsettling, with the police openly demonstrating once again, that they were not upholding the rule of law in the country.

....

Every Friday the national newspaper, *The Herald*, published a list of farms that were to be taken by the government for land re-distribution. If a farm listed had been purchased after independence, and with permission from the government, the owners would rush to their lawyers, and get it de-listed. A couple of weeks later it was re-listed, and the farm owner would have to go through the whole costly process again.

So far, there had been a lot of pegging and squatting, but very little sign of farming, by the land-hungry war-vets.

For a while, there would be no acts of intimidation or violence, but then, as if someone had stirred them into action, the squatters would rise up and wreak havoc again. Tom received reports from his gardener, Samuel, that they were having meetings at night.

Then the fires started.

****

Chapter 41

Bush-fires burned everywhere, and a blanket of smoke covered the countryside. The destruction of the natural forestation, so carefully preserved for years by the conservation conscious farmers, was rapidly being destroyed. The squatters would light the fires to smoke bees out of dead trees and to flush wild animals into their snares.

One lunchtime, a group of the youth militia brigade, appeared at the kitchen door with one of the security guards.

"You must come with us," the oldest of the group said to Tom.

"Why? You have no right to come to my house and make demands."

"There is a meeting, and you must attend."

"When you need me to attend a meeting, I must be warned in advance."

"If you are warned of a meeting, it will give you time to prepare. We guarantee that you will be safe."

Knowing that there was no chance of refusing their demand, Tom turned to Maria and said. "Tell the office that I will be late getting back, and let Ted know what is happening here."

Trying to appear calm, Tom was marched off into the bush by the bunch of hired thugs. He had not heard of this happening to anyone else in the district, and the further he walked the more worried he became. He started to sweat, his nails bit into the palms of his hands, and his eyes danced around searching the bush for signs of danger.

The only farmers he had heard of being taken away had been either killed or badly beaten. However, he knew that if he showed any sign of weakness, it would be the end of him. Eventually, they reached a spot in the middle of the bush, where a group of about fifty war-vets was gathered and seated on the ground in the shade of the Musasa trees.

Tom was told to sit on a rock, in front of the gathering. The meeting began with the usual raising of clenched fists and shouting of the slogan "*Pamberi Zanu.*" Tom knew they expected him to follow suit, but they knew he did not support their party and had he done so it would have displayed weakness, and so he did not salute.

He was asked by various members of the group, what his intentions were on the farm. He explained to them that, as they had taken over the farm, he had stopped his farming operations and was now running his business in Msoneddi, but that he was not leaving the farm. Tom needed to exert a lot of self-control not to show the anger and frustration he felt at being ordered around and questioned by these people. It was his farm, and he was the man in charge, not them. They had no right to be there.

During the proceedings, Samuel arrived. He had been running, and was out of breath and sweating when he stopped next to Tom. After making the ZANU PF salute, he asked for permission to address the meeting. He then proceeded to explain to them that Tom was a good man; that he did not interfere with them, and had supplied them with water, pumped from the borehole at his expense.

Eventually, after a lot of discussions, and much to his relief, Tom was allowed to go, but was told he could stay on in the house 'for the time being.' They were making a point - they were in charge now.

Maria, in the meantime, was in a state; she did not know what to do, and could not raise anyone on the radio. But, thanks to the intervention by Samuel, Tom returned unharmed albeit a little shaken by the experience. From then on the war-vets made more and more ridiculous demands. Tom was marched off to meetings now and then, and there were even threats of joint occupation of the house.

The incidents that were taking place almost daily, must have been organized by the senior member in the area. With so many of them claiming to be local leaders, nobody knew who the main instigator was.

One of their neighbors was away in Harare when his wife and children got a nasty shock. They were out walking on their farm when they were accosted by a group of youths who chased them back to the house. They locked themselves in, but the youths proceeded to slaughter all their poultry and throw stones through the windows. On the husband's return, he was beaten up and required twenty stitches in his head.

An elderly couple, both in their seventies, was attacked in their garden by a gang of 15 youths wielding sticks and machetes. With the help of their gardener they were able to beat the attackers off, but not before all three had been quite badly injured. The matter was reported to the police, who did nothing.

Another family was forced to take refuge in their 'safe' bedroom, while an angry mob ransacked their home, killed their dogs, and stole all the food and valuables from the house. This invasion lasted most of the night. Farmers from the area waited helplessly at the farm gates for the police, who never arrived. They claimed they had no transport.

In yet another attempt to incite the farmers to react violently, war-vets pegged the Mvurwi Cemetery. This enraged the community who were unable to get the police to intervene. On some farms, the war-vets were known to have hamstrung cattle (cut tendons on the hind legs with pangas).

Tom and Maria, along with most farmers, got involved with promoting the opposition party, the Movement for Democratic Change (MDC). They had to try to get Mugabe and his ZANU PF out of power if there was to be any hope of restoring law and order. In the build-up to the elections, they were lucky to escape arrest. They scattered leaflets, and painted slogans on the road signs along the roads and in villages. Tom's drivers bravely volunteered to assist.

On Election Day a 75-year-old farmer from Mvurwi was arrested for assisting in the monitoring of the elections. He was in possession of the portable radios they had planned to use to monitor the polling stations, to prevent interference with the ballot boxes. It was yet another display by the police of their non-adherence to the rule of law.

Some believed that during the counting, Mugabe was in hiding in Libya, and only returned after the announcement of the bogus results. With rigging, ZANU PF won the election, but only by a narrow margin. Mugabe was furious and vowed to teach all those who supported the opposition a lesson.

With 20000 of its citizens in Zimbabwe and the possibility of mass slaughter, Britain spoke of rescue plans. If it became necessary, the UK Consulate advised that they make their way to South African, where planes would be waiting to fly them to England. They were further advised, however, that on arrival in the UK they should not expect any assistance from the government, and would have to fend for themselves.

From Harare to the South African border was 600 miles, and after losing everything they owned; including all their funds, it was hard to see how they would manage in England. All they were being offered was a free passage. It was better to stay put and ride out the storm.

With ZANU PF once again firmly entrenched, the war veterans were motivated into a huge increase in their effort to get the whites off the land. Farmers and their families were locked in their houses, terrorized, their pets killed, their homes and farms ransacked, their cattle hamstrung, and they were continually harassed and intimidated in every possible way.

And the rest of the world did nothing to help.

....

One morning, not long after the election results were announced, Tom drove up to the security gate leading out of the homestead yard and was confronted by a group of thirty to forty individuals. As usual, most of the men were youths and the women middle-aged. They were in an aggressive mood and blocked the gate.

Realizing what was about to take place, Tom quickly reversed back to the house and parked his van in the garage. Calling the dogs into the house, he locked the garage doors as he shouted to Maria and the domestic staff to lock all the doors and windows. Then he went to the radio to report to the controller that a '*Jongwe*' was about to take place on Outlook.

Within minutes, the mob of angry individuals, all armed with sticks and pangas, broke through the gates, surrounded the house and started shouting demands for food and drink. The war-vets dragged dead branches and firewood to the middle of the lawn where they made a big fire. Tom, Maria, and their domestic staff barricaded themselves in the main bedroom, which was reasonably secure and where the radio was. This was not a situation that lent itself to 'Staying Calm.' They were all terrified and knew there would be no physical help, only the usual show of support in response to their call for assistance.

"Tom you must all try to keep calm. We are doing all we can to help," the duty controller said.

"Are you chaps safe?" Ted asked, also responding to the call.

"We are for the moment. We are locked in the bedroom. There are about forty of them dancing and singing around a big fire on the front lawn."

"Ok Tom. I am gathering the troops. We have sent a vehicle to collect a policeman, and the other chaps will be here shortly. Then we will come down to show our presence and support. We will be there as soon as possible."

They huddled together, peering through the curtains now and then at the now volatile and aggressive mob cavorting in the garden. One of Tom's sheep was dragged bleating across the lawn to the fire, where it was slaughtered, disemboweled and skinned. The carcass was tossed onto the fire to cook. They had managed to get liquor from somewhere, and were drinking as they danced; chanting, clapping their hands and singing war songs, while they waited for the meat to cook.

"*Pasi ma British settlers*," they chanted. (Down with the British settlers) and "*Pasi MDC*." (Down with the Movement for Democratic Change)

Inside the house, the small group waited for Mvurwi Security and the farmers to arrive with the police, in the hope that they would be able to get the crowd to disperse. It was difficult keeping the dogs quiet inside the house; they were getting quite frantic wanting to get outside to chase the intruders away.

The housemaids, Catherine and Joyce, clutched each other's hands, sitting wide-eyed on the floor in the corner of the room. Tom and Maria kept watching at the windows.

"Where are Darakin, Samuel and the gardeners?" Maria asked the young girls.

"Madam, I saw them running to their houses when you called to us," Catherine replied.

"I am sure they will have got out of the way. If I know Samuel, he will be halfway to Msoneddi to report to Ted," Tom assured Maria.

It seemed like hours before help arrived at the front gate, and a policeman approached the noisy mob. After speaking briefly to the ringleaders, he went back to the vehicles at the gate. Taking no notice of anything the policeman might have said to them, the 'war-vets' continued with their '*Jongwe*,' sitting around eating the half cooked meat.

"Come in Outlook," the radio crackled to life.

"Go ahead," Tom responded

"You must just sit tight for now. They refuse to disperse, but we will wait here until they have calmed down," John, the Mvurwi Security manager, assured him.

"Thanks, John. There's not much else we can do. The bastards are so unpredictable you don't know what they are planning to do next."

Once they had satisfied their hunger, and their lust for violence, they calmed down, lost interest and started to move off, leaving the garden trampled and full of rubbish. They took the intestines of the sheep wrapped in the skin with them. Some of them even used Maria's garden as a toilet, a sign of their disdain.

Tom and Maria were lucky. They had not had their house broken into, they had not had their dogs killed or maimed, and they had survived the ordeal without being injured in any way. It was a frightening experience for them and their staff. They knew that things might have been different, and a lot more unpleasant if the farmers had not arrived to show support. The policeman had merely asked them to finish their '*Jongwe*' and then to 'please' disperse.

They felt like they had gone through the worst now. If the 'vets' had intended to do them any harm, surely this would have been the time. Perhaps it was another attempt to force some sort of reaction. Instead, what it did was to strengthen Tom and Maria's resolve, and make them even more determined not to give in and leave their farm.

Tom noticed that from then on Maria became a lot less tolerant of the war-vets, even refusing to speak with the local 'Chairwoman,' an unpleasant character who seemed to enjoy antagonizing her.

They joined a group of farmers and their wives and went to Kanyemba, on the banks of the Zambezi River, for four days of Tiger fishing. While they were there, Tom and Maria were introduced to the Vadoma tribe or 'Ostrich People' who had always lived in the area. Because they were forbidden to marry outside the tribe, one in every five born had the three middle toes missing, and the two outer toes turned inward. It gave their feet the appearance of 'ostrich feet.' It is a defect that has been passed on from generation to generation.

These people spoke Portuguese, and so Maria was able to communicate easily with them and learned a bit about their culture. Apparently, in pre-David Livingstone times, there had been a Portuguese trading post at Kanyemba.

In May the farmers were all given 45 days to stop production on their farms, and another 45 days to leave their properties. Tom, along with most of the other farmers, took this order to the courts, again in the hope that the law might prevail. Meanwhile, representatives of the Commercial Farmers Union were engaged in talks with senior government officials, in a last-ditch attempt to resolve the standoff.

As time went by, more and more farmers rented or purchased houses in Harare, and other towns and cities around the country. They moved what equipment and possessions they had left to these houses, and when it became too unbearable, many of them moved with their families. The men commuted back and forth, managing their farms as best they could. Although most of them had stopped farming operations, they still had to show they had not abandoned their land. Some of them did eventually give up the struggle altogether and left.

The war-vets were constantly at the back gate demanding one thing or another. If it was not for the use of the barns, it was to carry out an inventory of all the equipment. They wanted to graze their cattle in the garden as it was a fenced area. They wanted to store what little maize and pumpkins they had grown in the grading sheds.

They wanted to slaughter stolen cattle on the loading ramp, and on several occasions, while Tom and Maria were at work, they did just that. They wanted Tom to plow their lands for them and to plant their crops at his expense. They wanted Tom to supply electricity to their homes. They wanted to chase the domestic staff out of their houses because they were supporters of the opposition so that they could move in themselves.

"We demand" and "We want" and "You must" every day. It began to wear everyone down, and it was not surprising that some farmers gave up.

The situation got worse by the day. With all the farm stoppages, food production in the country fell by 70 percent. The farm workers were not being paid a full wage because they were not working, but were fortunate to have housing, food and some pay. Those on farms whose owners had left were less fortunate; they had nothing and were forced off the land by invaders. They were supporters of the opposition party, and according to the war-vets, were not entitled to stay.

....

Tom and Maria were on their way home from Harare and approaching Msoneddi when Maria suddenly said, "Tom, stop the car. There's the goat."

"Where is he?" asked Tom, as he pulled up on the side of the road.

"There he is up on top of that big rock," Maria pointed to the top of a small koppie.

"Hell, look at the size of him. He must be the biggest goat I have ever seen," Tom said, admiring the animal.

"Do you think he is the one they say is the guardian of the district?" Maria wondered.

"By the size of him, and by the way, he is gazing around as if it were his kingdom, I would say so."

"What a magnificent long black coat and beard he has," Maria observed as they drove on. It was the first time they had seen the 'Guardian of Msoneddi.'

A couple of weeks later Tom heard from one of his laborers that the goat had disappeared, and it was suspected that it had been killed and eaten by the war-vets.

Tom decided it was time to get rid of all his livestock, and sold all the cattle and sheep on the next auction at the sale pens. The low price he received was better than the risk of having them all stolen, and slaughtered by war-vets.

It was the middle of summer with the warm days usually followed by afternoon showers of rain. But there had been very little rain for some time, and the countryside was dry. In the past week, it had been building up for more than a shower until one night the heavens opened up with a tremendous thunderstorm. Tom and Maria sat on the veranda, having their sundowners, watching the approaching storm, with dark clouds and lightning rolling in their direction.

Loud crashes of thunder, accompanied by heavy rain falling on the roof, made it almost impossible to speak and drove them indoors. The thunder was preceded by a series of spectacular, violent flashes of lightning; attracted by the granite surrounding the house. The jagged bolts sizzled as they struck the rocks. The storm lasted most of the night with a lot of rain falling.

"After that storm last night, I'm surprised we haven't come across a few *nyokas* (snakes) hiding in the house. Do you realize that in all the years we have been on this farm, we haven't had a snake anywhere near the house?" Tom said when the storm had finally passed. "I think the staff should check everywhere in the house."

"I have already instructed them to do so. But yes, you're quite right, come to think of it I haven't even seen any snakes in the garden either," Maria said.

"With the granite koppie just behind the house, and the rocks all around us you'd think it was a perfect haven for snakes. It just seems strange that there are none about; the dogs and cats must be doing a good job in keeping them away," he concluded.

"Well, I'm quite happy not to have any around. I hope they continue to keep away," Maria said.

It was as if they had wished snakes on themselves. In the week after the storm, three snakes were killed trying to slither into the house - a large puff adder followed by two cobras. The last cobra was nearly three paces long and very aggressive, charging quickly as soon as it saw them. It was a Mozambique spitting cobra with deadly venom. Samuel disposed of it with a long stick, before it could strike or spit venom at them or the dogs who were eager to help kill this nasty creature.

****

Chapter 42

Maria had trouble sleeping at night. Every time Tom was forced to march off to attend meetings in the middle of the bush, she had visions of him being killed by the war vets. The ringleader on the farm, who had taken the place of Gurupira, was a woman claiming to be the chairman. She stopped them on some occasions, to ask for a lift to Mvurwi.

Maria never wanted to oblige her, but Tom said that it would only antagonize her, and make matters worse if they refused. And so, as much as he hated it, he always gave her a lift as far as Msoneddi. Whenever possible, she seemed to take great delight in trying to annoy Maria.

"One of these days, I will share your dining room table with you," she said, to Maria, on one occasion.

"No, you won't. I will never sit at a table with you, and you will never come inside my house."

"Your wife is too cheeky," she said to Tom when he dropped her off at the crossroads.

Business was not good. More than half the farmers in the district had left, and so the demand for spares and equipment had almost stopped. Their service stations were not as busy as they had been, but because of fuel shortage in the country, continued to run dry.

Tom spent most of his time sourcing fuel in Harare and then having to accompany the tankers back to their service stations. It was far easier for them to offload at stations in or near Harare. The fuel had to be paid for in advance, and the only guarantee that it would arrive was to stay with the tanker from filling to delivery.

Not wanting to spend time alone at home, Maria spent most of her time in the office. She kept herself busy controlling the finance and chasing account holders who also had to pay in advance for their estimated monthly usage. Now they had a new breed of customer; those who tried to get everything for nothing – the war-vets.

Tom was in Harare. He had just called to let her know that he was on his way home, and would be back in an hour. Maria wandered out of the office to the forecourt, to make sure the attendants were checking the tires and windscreens on the customer's cars after topping them up with fuel.

As she was about to step outside, she froze in mid-stride. There, sitting in the passenger seat of a Land Cruiser, parked at the pumps, was the man responsible for her nightmares all of these years. He sat there with his dark glasses on and a hat with the side turned up, looking very important. It was Mamba.

Turning quickly, and almost tripping up as she did so, Maria hurried back into her office. She had gone cold. She prayed he had not seen her, and that he would not follow her inside. Tom must not get back before he left. What was the monster doing here?

No sooner had she got her emotions under control when Kelvin, one of the petrol attendants, knocked on the door of her office.

"Excuse me, Madam," he said. "This man wants to open an account for fuel. I have told him that he must pay a month in advance," he said, ushering the man into her office. Mamba stood in front of her desk wearing his dark glasses and with the hat still on his head.

"Yes, that is the way it works. You must pay us a deposit to cover what you think you will use in a month," Maria managed to blurt out, hoping her shaking voice would not give her away.

"Why must I pay for one month in advance?" he asked aggressively.

"Because when there is a shortage of fuel the people with accounts get preference," she explained.

"Do you know that I am the leader of the War Veterans in this whole area? My name is Comrade Titus Mamba."

"I am sorry, but those are the rules. We have to pay in advance for fuel, and if you want an account, you must pay a deposit."

"Do all the white people pay for fuel in advance?"

"Everyone who has an account must pay in advance. The rules apply to everyone. If you want to have an account, you must pay a deposit. I do not make the rules." Maria was starting to get angry but knew she could not show it; this man was dangerous.

Maria turned to Kelvin and said, "Will you please take Mr. Mamba to the front office and if he pays the deposit, open an account for him," she said wanting him out of her office as quickly as possible.

"Ok Madam," Kelvin replied as he turned to escort the man out. Mamba took a long, hard look at Maria, before turning to limp behind Kelvin.

Surprised that she had managed to keep her composure and her emotions under control, she started shivering and felt the bile rise in her throat. She ran to the toilet where she retched violently. Why had this beast come back to haunt her? He had murdered her mother, and now here he was in the district. She started to panic.

She desperately needed Tom, but she did not want Mamba to see him and recognize him. She knew that he would be there in less than half an hour. She tried to call him on his mobile phone, but he did not answer - the signal was bad along the road. What was Mamba doing here? He looked very cocky and sure of himself and said that he was the king-pin in the region. What was his role in this whole mess?

Was this ever going to stop? There had been many good years followed by the last three years of hell on the farm. Why? What had they done to deserve this? What were they going to do?

****

Chapter 43

Where had he seen the woman at the Service Station before? Mamba wondered as they drove away from Msoneddi. There was something familiar about her that worried him. He would have to find out about her the next time he was in the area.

Back at his headquarters on the farm in Concession; he had taken over the previous white owner's furnished home when they had chased the cowering dog off his farm the previous year, Mamba was surprised to find he had visitors. Two high-ranking army officers were standing beside their vehicles in the driveway and greeted them cautiously.

"Comrade Mamba. We have brought bad news. We thought it would be better for us to tell you before you hear it elsewhere," Colonel Sithole told him.

"What has happened? Is the President okay?" Mamba asked.

"Yes. Yes, he's fine. It is Comrade Hunzvi; he died last night in the hospital," Sithole told him.

"Was he in an accident?"

"No, he died from malaria. As from today you will report directly to me," Brigadier Makoni told him. "You are to carry on as you are for the time being. We will advise you of any changes. If you have anything to report or any problems you will contact me." Getting back in their cars, they drove off.

Mamba was surprised; he was not even aware that Hunzvi had been taken ill. He was worried by the news and wondered how the army would interfere with his operations. He would have to wait until after the funeral to see what was going to happen. By rights, he should become the new leader of the 'Brown Shirts' (war veterans)

Although not a veteran of the war, Hunzvi was buried in National Heroes' Acre outside Harare. At the funeral, President Mugabe lavished praise on Hunzvi, as leader of the War Veterans' Association, and for his role in Zimbabwe's land reform programme. But his death would not change the fast-track resettlement program Comrade

Mugabe stated; the eviction of the enemies, the 'White Settlers,' would continue.

Satisfied that there were going to be no immediate changes, Mamba continued as before; orchestrating violence and harassment of the remaining white farmers; as well as one or two black commercial farmers who were known to support the MDC.

Two months after Hunzvi's burial, Mamba was in the Mvurwi district, and stopping for fuel at Msoneddi on the way back from Centenary, he remembered to ask about the woman.

"She is Mrs. King. Her husband is the manager here at the workshop," the attendant told him.

"Where are they from? Where do they live?" he demanded.

"They live on their farm at Outlook. It is about 4 miles from here."

Mamba decided to visit the war-vets on Outlook farm to investigate the Kings. He paid a visit on the woman in charge of the war-vets on the farm. After inspecting the progress they had made, he asked her what she knew of the farm owner and his wife.

All she knew was that they had come from South Africa, about ten years previously, when they had purchased the farm. She had heard, however, that they had lived near Chiredzi during the Chimurenga.

"The man who owns Bushlands farm knows them well. I have seen him visiting here on many occasions," the woman told him. "He is a black man. I heard that he was a '*majoni*' (policeman) with the Smith regime."

"You have been of help. I will be visiting you again quite soon," Mamba said, rewarding her with money.

Needing fresh meat, Mamba drove to the cattle section on Valley Estates, not far from Outlook farm. His war-vets liberated and slaughtered a beast every month. With a bag of mealie meal, a pile of vegetable, two bags of oranges and a huge chunk of meat, he made his way home.

Passing Bushlands Farm on his way, he stopped to see the war-vets there and learned that the owner, Lucas Mpofu, had been a policeman stationed in the Lowveld many years before.

The pieces were starting to fit, but he would have to see what the man looked like if he was to confirm his suspicions. Waiting under the shade of a large Jacaranda tree near the farm entrance, Mamba decided that the man was the person he thought it was, he would get rid of him and his friend for good.

An hour later, a van drove up to the gate. As the driver got out of the vehicle to open the gate, he glanced in Mamba's direction. It was him! There was no doubt in his mind that it was his old enemy from the early days in Stodart, and later during the Chimurenga when he had been operating in the South East.

His hatred of the man was so intense that his leg immediately started throbbing. Unable to speak properly, he signaled his driver to move on, and they drove back to his lair.

He now knew who the two men were, but he still did not recognize the woman, and it worried him. For the next few weeks, he became totally absorbed with his plans to rid himself of these two men who were responsible for the loss of his leg, and his imprisonment. The pain in his leg became worse the more he thought about them.

This time, they would not get the better of him. The situation had changed, and now he was the one in charge. They were going to pay for what they had done to him. If it were not for his amputated leg, he would most certainly have been one of the 'top dogs' in the army, perhaps even a Brigadier.

The white settler's wife would be his prize.

****

Chapter 44

When he arrived back at the office from Harare, Tom was shocked to see Maria sitting at her desk staring into space, with tears running down her pale cheeks.

"What's the matter?" he asked, rushing to her side and putting his arm around her shoulders.

"Mamba is back. He was right here in my office," she sobbed.

"Are you sure it was him? What the hell did he want?"

"Yes. It was him alright. He even gave me his name. I could never forget him. He wanted to open a fuel account, and when I told him he had to pay a deposit, he got quite aggressive."

"Did he recognize you?"

"I don't think so. I tried not to show that I knew him. Tom I am so scared."

There was no time to lose. Tom had to move Maria to their house in Harare, and quickly. He was not going to have her worrying. It had been a nasty shock for her being face to face with that monster. Contacting Lucas, Tom told him about the sudden appearance of Mamba. He too was shocked by the news.

"Tom. This man is going to cause us a lot more shit when he discovers who we are and that we are both farming here. It sounds like he is the main war-vet leader in this part of the country," Lucas expressed concern.

"I know Lucas. But what can we do about it?"

"Put a bullet in his bloody head, like we should have done a long time ago."

"Well, I am moving Maria to Harare. I don't want him coming anywhere near her."

"Yes, I think that is a damn good idea. Maybe I should move Tandi into town as well."

"I think you should. Once this bastard knows who we are, he is going to be coming for us. He seems to have the police unofficially on his side and has total disregard for the law; we must be prepared."

A year after the farm invasions started, Tom and Maria had purchased a house in Harare. In the past year, they spent most weekends there. It was a welcome break from the continual pestering and pressure by the squatters. Many of their friends had done the same. There it was still possible to have some sort of social life, without having the squatters prying eyes watching their every move. The Mvurwi Club had been closed for a couple of years; ever since war vets had occupied it, and so nothing was happening on the social or sporting scene out in the country.

Loading the dogs, the cats, and the housemaids, they drove to their house in Chisipiti, a suburb of Harare. Lucas phoned later that evening, to tell them that they too had decided to move into town, and would move to their house in Mount Pleasant the following week.

Knowing that his friend would not be exposed for much longer, Tom relaxed and felt a lot better. He did not expect Mamba to plan any nasty mischief for a while. They did not even know whether he had recognized Maria and if he had, did he know that they were married? It was not worth taking a chance with that devil. One thing was certain - once he knew who they were, he would plan some his revenge.

On Monday Tom returned to work and stayed on the farm by himself. He looked forward to joining Maria at the weekends. Although not ideal staying alone, it was essential to maintain their presence the farm; the squatters must not be allowed to think that they were about to leave. He was determined not to give up or to give in to their demands.

Apart from small patches of maize, grown around the huts they had built on the plots of land they had been allocated, Tom did not see any war-vets attempting to grow commercial crops – not even where some farmers had plowed for them. The government gave them the seed – some of it was planted, but the rest was ground up and used for maize meal. The fertilizer also given to them by the government was sold by most of them to genuine farmers in the Tribal Trust areas.

What was Mugabe going to do with all the arable, highly productive land? It was all well and good giving it to the war veterans, but they were not going to farm it efficiently. Did he honestly expect these masses of untrained people to produce sufficient food to feed the nation?

The majority of farmers and their employees supported the opposition MDC; as did most working people. It seemed that the only way to stop the farm invasions was to get rid of Mugabe and the ZANU PF. The farm workers were not all happy with the land being taken from their employers, because it meant them losing their jobs and being thrown off the farms by the war-vets. Their 'support' for the opposition, meant they would not even be included in the redistribution of the land.

Still, the MDC was growing in strength, and so ZANU PF youth gangs roamed the district, forcing the workers to run long distances at night to attend re-education sessions in the middle of nowhere. Then, in a bid to win them over, Mugabe, as wily as ever, came up with a plan that he hoped would turn them against their employers. A retrenchment package, called a 'SI 6', was announced in favor of the workers. The war-vets then stirred up more trouble, by telling them that their employers were going to abandon them without pay.

Tom had not been able to carry out farming operations for a couple of years now and so he did not have the Z$10 million or US$200,000 he was forced to pay his workforce. He called a meeting with his workers to explain that they would have to wait until he had the funds to pay them and that he had no intention to leave the farm.

....

It was time to start looking at escape options, just in case they needed one.

Maria, who still had not recovered from the trauma of coming face-to-face with Mamba, was wound up tight like a spring, and ready to snap. She and Tom agreed that she needed some respite, and so she went overseas with a friend, for a break and to see what the UK looked like as an option.

At the beginning of July, while Maria was away, all the farmers were once again served with eviction orders, which most of them ignored; including Tom. The following week, on the day before the long weekend of what used to be called Rhodes and Founders, (now nicknamed 'Rogues and Scroungers' or 'Gooks and Spooks') they were told they had to get off their farms by midnight, or face a two year prison sentence for defying the law.

Tom went to town for the weekend and on his return, was confronted by a very worried Samuel. He had heard that the war-vets intended arresting him early the following morning and insisted that Tom leave the farm before six in the morning, and go back to Harare until it was safe for him to return.

A week later when Tom went back to Msoneddi, he was met by Samuel, who told him that the war-vets were waiting on the farm to abduct him. He said he would contact Tom when it was safe for him to return.

There was nothing Tom could do but wait until things died down. Leaving Ted to look after the business, Tom traveled to the UK to join Maria. He had never been to England before, and could not get over how everyone lived in such cramped conditions.

The roads were narrow; the houses tiny and most of the farms no bigger than small holdings in Africa. There were millions of people all crowded onto a small island, and judging by the number of pregnant women and their strings of small children; they seemed intent on creating a massive overpopulation problem for themselves. Tom could not imagine how he and Maria could survive here after a lifetime spent in the wide open space of Zimbabwe and Southern Africa.

....

Tom and Maria returned to Zimbabwe, hoping that by the time they got back, there would be a resolution to the Fast-Track land grab. Maria stayed in the house in Harare and Tom went back to the farm.

It was heartbreaking to see the squatter's huts all over the farm and in the middle of his once productive lands. It was not farmers or even war-vets who were occupying their farm, but a bunch of paid youths who wandered around wearing yellow t-shirts with 'ZANU PF' printed on them. The atmosphere was very tense. What a homecoming!

The morning after he returned, a crowd of about 15 young squatters confronted Tom at the gate. They told him that the farm now belonged to an army officer and that he had no right to be there. Before returning to the farm, Tom had obtained a court order in Harare declaring that the squatters had no right to be on the farm. He showed them the document and explained that they should follow the law. It threw them off balance, and they withdrew to their meeting place under the Marula tree, to consider their next move.

Every day they were at the fence wanting Tom to sign pieces of paper, declaring that the farm had been handed over to them; wanting to break open the gates to come inside; wanting to inspect the house; wanting to be supplied with vegetables. They were always armed with sticks, clubs, iron bars and machetes.

The crowds at the gate became bigger and bigger each day, until there were well over fifty of them, with others patrolling the fence, like a pack of hyenas waiting for their share of the spoils. After they dispersed that afternoon, Tom packed the remaining items of value and the farm books and went to Harare. Maria had already taken all her precious belongings; her photos; valuable documents, their passports, pictures and anything else she wanted to keep with her when she had moved. Tom had been ferrying bits and pieces, each time he went to town, and so now only the bare essentials remained on the farm.

Tom sold his share of the business to Ted, enabling him to pay the 'SI 6' to his labor, and was ready to leave the farm at a moment's notice. He could not believe it had come to this!

****

Chapter 45

There was a problem with Lucas moving Tandi to Harare. Their house in town had been let out, and they had to give the tenants notice, meaning she would only be able to take residence after four weeks. When Tom discussed his concern about their safety, Lucas reassured him that there were no problems with the squatters on his farm. He was positive they would be left alone.

Three weeks later Lucas phoned Tom with some disturbing news.

"Tom. When I came home at lunchtime today, a vehicle was parked under the Jacaranda Tree near the front gate. I couldn't see who was in the vehicle, but the man in the passenger seat was wearing dark glasses and a bush hat. As soon as I locked the gate behind me, it drove away," Lucas sounded worried.

Tom didn't have to ask Lucas to explain. "Perhaps it would be wise for Tandi to stay with Maria," he said.

"Thanks, Tom. I will speak to Tandi, and get her packed up and ready to move." Lucas's relief was audible.

"Good. I will tell Maria to expect you later on today or tomorrow sometime."

Tom was in his office the following day when picked up an urgent call from Lucas. There was an angry crowd of about 100 squatters and youths armed with sticks, iron bars, and machetes, threatening to break down the gates and demanding to speak to him. The duty controller told Lucas that he was sending Mvurwi Security Services to collect a policeman, and then would rush to his assistance. In the meantime, he was not to speak to them, and they were to lock themselves securely inside the house.

Tom called Lucas on his cell phone to find out exactly what was happening on Bushlands. "Are you under attack? Are you guys alright?" he asked.

"I don't know what has got into them. I have had no trouble recently. At the moment we are safe, but the war-vets are getting pretty violent, and it looks like they might break the gates open."

"Is Tandi with you?" Tom asked, concerned for their safety.

"Yes, she is still here. We were about to leave for Harare when they arrived at the gate."

"Well hang tight my friend. Don't do anything stupid. Help is on the way, and we are coming to give you support," Tom assured him. "They must have got a bee in their bonnet about something."

"This has got to be something to do with Mamba."

"Why do you think that?"

"I heard that he is based on Rocky Grange farm, in Concession, and I saw his car here again this morning."

"Is he still there?"

"No, I don't think so. I didn't see his car when I came in from the lands, an hour ago."

"Okay Lucas, we will all be there shortly. Just keep calm."

Fifteen minutes later the group of farmers that had assembled outside Tom's office was given the go-ahead by the controller to move to Lucas's. The Mvurwi Security team had collected a policeman and were on their way to Bushlands.

A frantic voice came over the radio. "Control this is Bushlands. Please come quickly. They have now broken the gates open and are surrounding the house," it was Tandi, and she was in a panic. "Lucas has gone outside to try and calm them down." Then after a brief pause.

"Control this is Bushlands. There is no chance of stopping them. They are on the front veranda and have already hacked one of my dogs to death. This is serious," this time it was Lucas, and Tom could hear the fear in his voice.

"Bushlands this is Control. Help is on the way. Security will be there within minutes, and the farmers are also coming to give support. Hang on and try to stay calm."

"Please hurry. The mob is stirred up and very violent."

Ten minutes later when they arrived at the gates to the Bushlands homestead, Tom was horrified to see a large crowd milling around outside the house. They were waving their weapons in the air, while they danced and chanted slogans. Some of them seemed to have lost interest and were starting to drift off in the direction of the compound.

"Sell out. Sell out. *Pamberi Hondo*." (Forward the war)

The Security van was parked outside the broken down gates, with a police constable standing beside it, observing the antics taking place in the yard. Seeing the farmers drive up to the gates, the crowd broke up and ran chanting back to their collection point, near the main farm entrance.

The house was a mess. From the broken down gate, they could see that the windows had been smashed, the door was broken, and a dead dog was lying on the veranda. A police inspector and three security men emerged from the house as Tom and Ted approached. There was no sign of Lucas or Tandi.

"What has happened here?" Tom asked, addressing the Inspector.

"You must return to your vehicles immediately. There is nothing for you to do here," he ordered.

"I want to speak to the owner of the farm, Mr. Lucas Mpofu," Tom insisted.

"You must leave now!" the inspector shouted.

"We are not leaving until we are satisfied that Mr. Mpofu and his wife are safe," Tom responded, also getting angry.

"I am sorry Mr. King. The owner of the farm and his wife, have both been killed by the war vets. They broke into the house and killed them," the section leader of the security service informed them in a matter-of-fact tone. "We were too late to help them," he continued, this time apologetically. His voice sounded like a drone to Tom.

"Oh my God!" shouted Tom. Then turning angrily on the police inspector he said "This is your bloody fault. It should never have been allowed to happen. You are supposed to protect people from being attacked by these monsters!"

"Mr. Mpofu must have done something to anger the war-vet settlers," declared the inspector, lamely backing down.

"No he bloody well did not, and you know it! Those people have no right to be squatting on his farm. You have allowed decent people to be murdered by bloody criminals," Tom spat back at him.

"You must not talk to me like that. I am the authority here, and I will take care of matters," he told Tom. "Now will you please leave this farm?"

"I want to see Mr. Mpofu and his wife before we go anywhere."

"I will have you arrested if you do not leave now."

"Who is going to arrest us? You are here in our vehicle with our security men. We are going into the house, to see exactly what has happened," Tom said, as he proceeded to push past him, entering the house followed by the other farmers.

The war-vets must have used heavy iron bars, to force open the steel gates into Lucas and Tandi's bedroom. Tom was horrified, sickened, and overcome by a huge wave of sadness, at the scene that greeted him. Lucas was lying on the floor near the door with his head staved in, and wounds all over his body; he had been bludgeoned and hacked to death; Tandi was spread-eagled on the bed, with her throat cut and the clothes ripped off her; it looked like she had been raped before being slaughtered.

There was blood everywhere; her suitcases were lying on the floor where they had been broken open, and all her clothing was scattered around on the blood covered floor. Walking over to Tandi, Tom gently covered her body with the bedspread before turning away in a daze.

"What do you intend doing about the murder of these people. Are you going to arrest them, or just let them get away with it?" Tom shouted at the police inspector, knowing full well that there would be no arrests, but he could not contain his sadness and rage.

"We will carry out a full investigation. Those responsible will be arrested and charged," he replied.

"I very much doubt it," Tom said, getting into his vehicle and driving away, his heart full of sadness, grieving for his friends.

There was no doubt in Tom's mind that this was the work of Mamba. He swore that the monster would pay for this dreadful murder of his dear friends.

How much did Mamba know about them? If he knew about Lucas, then he most certainly would know about Tom. But what about Maria? Did he know who she was? Realizing that Mamba would go to great lengths to get rid of his enemies, Tom decided the time had come to get her out of the country.

From Bushlands, Tom drove to Lucas' parent's house, in Mvurwi, and broke the news to the old people as gently as he could. The old man said that he would notify Tandi's parents, and then go to Harare and collect the two children, who were now his responsibility. Together with Tandi's parents, they would collect the bodies, and make funeral arrangements.

This was too close to home, and had now become very personal. Mamba had to be stopped.

****

Chapter 46

Mamba drove away from Bushlands a happy man. He had arranged for one of his enemies to be killed, and nobody was going to stop it happening. He had moved a group of his more trusted militia youths to lead the attack and would move them away again, as soon as their mission was accomplished.

He had promised them and the war-vets on the farm, a handsome feast, and a pay-out after they successfully carried out the attack, and the black owner of the farm was dead.

They could do what they wished with his wife; preferably kill her as well. He would get a phone call from his contact at the police station to confirm that the attack had been successful.

. . . .

Moving quickly, Tom went from Mvurwi directly to Harare. Maria was not there, and when she did not answer her mobile phone, he started to panic. Had the monster beaten him to it; did he already have her in his clutches? As he was about to start phoning their friends, she drove in through the gates. The battery on her phone was flat!

"What is the matter, Tom? You look terrible."

"The bastard has killed Lucas and Tandi, in their own home!" he burst out.

"Oh my God! What happened?" Maria asked, horrified.

Tom relayed the horrific tale, leaving out the part about Tandi having been raped. "I know Mamba had a hand in this!"

"We must go to their children and bring them here to stay with us," Maria blurted out as tears welled up and started to run down her face.

"No Maria. I have already arranged everything with Lucas's father. He will break the news to Tandi's parents and the children. They will all move to Lucas's house in Harare and will take care of the two children. Ted will help them," Tom took her in his arms.

"What about the funeral? What arrangements are being made?"

"Old man Mpofu is organizing it all. I have explained that we will not be able to attend, and he fully understands our situation," Tom explained.

"They were good friends. We should be there."

"Under normal circumstances, I agree with you. But right now we must move fast. I am taking you to South Africa today. We will fly down as soon as you have packed."

"Then what's going to happen?"

"Right now, I don't know. We'll discuss that on the way. But I want you out of his reach."

"No Tom. I am not going to let him control our lives like this. We will attend the funeral, and then I will be prepared to go to South Africa." Maria put her foot down.

Tom realized how important it was to Maria to lay her friends to rest; he owed her that much.

"Very well then," he softened. "But we must be very watchful and take all the precautions necessary. He hurt you, he murdered your mother, and now he has murdered Lucas and Tandi, I am not going to let him come anywhere near you."

....

Lucas and Tandi's funeral was held in the Mvurwi cemetery three days later. The war-vets had decided to remove their pegs a year ago as a sign of respect – they proclaimed. Two policemen were stationed at the entrance to prevent any unwanted intrusion, and Tom kept a wary eye open to make sure that Mamba was not lurking somewhere in the background.

It was an overcast day with a light breeze rustling through the trees pushing the mist away into the valley below the cemetery. Most of the remaining farmers in the district came with their wives to pay their last respects. The men looked uncomfortable in their suits and ties, and the women were smartly dressed.

Lucas and Tandi had been well respected and played a large role in the community by being active in the club as well as helping at the Old Age Home. The mood was somber; everyone was angry as Lucas and Tandi were the first farmers in the community to have been murdered.

Tomas and Sarah, Lucas and Tandi's two children, were dressed in their school uniforms and stood at the graveside in front of their four grandparents. They all looked bewildered and frail. The two elderly women and the children wept quietly as the service continued.

To one side, a group of workers from Bushlands stood with bowed heads – their future now uncertain. A choir of children from the farm school sang 'I Believe' as only Africans can; it was a fitting farewell.

Later that day Tom and Maria flew to Durban.

. . . .

Flying back alone five days later, Tom had plenty of time to think. He had left a very worried Maria with Stuart and his family. There he knew she would be safe. Maria was comfortably settled in the self-contained cottage in their garden. Now Tom could stop worrying about Maria and apply all of his thoughts to planning the demise of his old enemy.

Back at Msoneddi, Tom discussed the situation with Ted. During Tom's absence most of the mob, that had attacked Lucas and Tandi, had hurriedly been removed from Bushlands, and taken to another location - no doubt to create havoc and misery there. It appeared that they were Mamba's private hit squad, and he could move them around to wherever he wanted to apply pressure or worse.

Convinced that Mamba would launch some an attack on him within a couple of weeks, Tom realized he would have to make Mamba come to him; when he was ready. And it had to be finished quickly as he had no intention of having to watch over his shoulder, day and night, for weeks or months on end.

The day after Tom returned from South Africa, Samuel, gave him more disturbing information. While he was away in South Africa, a senior war-vet had been in the compound asking questions about Tom.

The man had wanted to know where Tom came from, and whether he had ever worked in the Lowveld.

"I saw this man Ishe. He is a bad person," Samuel told him. "You must be very careful. Maybe he wants to kill you now."

"Thank you, Samuel. I am sure he does. He is the same man who attacked our house in the Lowveld, and who killed Lucas and Tandi. We must make a plan to stop him," Tom said.

"Yes, Ishe. I will help you for sure," Samuel responded eagerly.

"Good. I will think of a plan and let you know what to do. Thank you, Samuel."

Mamba, it seemed, was moving quickly, and had already begun to stalk him. Tom would have to move as quickly to put the idea he had been working on into action. There was not much time.

Spending most of the day with Ted and Jack, another friend, they finally agreed on a plan. The whole thing would depend on Mamba taking the bait that Samuel was going to offer.

The bait was Tom.

****

Chapter 47

Now Mamba had to deal with the most important one. He had crossed paths with this man on many occasions, and Mamba had always come out the loser. But not this time; he would plan his attack carefully, and would carry it out personally. He wanted the pleasure of seeing his victim beg for his life before he slowly killed him. He was not in any hurry and would bide his time until the right opportunity presented itself.

He would go out to Outlook as soon as the dust had settled after the Bushlands killings.

His connection in the Chiredzi area of the Lowveld had found out about Tom Owen. He had worked as a farm manager in Triangle. His wife had been killed in an ambush on a convoy, after Mamba had been wounded, in the failed attack on King's home, and put into prison without trial. Shortly afterward, King had left the Lowveld, and a Portuguese woman by the name of Maria da Silva had gone with him.

He was amazed and could hardly believe that this could be the same woman he had been at school with all those years ago. It was a huge coincidence, and he would have to have another look at her to make sure. With luck, he would be able to kill them both at the same time. He might even be able to have his way with her, while her man watched. That would certainly give him great pleasure. If she were not the woman he thought she was, it would not matter in any case; but it would be a bonus.

Two weeks after the attack on Bushlands, Mamba went to pay the bonus to his 'soldiers.' They had moved them to a farm in Centenary, where there was a problem farmer who had to be dealt with. On his return trip, he stopped at Outlook, to get information on King's movements. This had become part of his daily routine and usually yielded no information. But today was different; today he had a breakthrough. The 'chairwoman' on the farm, informed him that a member of King's staff wanted to speak with him.

"What do you want?" he asked gruffly as the man cowered in front of him.

"I am told that you have been asking about my boss and that you might want to deal with him like what happened to his friend on Bushlands," the man answered him.

"What business is that of yours? Are you not loyal to this man? Are you not an MDC supporter?" Mamba stood so close he could see small splatters of his spit land on the traitors face.

"Yes I have worked for him for many years," the weasel stammered. "And he has promised me some land. But you now control the land, so he will not be able to give me what he has promised, and what I am due," Samuel told him. "I have had a ZANU PF member's card for five years now. I do not belong to the MDC," he said producing his card.

"So what is it that you want from me?" Mamba stepped back and lowered his voice slightly.

"I will help you to get rid of my boss if you will arrange for me to be allocated a piece of land on this farm, which I will choose."

"How will you be able to do this?"

"He trusts me. I will be able to get you into the house."

"Why must I use you to help me when I can easily bring in my soldiers to do the job for me?" Mamba sneered.

"Because he is an old enemy of yours from the Chimurenga, and I think it will give you more pleasure to deal with him yourself. Is he not the one who injured you?"

"Yes, that is so." Mamba was beginning to like this man – they thought the same. "I will think about what you have said. The next time I am here, I will send for you. If I hear that you are trying to deceive me, I will cut off your genitals and make you eat them," Mamba warned, just in case.

"No. I will help you. I want some land."

"Go now. I will be back soon," Mamba said dismissively.

This was the opportunity he had been waiting for, and his excitement was growing. He made up his mind instantly regarding the worker's offer. Revenge would be his. He didn't want to wait. He had lived for so long with his anger and hatred of this man that he was prepared to take a chance.

Two days later he was back on the farm. Sending for Samuel, he agreed to give him land once King had been dealt with for good. Together they hatched the plot. Samuel would get him into the yard without being detected, and then he would attack and kill King and his wife in the early hours of the night. He would not go there in his official car but would use an old van in which he would remove their bodies and dispose of them.

Mamba did not want anyone to know about this killing; it would not be wise to be linked in any way to two separate killings in the same area. It would make him far too vulnerable to jealous lower ranking war-vets who would like to unseat him, and to criticism by army officers.

Mamba's driver was trustworthy, but he would have to eliminate this man Samuel, as soon as he had dealt with King. This time he knew he would not fail.

....

It had to be a night-time attack; the whole plan rested on it. Tom was never there at the weekend, and during the day he was at work at Msoneddi. There was to be no noise or as little as possible; they did not want to alert the resident war-vets, and nobody, apart from those involved, was to know what was going on. The possibility of the whole thing backfiring, and their plan being compromised had to be factored in.

Before dangling the bait, Tom had to have everything in place. Once the bait was put out, there was no guarantee that Mamba would get hooked. He was devious, unpredictable, cunning, and could very easily change the plan to suit him. Tom had put Samuel into danger, and this worried him, but he had seen no option. If anything happened to Samuel, he wouldn't be able to forgive himself. He couldn't stand the thought of losing another loyal and trusted friend.

Somehow, they had to ensure that Mamba did not get any of his war-vets to assist him. It meant he would have to be persuaded to approach the homestead via the road leading from a neighboring farm, to the west of Outlook, and not use the normal entrance road. The track was away from the main road and on the opposite side of the homestead from where the war-vets were camped. On the agreed day, and at a specific time, Samuel would have to arrange to meet him on the back road.

Mamba would then be coming into the yard via the front gates. A high wall from the garages around the side of the driveway offered protection to the main living area in the house. Samuel would lead him through the gate in the wall, allowing him easy access to the front of the house, where Tom would be waiting.

Tom was also aware that Mamba most certainly would want to kill Samuel as soon as he had let him into the yard, and so they had to have protection in place to ensure his safety. He would be the most exposed person. Ted and Jack would take care of that the moment Mamba had been let into the yard. They would also take care of the driver.

．．．．．．．．．．．．．．

After three days of careful planning, preparation and rehearsals with Ted and Jack, they were ready to spring the trap. Samuel met with Mamba, who seemed interested in the proposal, but did not show too much enthusiasm. He returned two days later, and together they planned an attack on Tom and Maria, who had supposedly returned from Harare.

"Do you think we will be able to pull this off without being caught?" Jack asked in a moment of fear. "We are not as young and fit as we were back in those days."

"No, we most certainly are not, but nor is Mamba, and he is not used to resistance anymore," Tom said. "Yes. I do think we can pull it off; as long as he doesn't bring in extra thugs, and only comes with his driver to do his evil work. I am betting that he will want to do the job himself, and not get the blame. After they pass Jack's position, we will have to finish them off, no matter what happens. Mamba and his driver must not be allowed to escape the trap, or we are dead men."

"What do we do if there are others with him?" Ted said.

"Samuel will tell him that I have gone out unexpectedly," Tom said. "If they still carry on past you and Jack, and you see that he has brought more troops than expected, give a wolf call and then get the hell out of the area. Ted will hide in the rocks on the koppie, and I'll barricade myself in the storeroom. They will think there is no one at home, and Samuel will have to try and persuade Mamba to come another time."

．．．．．．．．．．．．．．

Mamba planned his attack for Friday night. To keep his identity safe, and to be able to remove the bodies, Mamba agreed to keep the operation quiet, and not use his official vehicle. He would meet Samuel half a mile from the homestead, on the road from Tennet Farm and Concession, at 8 pm.

At five o'clock on Friday evening, Ted and Jack also using the Tennet farm road so as not to be seen, arrived and locked their vehicle in Tom's garage. After carefully running through every detail of the plan, they smeared their faces and hands with charcoal and moved into their positions. Each of them was armed with a 12 bore shotgun; it was the only weapon a farmer was permitted to keep and the best for this purpose. They would only be used as a last resort. Jack went off down the road a little way, and Ted positioned himself near the entrance gate.

After switching on lights in most of the rooms in the house, and leaving the French doors that lead from the lounge onto the veranda wide open, Tom armed himself with his shotgun, a sheath-knife and his cross-bow with four bolts. He took up his position in the flower bed under the large peppercorn tree, about 20 paces from the entrance gate in the wall, and the front door into the lounge.

Making sure he had a clear view of his target area, and had space to move without rustling the leaves of the small shrubs and plants, he put his shotgun within easy reach and settled down to wait.

A light breeze blew from the south but the sky was clear, and a myriad of stars twinkled. The moon would rise in an hour. It was quiet as Tom lay in the dark, waiting for the signal. He would know Mamba was approaching when Jack gave a double owl-hoot.

But what if his signal was drowned out by the sound of the vehicle or the wind?

It was a long time since Tom had lain in ambush, and he soon became uncomfortable, wanting to change his position. As quietly as he could, he rolled from side to side to ease his discomfort. He would need to have steady arms when the time came - he had a bolt ready to slot into the cross-bow.

....

Jack saw the lights of the approaching vehicle come up the hill, and stop at the spot where Samuel was waiting. Jack's eyes had become adjusted to the night, and so it was easy for him to see the silhouettes of the driver and the passenger when the headlights were dimmed. The vehicle started to move again and came on slowly without any lights.

As it passed his position, he saw Samuel, standing in the back of the van on his own. Jack gave two loud owl-hoots that didn't sound as good as they should have because his nerves were on edge and his mouth dry. Not wasting a moment, he left his position and followed the van to the front gates.

....

Tom heard an unusual sounding owl-hoot, followed immediately by another, which warned him of Mamba's approach; and then came the hum and rattle of a vehicle approaching slowly. Slotting a bolt into the cross-bow, and making sure he would be able to get up in a hurry, he waited. His stomach was in a knot, and adrenalin started coursing through his veins. His mouth was dry, and he started to shake.

The faint rattle as the front gates were opened a short time later told Tom that it would not be long. Suddenly he calmed down as the contact became imminent; his senses sharpened, and he concentrated on the inner garden gate in the wall.

A shadow appeared like a ghost, and then there was a squeak as the gate was opened. The dark figure came through the gap and stopped briefly half turning towards the gate. A moment later he continued walking slowly and cautiously towards the front veranda. Tom knew it was Mamba because of the limp.

In the light cast by the veranda lights, Tom could see he was armed with an AK47 rifle. If he saw or heard Tom hiding in the garden, he would be killed in a hail of bullets. With his heart racing, Tom watched the monster limping closer and closer to him as he approached the house.

....

Ted, hiding near the entrance gate, saw Samuel jump off the back of the van, and Mamba get out of the passenger side. Together they opened the gate and walked up the driveway towards the house. The driver got out of the van and leaned against the fender. He did not see or hear Ted, creep up behind him and stick the barrel of his shotgun into the back of his neck. He closed his mouth with his other hand. By then Jack had arrived and, without hesitation, knocked the driver out with his knobkerrie. He fell to the ground with a groan and was quickly gagged and trussed up with rope and cable ties.

....

A muffled groan from the direction of the gate made Mamba hesitate again. He half turned, presenting Tom with a perfect target in the veranda light. Not hesitating, Tom pulled the trigger and released a bolt. The missile ran true, and with a dull 'thunk' struck Mamba in the chest, throwing him over backward. The AK47 he was carrying fell from his hands and clattered onto the pathway.

Casting the bow aside, Tom grabbed his shotgun, leaped to his feet and ran to where the man lay writhing on the ground, struggling to get up. Clutching his right shoulder, Mamba tried to crawl towards his weapon. Tom kicked the AK47 away and put his shotgun down out of Mamba's reach. The bolt from the cross-bow was embedded in the upper right-hand side of his chest.

He stood over the injured man with his knife at his throat.

"Move one inch, and I will put this piece of steel through you, you bastard," Tom warned him. "Now put your hands in front of you where I can see them."

Once he had tied Mamba's thumbs securely together with cable ties and with his knife still in hand - Tom searched his victim thoroughly. It was not a pleasant job; his stench was almost unbearable. The only thing he had on him was a pair of dark glasses tucked in his shirt pocket. Without pulling the bolt out, Tom rolled his victim over, took a length of rope from his pocket and tied Mamba's arms tightly to his body at the elbows. Satisfied that he was secure, Tom squatted beside him and shone his torch into Mamba's angry bloodshot, smoldering eyes.

"When you killed my friends, you signed your death warrant, you dirty murdering rapist," Tom spat. "You should have known better, you useless piece of shit."

Mamba laughed. "They will get you for this. You whites do not run this country anymore. My men are coming to get you. I should have shot you when I saw you at Sabi," he tried to spit at Tom but his saliva, mixed with blood, just ran out of his mouth and down his bearded chin. His breath smelt of putrefying meat. It was Tom's turn to be surprised by this revelation.

"Your thugs do not know where you are, and they are not going to find you, or your driver. You are going to disappear for good," Tom told him flinching at the smell and pulling his head back.

"My men will be coming to rescue me soon. You will not kill me. You do not have the right."

"Oh yes I do have the right. I am sorry I did not finish you off many years ago, and saved myself all the trouble now."

"My driver has gone to get assistance. He will be back soon."

"No, he has not. We have him tied up."

"You are finished, white man. You must pack your things and get out of our country. Leave your white bitch behind. I want to show her what a real man is like, as I did many years ago," he hissed. Tom struggling to control his anger ripped a piece of his bloody shirt off and used it to gag him.

Just then Samuel appeared from behind the garden wall, and after picking up the AK47 rifle, helped drag Mamba to the van parked at the gate. Mamba's wide-eyed driver was gagged, trussed up like a turkey and lying in the back when they pushed Mamba in with him and tied his legs together above and below the knees.

Ted and Jack stood beside the vehicle looking very pleased with themselves.

"By the looks of it, all went according to plan," Tom said.

"When I heard the small gate in the wall squeak, I jumped the bloody driver. He has grown fat and lazy and was easy to capture," Ted said proudly.

"I thought I might have blown it when I made the off-tune owl hoot," Jack said absent-mindedly as he prodded Mamba with his club as if studying some previously unseen animal secured in a hunt.

Tom pulled him back to the urgency of the moment. "We'd better not waste any more time. We need to finish the job. Are we ready to move off?" he spoke quietly as he looked around anxiously. The others were busy cleaning charcoal off their faces and hands with a wet towel.

As a precaution, the shotguns and the cross-bow were hidden in the garden, to be retrieved later. It would not be good for the three of them to be caught with firearms and blackened faces. Before moving off Mamba's driver was knocked out again, to stop him wriggling around. Tom wanted Mamba alive and awake to suffer every bit of his demise.

Samuel was left to clear up all signs of their activities, and to wait for Tom's return. Ted, who knew his way around the mining areas on the Great Dyke better than anyone, took the lead in his van. Jack drove Mamba's van with Tom guarding the captives in the back. Moving slowly, and leaving the car lights off until they were well away from the farmhouse, they made their way back along the Tennet road before heading towards the distant hills to the west.

They followed an old unused road for an hour or so, seeing nobody along the way. Finally, they reached a high ridge at the top of the Dyke and turned off their lights. They could still see quite clearly in the moonlight as they wound their way slowly over the crest and along the road, towards an abandoned mine shaft in the side of the hills. Leaving Ted's vehicle parked on the side of the road, they took a smaller branch road that led them quickly to their destination.

There they stood beside the vehicle quietly listening for any sounds that might indicate there was someone else in the vicinity. The bare, barren hills were colored grey in the light of the moon; only the remaining rigging at the head of the mine shaft cast a long shadow over the dark hole below.

At last, satisfied that they were alone, they dragged Mamba and his driver from the back of the van. Mamba, who had lost a lot of blood, was weak and not quite so aggressive when they dumped them at the edge of the big dark hole which went 200 feet straight down into the heart of the mountain.

The driver, who had regained consciousness, was terrified and his eyes were bulging out of the sockets as he struggled against his bonds. He was the first to be pushed over the edge and was heard thumping against the sides of the shaft as he fell to his death.

The fight and anger in Mamba was replaced by fear when he realized that there was no escape. Like all bullies, he was a coward and started to cry, and urinated in his trousers. He looked pleadingly at Tom who, after wiping all fingerprints off it, tossed the AK47 down the shaft before turning his attention to the pitiful, stinking excuse of a human being lying at his feet.

"Is there anything you want to tell us before you die?" Tom asked his victim, as he removed the gag from around his mouth.

"Please, please. You must not kill me. I did not kill your friend," Mamba managed to say as he cried and begged for his life.

"We know exactly what you have done. You have been raping and murdering people all your life. Now you must pay for what you have done."

"I am an important man and my people will get you. I will get all the war-vets to leave you alone and to leave your farm."

"You're not so brave now, are you? Goodbye, you bloody murdering arsehole. You are going where you can't hurt anyone anymore. You are going to burn in hell."

"No. No, it was not me. Please spare me. You cannot do this."

Feeling nothing but contempt, Tom suddenly wanted to get it over with so he rolled the now terrified Mamba, whose bowels relaxed, to the edge of the shaft, and then gave him a final shove over the edge of the gaping hole with his foot. They heard him screaming all the way down as he too fell to his death at the bottom of the shaft.

****

Epilogue

Back at Ted's house, an hour after pushing the war-vet van into the shaft and carefully sweeping away their tracks, they cleaned up and settled down with a drink to unwind. After all the pressure and hardship they suffered at the hands of the war-vets, none of them felt any guilt; but still had emotions to deal with, and had hardly said a word on their way back from the Dyke.

"Thanks for your help, you guys. That bastard has been hounding Maria, Lucas and I for years. I am only sorry that we didn't fix him before he got to Lucas and Tandi. He also murdered Maria's mother you know," Tom said, surprising both Ted and Jack.

"It's about time someone did something about these swine that have ruined our lives and threatened our families," Ted responded.

"Too bloody right! Perhaps from now on the war-vets might be a little less aggressive when they find that their local leader has gone missing," said Jack, raising his glass.

"It felt a bit like the old war days. Let's hope nothing ever gets out about this business. I would hate you guys to be locked up in Chikirubi Prison with me."

"Well, we'll most definitely not be telling anyone. What about old Samuel?" Jack asked.

"I'm going to move him to our Harare house first thing in the morning before anyone starts asking questions. He will not know what happened to Mamba in the end," Tom assured them.

"Mamba shouldn't be missed for a while anyway. I don't think he will have told anyone where he was going, or that he was on a mission to do away with Tom," Ted surmised.

"Not bad for three old PATU fossils," Jack grinned, and they all let out a much-needed chuckle.

"I'll get your firearms back to you in the morning," Tom said, starting to relax and unwind at last after their nerve-racking mission.

Arriving home an hour later, Tom found Samuel waiting there for him. He had cleaned up and cleared away all signs of their unwanted visitors.

"Did you find a good place for Mamba sir?"

"Yes Samuel. He won't give us any more trouble. We have handed him and his driver over to the right people."

He did not know that Mamba and his driver had been killed. They had been wounded but alive when they were loaded onto the back of the van. for his own safety it was best kept that way. Samuel must just believe that they had simply disappeared.

In the morning, after a thorough inspection of the house to make sure there was no evidence of the previous night's activities, Tom went to the office to return the shotguns to Ted. Samuel went to speak with the war vet chairman on the farm. Mamba had arranged to meet with him the previous day and had not turned up, he told her. He asked if she had seen or heard from him. She said she hadn't, and that she would call him when next Mamba was there.

"Ishe. The *mawiri* (war-vet) woman did not know that Mamba was coming to the farm yesterday. He did not tell anyone. Nobody suspects anything," he said, reporting back to Tom.

"That is good Samuel. When you disappear, they will think that Mamba has taken you somewhere. You will be quite safe, but you must not tell anyone what has happened here."

"What should I tell the farm staff?"

"Tell them you have matters to attend to at home, or that someone is sick, and you are taking your leave."

Later that day, with Samuel hidden in the van as they left the farm, Tom moved him to the townhouse in Harare. He would be safe there. He had been the main player in their ambush and what he had done had taken a lot of courage and loyalty. He would be well rewarded for his part.

Tom, Maria, and Lucas had crossed paths with Mamba, on and off, for nearly forty years. He had always been in the background of their lives and a continual threat. It was over now, and he would go to Maria, as fast as possible, to tell her that her nightmare had at last ended. He could not risk telling her anything over the phone.

After leaving Samuel at the house, Tom drove out to Mount Hamden, fuelled his plane and flew to Durban.

The debt was settled, and Mamba would not be hurting anyone again. Tom felt it might be a good idea if he stayed out of the country for a while.

....

As he flew over the great plains of the Highveld, and later the Mopani covered scrubland of the Zimbabwe Lowveld, Tom was engulfed by emotion for all they had had to deal with over the past six years. Mainly, he felt a deep sadness at what had become of a beautiful country – but at least they were alive.

....

Two months of relaxing and enjoying a holiday near the sea worked wonders. It was as if a burden had been lifted from their shoulders. Flying over the country on their way home, they were horrified to see from the air, the extent of the damage that had been caused by people who had been given or just taken tracts of land in the Lowveld. They had hacked most of the trees down and burnt them to clear patches of land for their corn.

There were fires burning as far as the eye could see, and the smoke from the fires covered the entire countryside like a blanket. When was it going to be enough?

There was plenty of available land in the agricultural areas of the country, why did they have to destroy the natural vegetation and bush of the hot, dry ranching areas in the south and west? It was bad enough that they were destroying carefully preserved areas of conservation in the Highveld.

The people responsible for this destruction claimed that they were the original inhabitants of Zimbabwe. It was not true; they had moved down from the north, and killed or driven the San or Bushman tribes out. They had taken the country by conquest just as the colonial settlers had under the British flag. Why then had the world been so adamant that Rhodesia should be handed back to them? Why not hand it all back to the Bushmen? Why not hand England and America back to the original inhabitants?

It was an unpleasant feeling knowing that although they were going home, there was no real home anymore. Yes, it was good to be with the animals and have their loyal domestics around them in Harare, but that is where it ended. Their home was on the farm, and the squatters still inhabited it.

Without any farming activities and staff rushing busily around, there was an empty, deserted look to the place. The only sign of life was one or two squatters, who wandered around with homemade axes or '*demu's*' over their shoulders as they went off with their dogs to hunt for what little game there was left, and to cut down a few more trees.

Tom and Maria's return to the farm only caused mild interest. All the workers and staff were pleased to welcome them home, greeting them with broad smiles. They were anxious to bring them up to date with the latest developments.

It was a hopeless situation. Legally the farm belonged to Tom and Maria; they had purchased it with the consent of the government. They had invested a great deal on money into the farm and were reluctant just to walk away, and leave it to continue being destroyed.

By all accounts, the land grab was getting worse.

Rations supplied by donations from overseas countries were not being given to the needy, or any members of the opposition. Apart from fuel sales to passing road users, the business had virtually ground to a halt. There were very few farmers still working their lands, or on their farms and so there was no demand for bulk fuel.

A year later business had deteriorated to such an extent that it no longer generated sufficient funds to sustain two families. Reluctantly Tom handed all his affairs over to Ted and moved all their remaining furniture and staff to Harare. They locked up the house and left the farm. It had been theirs for fifteen years.

After a long six month holiday in South Africa and the UK, Tom and Maria returned to Harare, where they are determined to wait for a change in government and for Zimbabwe to recover from the mess created by the county's leader – Robert Mugabe.

. . . .

Five years have passed since Mamba disappeared. There has never been any investigation into his disappearance, and no questions have been asked. He seemed to have just gone missing, and nobody was in the least bit interested in finding him. It is believed, that he was getting too big for his boots, and had become a thorn in the side of certain army brigadiers. Perhaps they had a hand in his disappearance. At that time three or four senior politicians died in car accidents and others under mysterious circumstances.

The Mozambique project never got off the ground; the organizers disappeared, and Tom and Maria lost the money they had invested in the scheme. The young South African couple they met there, are still farming, and their two daughters have grown up and moved on.

Stuart and his family have moved to Canada, and Kyle has moved to Queensland in Australia where he runs a sugar estate. George and Megan moved to Botswana, Nick and Anne moved to Perth in Australia, and Gary and Judy moved to South Africa. John and Jill moved to Zambia to set up a Game Camp on the Luangwa River. Ted and Elsie are still in Zimbabwe and have moved to the outskirts of Harare.

Bushlands had been taken over by war-vets. Maria's lovely home on Outlook had been burnt to the ground, and her beautiful garden destroyed.

Samuel still works for Tom and Maria in Harare.

....

The fires are still burning in Zimbabwe, there is no '*Sadza*,' and the '*Nyama*' is finished. But there is still hope.

KT

(Sadza – the staple diet made from maize or corn. Nyama - meat)

Now read 'THE GOLDEN HORN' the next in this series. (Book 3)

Have you read 'BAREFEET and PAPERTHORNS' Book 1 in the 'TOM OWEN' series?

Zimbabwean Drums

The drums are calling old man, and they're louder by the day,
They are calling you to judgement and now's the time to pay,
For the wrongs you've done your country and the trust you have betrayed
So hear those drumbeats swelling, hear well and be afraid.
You came to power on waves of hope that you would make your mark,
In a land that shone in Africa like diamonds in the dark.
In simple faith the people put their trust within your care,
And were repaid by the Fifth Brigade and CIO and fear.
Thirty years of motorcades and lavish trips abroad,
A nation's heritage is lost through patronage and fraud.
The chiefs grow fat while people starve and famine stalks our homes,
On idle farms the weeds grow rank and cover cattle bones.
The youth are taught your slogans but even as they sing
The drums of change are beating for the truth is seeping in.
The demagogue had feet of clay and lies will not sustain
The shattered land that once seemed free and will be so again.
Too late to blame the drought, the Brits, the whites or the MDC
For all know where the finger points with cold finality.
So hear the drums, old man, and listen to them well,
They foretell of your end days and they have much to tell.
For he who sows the seeds of hate will reap the grapes of wrath,
So tremble in your bed at night, at the end of your sorry path.

by Alf Hutchison

The Call of Africa

When you've acquired a taste for dust,
The scent of our first rain,
You're hooked for life on Africa
And you'll not be right again.
'Till you can watch the setting moon
And hear the jackals bark,
And know that they're around you,
Waiting in the dark.
When you long to see the elephants,
Or to hear the Cougal's song,
When the moonrise sets your blood on fire,
You've been away too long.
It's time to cut the braces loose,
And let your heart go free beyond that horizon,
Where your spirit yearns to be.
Africa is waiting…COME!!
Since you've touched the open sky
And learned to love the rustling grass,
The wild Fish Eagle's cry.
You'll always hunger for the bush,
For the lion's rasping roar,
To camp at last beneath the stars,
And to be at peace once more.

With thanks to C. Emily-Dibb

Acknowledgments

It occurred to me that after having moved so much around parts of Africa and having had a somewhat bumpy but interesting ride, it would be a good idea to create a story based on our travels and adventures.

This book then is not a memoir but a story woven around facts and actual events and is intended as a tribute to all those people of Zimbabwe who continue to struggle for real freedom. The places do exist, and some of the characters are based on actual people; some of them still alive today. Any offending reference is unintentional and I apologize. I have used my patrol notebooks, personal experiences, and recollections as a basis for the story. Political events and persons named, as far as I am aware, are accurate.

At the time of writing, Zimbabwe remains unchanged. In twenty-five years since independence, the country that was once the 'Bread Basket of Africa,' with a very strong economy right up to the end of the Bush War, has become the 'Basket Case of Africa.' Under Mugabe's dictatorship and with his land grab policy, the people suffering the most are the blacks.

Thousands of opposition supporters have been murdered. Thousands of farm workers have lost their jobs and with their families have been thrown out of their homes on the once productive commercial farms. With very little being produced on farmland, the nation is starving to death. Still, the Western World turns a blind eye, and nothing is being done to help some very brave people, who are trying desperately to change Zimbabwe and start the recovery of a once great country.

Jealousy (Majerasi) is the main cause of most problems in Africa.

I must start by thanking Collette, my wife, and probably biggest critic during my writing, for her patience and understanding. She has slaved away to 'keep the wolf away from the door' while I have been writing. Without the help and support of my entire family, I would never have completed the book.

I want to thank Phil Graham and Peter Russell for their contributions and help; without their input, a lot of the 'meat' would have been left out. They both gave me a lot of encouragement for which I am most grateful.

A special thank you goes to Chonell for the first edit of the story, and to Natalie Uhlarz, who battled tirelessly through the manuscript, correcting a myriad of errors.

Thanks must also go to all our friends who have encouraged me and offered their support.

Last but by no means least I thank our very good friends, Ant and Elise Hiscock for everything they have done and continue to do for us in Zimbabwe. 'Tatenda'

The book is intended as a tribute to the people of Zimbabwe, both black and white, who have bravely 'soldiered on' through extremely difficult times and who have suffered at the hands of a ruthless dictator and his thugs who have bullied, beaten and killed many of them.

Above all, Zimbabwe is a wonderful, magical country. It is full of genuine, honest people whose only desire is for peace and prosperity. It is God's own country and the place I love and dream of one day returning to.

GLOSSARY

Ambuya – Elderly woman
Amayi - mother
AK47 –Russian made automatic firearm used by terrorists/insurgents/guerrillas
Aieewe – exclamation of astonishment or surprise
Black South – Townships to the south of Salisbury
BSAP – British South Africa Police
Bush War – Rhodesian civil war
Bright Lights – homestead guards from the city
Bombshell – spread out to sleep in the bush
COMOPS – Command Operations Headquarters
CFU – Commercial Farmers Union
Chete – only
Chimurenga – 1st Ndebele v Pioneers. 2nd. Militant rebellion v whites
Dad's Army – the over fifties
DC – District Commissioner
Demu – axe made from a piece of motor car spring blade inserted in a club
Fire Force – helicopter-borne troops
Gooks – terrorists, insurgents
Gomo – hill or koppie
Gona-re-Zhou – Place of Elephants. Game conservation Area
Gonna Stagga Inn – pub in the police mess at Vila Salazar
Hondo - war
Hout – munt, floppy. Black layabouts.
Ishe – Sir or boss
Insurgents – illegal infiltrators' and indoctrinators
JOC – Joint Operations Command
Ja - Afrikaans for yes
Jambanja – hostile gathering intent on no good
Jongwe – same as above
Koppie – small rocky hill also Kopjie
Lala palms- bush like palms used for making booze
LZ – Landing Zone
Lekker – Afrikaans for very nice or good
Mukiwa – white man
Mawiri – terrorist or War Vet
Mabhunu – Boer or Afrikaans farmer
Mabritish – The Brits.

Mazwita - greeting
Makorokoto - beware
Majoni - policeman
Mama - mother
Meneer – Afrikaans for mister
Mevrou – Afrikaans for misses
Mombe – cow or beast
NAD – Native Affairs Department
Ngandanga – Shona word for terrorist
Nyama – meat on the hoof, domestic or wild
Nee – 'No' in Afrikaans
Ne Zvimba Wasungata Zvake – and his dogs or followers
Oom – Afrikaans for Uncle
PATU – Police Anti Terrorist Unit
Pamberi ne Chimurenga – Forward the Revolution or war.
Pasi Ne Smith – Down with Ian Smith
Pungwe – rally to work-up emotion (Pamberi'1 and Pasi's)
Putu – Swazi or Zulu traditional porridge made from maize meal
RV – Rondez Voux or meet
RL – Troop carrier
RBC –Rhodesian Broadcasting Corporation
Shuwa Bwana – for sure boss
SAS – Special Air Services
Selous Scouts – used for unconventional operations like SAS
Sitrep – situation report
Sharp End – where the action is.
Sekuro – Elderly man - Grandfather
Sadza – Shona traditional porridge made from maize meal
Stick – Unit of 4 to 6 men or troopers
Sommer – Afrikaans for in any case or just so
Tannie – Afrikaans for Aunt
Totsiens – Afrikaans for goodbye
Tatenda – thank you
Terrorist – attacks soft targets mainly at night
Terrs – as above abbreviated
Tango One – Call sign for Tom's unit (stick)
Unit – same as Stick
UDI – Unilateral Declaration of Independence
War Vet – War Veterans
Worvit – white farmers' children's name for War Veterans
Wilco – will comply
ZAPU – Zimbabwe African Peoples Union – Joshua Nkomo's party
ZANU – Zimbabwe African National Union – Ndabaninge Sithole's party

ZANU PF – amalgamation of two above
ZIPRA – armed forces of ZAPU
ZANLA – Zimbabwe African National Liberation Army

The Author

I first met the author of this novel, Kenneth Alexander Stanford Tilbury, in 1960 when he was sixteen years old and we have been close friends ever since.

He was born in South Africa of English parents and spent most of his life living and working in Southern Africa. Educated at St Marks School in Swaziland, he grew up amongst the local indigenous population learning to speak their language and understand their culture.

At the tender age of eighteen, he decided to join the British South Africa Police, in Rhodesia, as it was known then. After serving three years in the police, the author chose farming as a career and spent the next twelve years growing tobacco and sugar in Zimbabwe (Rhodesia). During this time he did service in the Police Reserve and was a member of the Police Anti-Terrorist Unit. Leaving Rhodesia at the end of the 'Bush War,' he farmed in South Africa and Swaziland for fifteen years before returning to Zimbabwe.

He experienced the horror of being thrown off his farm, under the threat of death, by so-called "War veterans" of President Robert Mugabe.

The experiences the author gained during his time in the region form the basis of this book.

Without taking any particular political stand, the book exposes the horror of war and terrorism as it is revealed in parts of Africa."

Phillip James Bruce Graham.
(ex-BSAP and author of 'Dare to Flee')
August 2010.

9 781699 789928